Karl Stieler, Herman Schmid

The Bavarian Highlands, and the Salzkammergut

With an account of the habits and manners of the hunters, poachers and peasantry

of these districts

Karl Stieler, Herman Schmid

The Bavarian Highlands, and the Salzkammergut
With an account of the habits and manners of the hunters, poachers and peasantry of these districts

ISBN/EAN: 9783744775175

Printed in Europe, USA, Canada, Australia, Japan

Cover: Foto ©Lupo / pixelio.de

More available books at **www.hansebooks.com**

THE BAVARIAN HIGHLANDS

AND

THE SALZKAMMERGUT

THE
BAVARIAN HIGHLANDS

AND

THE SALZKAMMERGUT

G. CLOSS, W. DIEZ, A. von RAMBERG, K. RAUPP, J. G. STEFFAN, FR. VOLTZ, J. WATTER,
AND OTHERS

WITH AN ACCOUNT OF
THE HABITS AND MANNERS OF THE HUNTERS POACHERS, AND PEASANTRY OF THESE DISTRICTS

BY

HERMAN SCHMID AND KARL STIELER

LONDON
CHAPMAN AND HALL, 193, PICCADILLY
1874

CONTENTS.

		PAGE
THE MOUNTAIN'S GREETING .	By HERMAN SCHMID.	
NEAR THE MOUNTAINS .	,, ,,	1
AMONGST THE MOUNTAINS. . .	. .	15
I. ON THE ZUGSPITZE . . .	By K. STIELER	17
II. ON THE WALCHENSEE	,, ,,	22
III. THROUGH THE JACHENAU TO LÄNGGRIES .	,, ,,	26
IV. A TOUR ROUND THE TEGERNSEE . . .	,, ,,	29
V. DORF KREUTH AND WILDBAD . .	,, ,,	33
VI. IN THE KAISERKLAUSE . .	,, ,,	40
VII. ON THE SPITZING	,, ,,	44
VIII. THE SCHLIERSEE	,, ,,	48
IX. FISCHBACHAU AND BAYERISCHZELL .	,, ,,	52
X. TO MIESBACH	,, ,,	56
XI. THE CHIEMSEE	By HERMAN SCHMID .	59
XII. ON THE KÖNIGSSEE . . .	,, ,,	64
XIII. FROM SALZBURG	By K. STIELER	71
XIV. TRAUNSEE AND ISCHL . . .	,, ,,	82
XV. ON THE SCHAFBERG . . .	,, ,,	87
XVI. GOSAUSEE	,, ,,	91
THE MOUNTAIN VILLAGE. SKETCHES OF MOUNTAIN LIFE	. . .	95
I. HOUSES AND CUSTOMS	By HERMAN SCHMID .	97
II. THE SCHUHPLATTLTANZ . . .	By K. STIELER	108
III. OF "DRIVING INTO THE OAT FIELD" . .	,, ,,	113
IV. THE POACHERS OF THE BAVARIAN HIGHLANDS .	,, ,,	116
V. THE BONFIRE OF THE SUMMER SOLSTICE .	,, ,,	129
VI. LIFE ON THE ALPINE PASTURES . .	,, ,,	135
MOUNTAIN CASTLES. AN HISTORICAL RETROSPECT .	By HERMAN SCHMID .	143
TOURISTS IN THE COUNTRY .	By K. STIELER	155
I. SUNNY DAYS	. . . .	157
II. WET DAYS IN THE MOUNTAINS .	. . . .	162
III. LAKE PICTURES	. . . .	166
ON THE ANIMAL AND VEGETABLE WORLD .	By HERMAN SCHMID .	169
POEM: GOD BLESS THEE!	,, ,,	181
APPENDIX. THE GEOGNOSTIC FORMATION OF THE BAVARIAN ALPS	By DR. KARL HAUSHOFER . . .	183

LIST OF ILLUSTRATIONS.

FULL-PAGE ILLUSTRATIONS.

		PAGE
On the Starnbergersee	By K. Raupp	7
Partenkirchen Before the Fire	,, J. G. Steffan	16
The Eibsee	,, G. Closs	20
A Moonlight Night on the Walchensee	,, ,,	24
Baggage-Horse on the Benedict Wand	,, F. Voltz	26
The Tegernsee	,, L. Höfer	30
Consecration of a Church in the Kaiser Klause	,, W. Diez	42
Goat Pasture	,, F. Voltz	46
A Haul of Fish—Chiemsee	,, K. Raupp	60
Ramsau	,, G. Closs	64
Mühlsturzhörner	,, ,,	66
Obersee	,, ,,	68
Wimbachklamm	,, ,,	70
Salzburg from the Capuzinberg	,, ,,	72
Salzburg	,, L. Ritter	74
Ischl	,, ,,	84
St. Wolfgang with the Schafberg	,, K. Raupp	88
Gosausee	,, G. Closs	92
Marriage Procession	,, J. Watter	102
Pursuit	,, W. Diez	126
Midsummer Day's Bonfire	,, J. Watter	130
A Luckless Case on the Alm	,, F. Voltz	136
Departure from the Alm	,, ,,	140
City People on the Alm. Sunny Days	,, J. Watter	158
City People in the Country. Rained in!	,, ,,	160
Boating	,, A. von Ramberg	163
Chamois	,, F. Voltz	170
Horses under the Umbrella-Pine	,, ,,	174
Eagle and Sheep	,, ,,	176

TEXT ILLUSTRATIONS.

		PAGE
Illustration to "The Mountain's Greeting" By *Watter*.		
Near the Mountains	,, *Closs*	3
Ammersee	,, *Steffan*	4
Wood-ship on the Starnbergersee	,, ,,	5
On the Starnbergersee	,, *F. Voltz*	6
The Castle of Starnberg	,, *Steffan*	8
On the Kochelsee	,, *Closs*	9
Castle of Schwaneck	,, *Steffan*	10
A Raft on the Isar	,, *Diez*	11
Valley of the Inn, near Brannenburg	,, *Steffan*	12
Reichenhall	,, *Frölicher*	13
The Wendelstein (from the Plain)	,, *Steffan*	14
The Valley of the Loisach, with the Zugspitze	,, ,,	17
Smugglers	,, *Diez*	18
Oberammergau	,, *Höfer*	19
Kloster Ettal	,, *Frölicher*	20
Road on the Walchensee	,, *Wopfner*	22
A Hermit in the Wood	,, *Closs*	24
Little Convent on the Walchensee	,, ,,	25
Procession of Marksmen	,, *Diez*	26
A Balcony	,, ,,	27
A Dead Peasant	,, ,,	28
Initial Illustration	,, ,,	29
A Style	,, ,,	31
Inn in the Valley of the Rottach	,, *Watter*	32
Churchyard in Kreuth	,, *Wopfner*	33
Woodcutters	,, *Diez*	35
Religious Procession	,, *Raupp*	36
Wildbad Kreuth	,, *Ritter*	38
An Invalid, Kreuth	,, *Diez*	39
Wooden Hut in the Forest	,, ,,	40
A Dog	,, ,,	42
A Winter's Night in the Forest	,, *Wopfner*	43
The Spitzingsee	,, ,,	44
The Herbs Collector	,, ,,	46
Schliersee	,, ,,	48
The "Leonhartsfahrt"	,, *Diez*	50
The Wendelstein, seen from Josephsthal	,, *Wopfner*	51
Guitar Playing in the Village Inn	,, *Diez*	52
Pasture on the Wendelstein	,, *Steffan*	53
Girl in the Balcony	,, *Watter*	54
Brawl in the Village Inn	,, *Diez*	55
Landscape on the Mangfall	,, *Frölicher*	56
Miesbach	,, ,,	57
Miesbach Fashion	,, *Diez*	58
Frauenwörth	,, *Closs*	59
Fisher Cottages at Frauenwörth	,, ,,	61
The Chiemsee—View of the Lords' Island	,, ,,	63
Königssee	,, ,,	64
Berchtesgaden	,, *Höfer*	65
Echo on the Königssee	,, *Raupp*	67
Boatman of the Königssee	,, ,,	68
Chapel in the Rock	,, *Closs*	69
Boatwomen on the Königssee	,, *Watter*	70
Salzburg	,, *Raupp*	71
Fountain at Salzburg (Hofbrunnen)	,, *Ritter*	74
Lovers under a Linden-tree	,, *Raupp*	77
Peter's Churchyard in Salzburg	By *Ritter*	79
Neu Thor	,, ,,	81
Storm on the Lake	,, *Raupp*	82
Gmunden	,, *Höfer*	84
Among the Rushes	,, *Raupp*	85
On the Schafberg	,, ,,	87
St. Gilgen	,, ,,	88
Approaching Tempest	,, ,,	89
Inn on the Schafberg	,, ,,	90
Initial Illustration	,, ,,	91
A Pair of Vultures	,, *Specht*	93
Houses and Customs	,, *Watter*	97
Dowry Wagon before the Bridegroom's House	,, ,,	100
Salting of the Soup	,, ,,	103
Alm-girls before the Sennhut	,, *Raupp*	105
The "Schuhplattltanz"	,, *Diez*	108
The Return Home	,, ,,	110
The "Driving into the Oat-field"	,, ,,	113
Ablutions	,, ,,	115
Initial Illustration	,, ,,	116
Unexpected Meeting	,, *Raupp*	117
The Nocturnal Journey	,, ,,	122
The End of a Career of Violence	,, *Diez*	127
Saved by a Twig	,, *Raupp*	128
The Bonfire of the Summer Solstice	,, *Watter*	129
The Duenna	,, ,,	133
Stone Alm on the Kampenwand	,, *Steffan*	135
Chamois Hunter in the Sennhut	,, *Diez*	139
Sunday in the Alm	,, *Watter*	141
Interior of a Hut in Winter	,, *Diez*	142
Mountain Castles	,, ,,	145
Schloss Hohenaschau	,, *Steffan*	148
Burg Falkenstein in the Innthal	,, ,,	149
Three Knights	,, *Diez*	152
Initial Illustration	,, *Watter*	157
City People in the Almhut	,, ,,	160
Village in Rainy Weather	,, ,,	162
Wet Days in the Mountains	,, ,,	165
Lake Pictures	,, *Bamberg*	166
Roses	,, ,,	168
Chapel in the Mountains	,, *Wopfner*	171
Smithy in the Forest	,, ,,	173
Primeval Forest	,, ,,	175
A Fox	,, *Specht*	176
A Mountain Stag	,, *L. Voltz*	177
Deer	,, ,,	178
Tatzelwurm	,, *Diez*	179
Illustration to "God Bless Thee!"	,, *Watter*	180
Wimbachthal	,, *Haushofer*	191
Englstein	,, ,,	192
Limestone	,, ,,	197
Limestone of the Watzmann	,, ,,	199
Dachstein Limestone	,, ,,	200
Funtensee	,, ,,	201
Blue Ice	,, ,,	203
Zürbe	,, ,,	205

THE MOUNTAIN'S GREETING.

WELCOME to the mountain-climber!
  Thee the heights in chorus greet.
As upon a temple's threshold,
Cast the dust from off thy feet.
Come, the forest tops are swaying,
Forest waters running free;
Com'st thou in the holy spirit,
Holy shall our plighting be.

When with striving Life outwearied,
And the sultry air below,
When thy limbs but drag a burden,
When thy heart beats faint and slow,
Come, the keen breath of the mountain
Shall revive thee and sweep through,
Till in thy new bloom of being
To thyself thou seemest new.

NEAR THE MOUNTAINS.

NEAR THE MOUNTAINS.

THE mountains, those pillars and foundations of the earth, are everywhere beautiful, whether their predominating character be that of wild grandeur or graceful softness; but it can scarce be denied, that the union of all these peculiarities and advantages is nowhere so complete and perfect in the beauty of ever-changeful variety as in that part of the German Alps generally described as the Bavarian Mountains. An equal charm is thrown over the country "Near the Mountains;" and, indeed, as its qualities form one of the chief beauties of these mountains, in this respect we are justified in first turning our attention thither.

The general character of these projecting spurs agrees in this, that more or less it bears the marks of their origin; of their dependence on the mountains themselves, which make them, and before whose feet they lie like children at the feet of their parents. The comparison is quite fitting for a great portion of the country near the mountains; for it was to the last upheaval from the surface of the globe that they owe their present shape, and that convulsion precipitated, rolled and poured down the masses of ice-stone and water, whose impact and pressure broke the banks of the lacustrine basins then generally to be found near the mountains; and these drained of their waters, the boulder-flats, clay bottoms, the peat bogs and reservoirs remained, which still speak to the inquirer of mighty revolutions, if, not content with the charming landscape, he desires to examine the ground whereon the magic colours of this picture are laid.

The mountains themselves, then, stand up in impregnable ramparts which, like the isolated advanced works of a gigantic central fortress, spread out and push forward on every side. It is not, indeed, impossible for human courage and strength to surmount them, as trenches are stormed and roofs climbed; but the calm and happy traveller and friend of Nature prefers to seek the doors which the world of mountains has itself left open, and through these—as it were living roads, which to the present hour maintain the ancient intercourse between hill and plain—to seek his diversion. These doors and highways are the rivers and the valleys which the former have hollowed out and dug in the heart of the mountains, and on that account lead by the nearest and safest way back to that heart.

With the mountain streams, therefore, we will commence our wanderings in the mountains—a way, to be sure, tolerably distant from the lines of railway; but we shall gain by it, for the mountain sprites are jealous and coy; they hate bustle and noise, and consent to display their hidden majesty to him alone who approaches them calmly and trustfully.

The first stream which comes under our consideration as a conductor into the mountains is the Lech; but here it is only the boundary which divides the proper Bavarian range from the very differently formed Allgaüer Alps, the Bavarian Oberland from Bavarian Swabia; more important are the Isar and Inn, with their subordinate tributaries and vassals, the Amper and the Loisach, the Mangfall and the Prien, the Traun and the Saalach, which are all connected with each other, and hasten in common to join the chief river of the region, the Danube.

In many of the mountain streams there is an ever-recurring peculiarity; viz., that their exit from

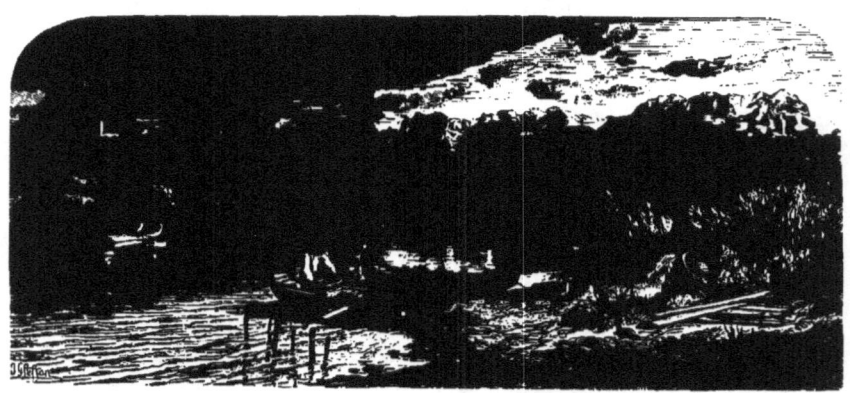

AMMERSEE.

the mountains is marked by a large basin, or lake, which they seem to form and flow through before commencing their proper course through the country. The basin formed by the Amper bears its name, the Ammersee, with its solitary and hilly banks. This lake, it is related, was once a fen or marsh; three noble maidens had attempted to fertilise the broad and desert land, and, having failed to get the mastery over the waters, they condemned it with curses to become a lake for ever: a tolerably clear indication of how long the remembrance of the time when the lacustrine basin was not yet full, survived amongst the people! He who, in a skiff of the simplest construction—often made of the hollowed stem of an oak—rows along on the mighty, wide-spread sheet of water, whilst he sees on his right the glimmer of the white houses of Diessen, will be hailed from the opposite height by the towers and gables of Andechs. This is the lofty baronial hall of the old Counts of that name who once held sway here, when the Roman province through which formerly the Romans conducted the road from Augsburg had become the Ambergau of the Middle Age of Imperial Germany. In front, as between two side-scenes, the mountains look down in the same majesty that they have displayed during all these ages, of which no vestige is found, except here and there a Roman castle, or a faded piece of embroidery which pious faith has rescued and honoured as the relics of a saint.

The road then bends over the lofty Peissenberg, with its pilgrim's church, its view, and its extensive coal-beds, which, perhaps, may secure it a greater future than both the former: it is one of the highest points in the whole district, which it commands like a watch-tower; for which reason it is used with success for meteorological observations. The mass of the Molassengestein, pushed forward in the formation of the mountains so far in its isolation, was too hard for the young mountain-child Amper; it preferred, therefore, to meander around it. This curve brings the traveller who ascends its course to the mountain-enclosed but broad and flat valley where the once considerable monastery Rotenbuch elevates its solitary and desecrated walls; then into the green space where Unter and Oberammergau lie, those lovely verdure-mantled spots with the trim picture-bepainted houses, their resident families of carvers, and the world-renowned decennial Passion Play; overtopped by the romantic giant peak of the Kosel (the Covelinens of the Romans), and gracefully embedded between the Ettaler and Hörnl-Mandl in rich meadows.

WOOD-SHIP ON THE STARNBERGERSEE.

In this highly attractive spot it is well worth while to lay down the traveller's staff for a couple of days, even if it be not the time of the Passion Play, to which the nations troop as in former days to the Olympic Games of the Greeks; for there is much original poetry in the simple people, and an exhaustless beauty in the Nature which they inhabit. But the Passion Play is, in its simple grandeur, a spectacle such as is to be seen nowhere else in the world. Apart from religious considerations, one is involuntarily impressed by the significance which a stage resting on such a foundation must have for the people, if it ceases to be an idle exhibition for entertainment, and, at the same time, has at its disposal the appliances which are here assembled in the theatre, which, with its fivefold stage, forms a most happy combination of the ancient Greek scene and the mystery-stage of the Middle Ages.

Here ends the region which may be described as lying near the mountains; beyond Oberammergau the road turns to the left towards Ettal, the remarkable old foundation of Louis of Bavaria (to which we shall return further on), and then descends, in long, steep mountain roads, into the territory of the kindred Loisach; but to the right, up the Amper and at the foot of the Kosel, opens out the beautifully green, solitary, mountain-shadowed valley where Graswang lies; that quiet, snug little village, the material home of all the idylls of mountain life; and, farther on, succeeds the still more solitary Linderhof, which the poetical King of Bavaria has transformed into one of those spots for profound meditation in which he so much delights, deep in the woody recesses of the Ammerwald.

A not less beautiful way offers itself to those who prefer to approach the mountains by the channel of the Loisach; the country passed through is amongst the most lovely to be seen on earth—it is that round Starnbergersee. It was a striking expression used by Julius Braun, the distinguished Egyptologist, who, after having travelled through almost the whole world, exclaimed, whilst surveying the lake and mountains from the position of Feldafing: "There is only one spot on the whole earth which can compare with this in lofty, various, and yet ever unalterable beauty—and that spot is the Golden Horn at Constantinople!" In fact, the Starnbergersee is like a fair and noble lady, who, though captivating in her grace and dignity at the first glance, becomes more and more attractive the longer one knows and beholds her, because every moment of her acquaintance unfolds a new charm, a new beauty. No one can forget the moment,

ON THE STARNBERGERSEE.

when, gliding on the flashing sheet of water, he surveys the beautiful outlines of the woody hills, covered with villas, whilst in the blue distance the Alps, like a half-revealed Eden, ever nearer, ever clearer, soar on high; in the centre, right away over the mossy plains and hills, is that prominent section of the mountains where the Kochelsee has buried itself at the feet of the Jocheralm and the Herzogenstand; beyond it are the gigantic limestone steeps of the Karwendel; whilst, away to the west, the mountain-chain of the Benediktwand, with its massive precipices and sharp-cut outlines, marks the commencement of the range of the more lofty mountains; but eastward the Wetterstein is massed up, rising ever wilder and wilder, at last to descend to the magnificent Zugspitze, which remains like a vacant throne waiting for its Eternal Ruler, and at whose feet the Algauer Mountains, and, further on, the Swiss, stretch away and vanish in the far distance.

In summer, the shining lake has its boats and small craft, as on land road and railway, its carriages of various sorts; and the cheerful people trudge along, often resting awhile at the pleasant spots on the bank to enjoy the splendid view. The rich and the travellers by profession, who desire to despatch their

pleasures hurriedly, make use of the neat little steamer to make the tour of the lake in half a day; but those who, perhaps, have less money and more time, wander along the magnificent banks, which, from Starnberg to Possenhofen and Feldafing, to Tutzing and Bernried, form a uniform and uninterrupted park, which, lavishly endowed by nature, ornamented by art in the best sense of the term, and with its lofty, mountainous background, may scarcely be equalled anywhere. Possenhofen is especially frequented; that ancient but modernised castle which belongs to the Dukes of Bavaria, and which was the nursery of the three sisters, one of whom now sits on the imperial throne of Austria. Above Possenhofen lies the village of Veltolfing, now called Feldafing, where an excellent inn stands on the best point for a view, and thus unites all enjoyments, both useful and pleasant, in the most enticing way. But Tutzing has also its friends,—the old castle with its brewhouses, and, still more, the old convent Bernried, with its beech-woods, whose trunks, in beauty, size, and age, have few equals in the world. There are many who prefer the left bank, because, taking a morning stroll between the castles and villas of Berg, Leoni, Allmannshausen, and Ammerland, one walks along in the cool shade, and has the opposite bank in full summer magnificence before one. Those who delight to connect the enjoyment of the present with that of the past, and to adorn the beauteous landscape with historical decorations, have also the richest materials here; they can speak of the little island in which King Louis rests under his roses; of the times of the Celtic pile-buildings, or of the later Germanic races who formed the ground of the island, on which once a heathen temple stood, into the shape of three burying-places, one above the other. It requires not much fancy to picture a stream of chivalrous champions rapidly descending from the gates of Garatshausen, equipped with crossbow and bugle for the chase, or, perchance, clad in steel for war, shield upon arm, and pennon flying above helm. Those who please may imagine the tones of an organ from the church of Bernried yonder, with the choral song of the monks sounding across the silent waters; or a line of black-cowled monks slowly moving along under the green shadows of the beech-wood. Such as prefer the modern and elegant, may call to mind one of those evening pageants, when the Bavarian Electors, imitating the pomp of Versailles, embarked on the gilded giant-ship for the chase of water-birds or deer driven into the water; and how the water-monster, spirting two jets of water above, and moving a hundred oars on either side like legs, swam majestically along among countless boats of various sizes—a world of brilliance, extinguished even for memory, like the fireworks which were shot up into the night for the celebration of gala days.

Landed at the end of the lake, the traveller moves on its former territory, to which the numerous little lakes around bear witness, into the district proper of the Loisach, through low or undulating land, to the old convent of Benediktbeuern, whose name in history not only brings to mind its great antiquity, but also its services to art and science and the numerous precious manuscripts which have here found a secure asylum. Not far off, the Loisach emerges from the so-called Rohrsee, the foremost and largest portion of the Kochelsee. This lake waters the surrounding country far around from its deep basin, into which the river seemed formerly to disappear entirely, till a canal was conducted through for the rafts; for the timber trade is not less carried on on the Loisach than on the Isar. Here we find repeated the phenomenon we remarked in the Ammersee, a lake placed at the river's exit from the mountains, which serves for a reservoir to retain the stream till it is itself full, thus acting as an excellent safeguard against inundations. This is especially the case with the Loisach, which frequently, when the snow melts, in the height of summer, fills with great suddenness, and causes vast devastation and damage. Fortunately, in this case the Rohrsee affords a respite of several hours, and gives time to the inhabitants of the upper course of the river to send tidings by means of so-called "water-riders" to those of the lower parts, that the "great water" is on the way. Thus precautionary measures can be taken, and the Isar, into which the Loisach flows, is the only river which at its flood times rushes on without warning, because it wants a similar safety-valve at its point of departure. The friendly, sober Staffelsee, near the town of Murnau also, and even the Würmsee, appertain properly, in this respect, to the Loisach district, for the traces of a former flood in this direction can be followed with tolerable precision.

It is not surprising that the prospect grows more and more charming as we quit the marshy plain. As a matter of course the more distant and lofty ranges become hidden from view; but, on the other hand, the more advanced ones are even more marked in the sharpness, distinctness, and beauty of their outlines, and present a more contracted, but more detailed and lovely picture. The broad and rocky brow of the Benediktwand towers like a giant, closely supported by the Jocheralm, whilst the Herzogenstand and the Haimgarten fill the interval between the Sonnenspitz, where the mountains slope again into the plain. There, hidden among the fruit-trees, lies the pleasant little village Kochel, in which may yet be found many of those pretty cottages with the low, projecting gables and flower-adorned

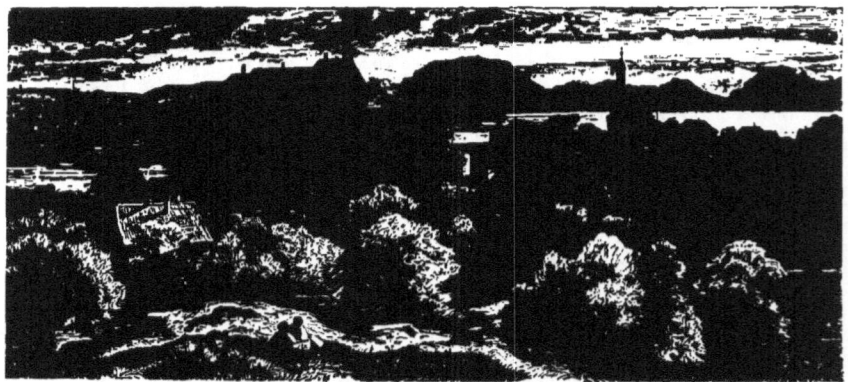

THE CASTLE OF STARNBERG.

balcony round the upper story (called the "bower") which are so distinctive of the country; alas! like the costumes of the people, ever more and more supplanted by the encroachments of town fashions, which will soon reduce the chief adornments of these mountain districts to a legendary tale. Schlehdorf, situated on the other side of the lake, serves as an example; it was destroyed by fire, and has indeed arisen again, not, like the Phœnix, in a more brilliant shape, but in an insipidity almost unequalled, giving the village from a distance the appearance as if a detachment of troops had pitched their white tents there.

The loveliest spot, which may be termed the conclusion of the hilly district in this direction, is the basin proper of the Kochelsee, not itself of any considerable extent, but for that reason can be taken in at one glance. It is a small, circular sheet of water, of a transparent, metallic green, which is explained by the reflection of the woods, which clothe the mountains on either side. Immediately behind tower steep precipices, called by the people "The Nose," on account of their curious shape; to the left, near the prettily hidden mill, runs up a spur of the Jocheralm, the precipitous Kesselberg, through mighty forests and past glorious waterfalls, to the height at whose feet the astonished eye descries the sober Walchensee spread before it; in the centre arises the oft-mentioned Herzogenstand, one of the most beautiful and remunerating points for a view, which King Max made of easy approach by a bridle-path. From this point both the plain and the neighbouring range of mountains can be overlooked, and in comparison with it the Rigi can boast of nothing but a renowned name. To the right, appears the smoothly-rounded Heimgarten, according to tradition a Germanic offering-place, adorned at its feet by a gently-ascending grove, in which the former canons of Schlehdorf have hewn a beer-cellar in the rock under the magnificent maples, thus in their matter-of-fact way proving what educated tastes they possessed.

Ascending the pebbly bed of the Loisach, we soon find ourselves between mountains which close in and scarcely leave room for the narrow line of road to wind along the bank; these are the Heimgarten, —this time from behind,—the Hirschberg, the Krottenkopf, and the Ettaler-Mandl, where, as already mentioned, it approaches the Ettaler-Berg, and enters the Ammergau. The whole of this diversified, wildly beautiful picture is closed in the background by the Wettersteingebirge and the Zugspitze; but

ON THE KOCHELSEE.

as this lies far beyond the limits of the district we are considering, we shall not follow the direction of the boisterous mountain-child into the Tyrolese mountains of Lermos and Ehrwald, but turn back again to commence the ascent of the mountains in the direction of a third and nobler conductor, to whom both the Amper and Loisach are subordinate, and towards whom they roll their green and brown waves in busy haste and meditative circumspection.

This conductor is the Isar.

Approaching the mountains by its banks, the traveller will arrive a little above Munich, at Schwaneck, situated near the narrow river-bed beneath the lofty banks, which are now bold and sloping, and now covered with beech-woods; in this town, the chivalric ideal of a genial artist, as in the charming plain, he will obtain a foretaste of the joys which await him. Although the road passes more than once through flat, marshy land until the confluence of the Isar and Loisach is reached, near Wolfrathshausen, yet it varies very prettily and richly between forest and hill; many a pleasant village greets us, and many a fair baronial hall, such as Eurasburg, looks cheerily down; but when the highest point is attained, and the glorious chain of the Alps lies yonder in all its extent, like a magic world—then indeed is the last fatigue rewarded and forgotten.

The extreme point of the country near the mountains is formed by the pleasant and much-frequented town Tölz, famous on account of the healing virtues of its mineral springs, and situated near the baths of Heilbronn. Tölz is well qualified, through its sloping situation on a ridge, to afford the traveller an idea of the mountain-world in the most beautiful sense of the word, and to permit him, as from a watch-tower built expressly for the purpose, a first glance into its secrets. It may confidently be said of those who have mounted the height with the Calvary church and the cross-road stations, looked down on the valley of the Isar extended at their feet, and never at the same time felt a glow beneath vest or bodice, that nothing is to be found there capable of an emotion. The view is one of the most complete, compact, and, for that reason, most lovely of landscape tableaus which are to be found; many a one who has stood here when the warm crimson of an evening sky veiled the dusky mountains, could

CASTLE OF SCHWANECK.

believe himself transferred to the charming valleys of South Tyrol, on the banks of the Adige, beneath the vineyards and chestnuts of Meran.

Those who ascend the Isar still farther into the mountains, will have, in the long Länggriesser valley, and still more so in the Riss, frequent opportunities of studying the peculiar nature and action of a mountain-stream: they will arrive at the musical Mittenwald, calmly established at the foot of magnificent but inhospitable Karwendel, as if there were no such thing as a winter, which, with its precursors and stragglers, not unfrequently wields an icy sceptre over it for fully nine months in the year together. This, however, belongs no more to this chapter than an excursion into the Jachenau valley, which branches off to our right; a long, broad, mountain-enclosed valley, whose few inhabitants, dwelling in scattered farms of considerable dimensions, according to the custom of the ancient Germans, are secure through their seclusion, and independent through their opulence: they yet preserve many of the old mountaineer habits, whose traces elsewhere are becoming obliterated through the influence of increasing intercourse.

Up the Isar, particularly in Länggries, is the especial home of those portly forms of mountaineers which strangers survey with so much delight in the streets of Munich, arrayed in their leathern breeches and (of course rapidly becoming rarer) stockings or "Beinhoseln," belt round waist, and axe upon shoulder, and the green hat, with its small cockade and hanging tassels, upon the brown, curly head. This is the race of woodcutters and raftsmen, who cut down trees and wood on the mountains, form rafts of them, and with a cargo of coal, lime, or deal boards, travel to Munich. There the cargo and raft are sold, and the raftsman returns home, axe upon shoulder, with the price in his pocket, to commence his trade anew. The invention of other means of communication, and the construction of magnificent saw-mills, may have injured the raft trade considerably, at any rate, in its magnitude; for, formerly, it was nothing uncommon to see a raft of this description travel as far as Vienna with conductor and cargo. Many a guest joined it on the way; many a travelling journeyman, who paid his fare by working at an oar, was found thereon; sometimes, too, a girl from the mountains, seeking employment in Munich;

A RAFT ON THE ISAR.

or a young monk desirous of shortening the tedium of his return journey from terms. A light shed in this case was constructed with boards on the raft, which generally had to serve as hostelry for the night at halting-places; before it burnt, upon stones, a cheery fire for the preparation of the simplest of meals; around the fire sat the motley troop of travellers, often to the sound of the guitar and song; and, standing on a bridge on the Isar when such a raft glided between its piles, one might reasonably take it for a joyous troop of pleasure-seekers.

Quite the reverse, though quite as lovely, is the picture which presents itself to those who choose to approach by one of the streams which belong to, and unite themselves with, the other leading river, the Inn. When the great, tiresome, monotonous plain of Munich, with its heaths and fir-woods, is once behind, the startling spectacle is presented, all at once, of the country sloping away into a deep valley, in which a very lively, light green mountain-stream brawls away; it is the Mangfall (so called by our forefathers on account of its tortuous course), the outlet of the Tegernsee and, in all probability, of the neighbouring Schliersee also; for, it speedily receives the tiny Schlierach, flowing out of the latter. These are a pair of charming guides, which one would willingly follow; but we cannot do so farther than, at the most, Market Miesbach, that pleasant village; for what entices us thither belongs to later pages, because it relates not to the exterior decorations of what we may term the mountain treasure-casket, but to two of the most beautiful jewels and precious stones placed in its innermost recess.

But the charming strip of valley watered by the Mangfall in its present course belongs to us now; for in the period of upheavals it flowed past Moosburg before pouring itself into the Isar; it has now pierced a way through the rock at the foot of Castle Altenburg; the former mansion of the powerful Counts von Falkenstein, and turns, in strikingly bold and tortuous curves, towards the broad valley, which, once a lake, now offers such a lovely picture, that, wherever the country near the mountains is famous, it must incontestably claim a foremost place. The view of the mountains may be more magnificent indeed from many another point; but it may be boldly maintained, that there are nowhere more picturesque and beautiful outlines, nowhere a more comprehensive and yet harmonious picture of the same, than that which presents itself to the spectator from the geometrical post on the Irschenberg, or opposite

VALLEY OF THE INN, NEAR BRANNENBURG.

from the church of Höhenraine. Not less happily situated is Aibling, a market-town, famed for the extraordinary virtue of its mud baths; since its neighbour Rosenheim has been admitted into the proud company of cities, no one will contest with it the glory, which once belonged to Rosenheim, of being the prettiest of the market-towns of the mountains. Gloriously the broad land extends itself in wide sweeping curve, like an immense garden adorned in rich variety with pretty copses, magnificent clumps of oaks, and dark woods of coniferous and foliated trees; at intervals appear shining villages, bright castles, and projecting battlements; the whole enclosed by the mountains, which stretch in a ring from the west along the south far away to the east. The Wendelstein is commonly indicated as a landmark or kind of centre of the district; but this is incorrect; for, although this giant, on account of his height and pyramidal shape, deserves preferment and a just homage, yet the characteristic marks of the Mangfall district are not found on him, but in the valley or indentation of the mountains from which the Inn, coming from the Tyrol, enters the plain. Boldly sloping away, the same shows itself as a broad and steep cleft, which the restless stream has slowly eaten and dug out in the mountains; in and above it, along its whole breadth, arises the long, low cliff of the "Fair Kaiser," which is overtopped and outdone in wildness, stiffness, and ruggedness by the Kaisergebirge itself, with its notched Trafoispitze, which, in contrast, has with justice been named the "Wild Kaiser." To the right rises the Madron ledge, with the little church of Petersberg upon it; then succeed the Wildbarn, the Riesenberg, the two weird Asenkopfs, ever ascending more and more as far as the Brunstein, the Haidewand, and at last to the Wendelstein, with which the Miesing, the Rothwand, and others connect themselves, and gently descend, to disappear in the Irschenberg. Opposite, as left side-scene to the valley of the Inn, the Kranzhorn (properly Gränzhorne) raises its remarkable peak, and the Heuberg elevates its phantastically formed head; in still bolder ascent follow the Samerberg and Hochriss, till they reach the shell-fish-shaped Kampenwand, and the Göttererwand, with its romantic peaks and points, sinks away in the distance. Farther still, the mountains of Traunstein and Reichenhall stretch away before the astonished eye, the Hochgern and the Hochfellen, with the massive Staufen and the Untersberg, which is often visible, and appears as if it were indistinct from the exhalation of its own legendary lore.

REICHENHALL.

From Aibling itself a very easy and charming road leads through meadows and woods to a small eminence, where stands the humble abode of a road-keeper, which is called pre-eminently the "Belle Vue;" and with justice does it bear this designation; for those who have once stood upon it and seen the mountains, the Kaiser Thor and the Wendelstein, with their crags glowing in the red light of sunset, will count the eve and the view among the jewels of his lifetime. It is true that a little pine-wood is placed so as to screen the easterly mountains, but even there the prospect is overpowering; those who wish to survey the entire mountain-chain can do so not far from Aibling; or they can wend their way northwards to the ancient castle Marlrain, whose history still waits for à properly descriptive pen. Here, under the shade of a clump of primæval oaks, a view of rare beauty discloses itself, which rouses thoughts that Paradise upon earth is not altogether lost—at any rate, as far as regards the beauties of nature.

The river Inn itself, whilst it yet rolls along between the constantly receding mountains, approaches the pleasant village of Oberau, the kindly Fischbach, and the ruin of Falkenstein, past the almost opposite strongholds of Brannenburg and Neubeuern, of which, perhaps, more may be said in the course of these pages; they belong, more or less, to the inner mountain region, whose limits we are attempting to skirt at a distance. When the Inn is crossed, we again see in the Chiemsee the phenomenon of a basin or reservoir, destined to collect and retain the waters of the mountains, unless, indeed, we have here the remains of a former gigantic lake, at one time covering the country on both sides the Inn, and of which we find unmistakable traces in the morasses of Rosenheim and Aibling. The most considerable confluents from the mountains are, of course, small; but, however unpretentious they may seem as guides, yet they are worth more than they promise; this will be experienced by those who ascend the clear Prien to the valley of Hohenaschau, with its hospitable inn and desolate, now inhospitable, feudal castle, or, still farther, to the frontiers of the Tyrol, near Sacharang; or, by those who prefer the brawling Achen, and follow it into serene Grassau, romantic Marquartstein, or mountain-guarded Kössen.

Beyond the Chiemsee itself, the Hochgebirge in a wide circle greets the traveller, who steams past the two islands on its blue waves; amongst them, the most prominent and remarkable are the Hochgern, the Kampen, and the awfully riven block of the wild Riss.

Farther eastward, the Traun conducts those who entrust themselves to its guidance from the lovely market-town Trostberg to the magnificently-situated convent of Baumburg; past the castle of Stain, with its romantic and chivalric reminiscences, into the pleasant little town of Traunstein, so brisk with its salt-works; farther on, to where the white and the red Traun divide, the one passing through the quiet valleys of Eisenarzt and Zell, the other through the picturesque, lonely valley of Innzell and past the mighty mass of the Staufen. We thus arrive again in a new district, that of the rapid Saalach, which storms down from the narrow Tyrolese mountains of Lofer and Anken, and leads to the niche in the mountains where Reichenhall, rich in salts, with its famous and frequented sanitary establishment, comfortably and cheerily extends itself.

With it the panorama of the country "near the mountains" must conclude; for the mountain prodigies which disclose themselves yonder in the country of Salzach and beyond Salzburg, like the country of the Lech, belong not to the limits we have here laid down, and also partly because they will find their place when we come to speak of the interior, the peculiar sanctuary of the mountains.

THE WENDELSTEIN (FROM THE PLAIN).

AMONGST THE MOUNTAINS.

PARTENKIRCHEN BEFORE THE FIRE.

THE VALLEY OF THE LOISACH, WITH THE ZUGSPITZE.

I.

ON THE ZUGSPITZE.

WESTWARD, the highest point of the Bavarian Alps is the Wetterstein. He is the King of the West, as the Watzmann is of the East; no head elevates itself higher than his, and no crown is richer in rocky spikes. Nature did wild work when she created this peak. The mountains are here more insolent and coarse than those around; like an assembly of princes, each demands his own throne and his own territory.

But most prominent of all is the Zugspitze, which is almost entirely torn away from the rest of the Wetterstein. On the right, the Eibsee has advanced up to its battlements; to the left, the Isar has cloven a way through the narrow valley into the plain. A world of unapproachable wildness dwells on these peaks; miles of desert stretch along these rocks without a tree or a plant; the vast solitude is primæval; but away below lies the plain, and the warm sun sheds his beams on the elevated meadows and golden cornfields.

Close to the Zugspitze lies Partenkirchen, built by the Romans when advancing into the German land. It was then called Partanum; their camp was situated here, and the flocks were pastured around it. Later also, when these times had long passed away, the road from Italy into the Empire led through it, along which numerous caravans of merchandise moved; and when the famous Fuggers and Welsers fetched the treasures of the South, their agents and porters held their night-camp in Partenkirchen.

The existing population of these districts is of another stamp, equally removed from the warlike spirit of the Romans as from the wealth of the old burgers of the Middle Ages. But few forms display the athletic build and haughty brow of the mountaineer; and even as their exterior is defective in beauty, so is their bearing devoid of that free and imperious air which lends to mountain people a natural nobility. There reigns a greater tendency to a sedentary than to a roving life, a preference of industrial employments to those of a hunter or shepherd. Of course we sometimes come across shapes which represent the herculean of mountain nature, but we must not look for them in the market-place itself; and then they form not a type but an exception to the general rule. Nature has lavished all her wild grandeur on the landscape, and the shapes of men have involuntarily assumed a somewhat tamer appearance.

In the good old times, when it was still worth the trouble, smuggling went on briskly in these mountains. Along the narrow path bordering the precipice the bold smuggler crept up, a hundredweight on his back and a loaded blunderbuss across his arm. Whilst he crept along under the overhanging rocks, the loosened stones gave way beneath his feet; it was a constant existence between life and death. Where the paths were practicable, a sumpter horse bore the hidden wares, and amongst the many loads, which evidently came from the Alm below, foreign valuables were smuggled in, which were then concealed among the rocks, and at night sent on farther.

SMUGGLERS.

The market-town Partenkirchen, formerly very attractive architecturally, has been several times fearfully devastated by fire. How it looked before this the numerous pictures of Bürkel and Peter Hess tell us; they are so strikingly true, and so much disseminated, that the remembrance of what was before the conflagration has been saved. In them we see the old well of the village, with the holy Florian (who has exercised his office badly); the houses are still of brownish wood, and have those pleasant galleries which are termed "bowers."

Since the last fire (1865), more solid buildings have been erected, and thus new Partenkirchen has become a Phœnix of cement.

Not far away lies Garnisch, with its famed Hussar Inn. But this martial appellation does not in any way indicate a cavalry occupation, but the solitary hussar one meets is a fresco on the wall, who disturbs the house neither by clash of sabre nor any other violence. The Civil Court holds its sessions also in Garnisch, which is then called "Werdenfels." This was the name of the ancient county, and thus it need not surprise one that the present district office will not willingly resign this proud designation.

Countless excursions of uncommon magnificence offer themselves to visitors who take up their quarters for the summer months in these two villages. There is the forest-house of Graseck, the Partnachklamm, the Rainthal, and the peasant on the Eck, who possesses the highest constantly-inhabited dwelling in Bavaria. If one presses farther into the Rainthal the blue Gumpe is seen before us, a little lake surrounded by the Partnach, like an amethyst set in the rock.

The ascent of the Zugspitze is rendered considerably easier since, by the liberality of a Munich family, the hut was erected which stands at the beginning of the so-called "Plattert" in the midst of the boulders; and which at least possesses a roof, although the rain drifts in through its numerous chinks. By the couch it contains a little fire-place, which a philanthropic professor from Würzburg has provided with a little iron oven. And yet men are profane enough to laugh at German professors. Thus it is evident that each must bring the wood which he may require, for up here Nature does not sit in the market-place with heaps of wood before her. During the summer, a strangers'-book lies there, but it is not forbidden to use also the wooden doors of the hut for the same purpose. At Herr Knorr's a spring offers its services for the refreshment of travellers; it bubbles up near the hut, and may be employed for all customary uses.

Upon the summit of the Zugspitze there is an iron cross fourteen feet high. It was first ascended

OBERAMMERGAU.

in the year 1820. The prospect which opens itself extends from Carinthia into Switzerland, and from the Danube to the Italian border. Far therein we see the indentation of the Brenner Pass; the Tauren chain lifts itself in long battlemented range; the Stubai and Ortler groups are before our eyes—snow, snow, a vast world of snow! Below glistens the fairer land—each house a sparkling point, each river a silver thread!

In Partenkirchen there is yet another object, lying in the depths; and though it cannot compete with the former in bulk, it equals it in grandeur of style.

We stand before immense rocks, which plunge perpendicularly into the abyss, torn as if Despair had created them. Mournful pines embrace their foot, desolate stones lie scattered round about, and in the midst lies a lake, as wofully deep, and unfathomably dark, as if there were no more Spring and no more joy upon earth.

These are the banks of the Eibsee, which was formed thousands of years ago by the subsidence of the Wetterstein; and even at the present time the immense fact stands, as if petrified, before our eyes. There lies a terrific power in this picture, a fearful fatality in the landscape; it is high as heaven, deep as hell, ancient and stony as eternity. Gazing up these steeps, ten thousand feet high, it appears as if dark spirits had been precipitated here into the abyss, as if one stood before their prison, in the midst of their domain. They are not annihilated by their fall, for the mind is immortal; they live still, and their torments have been stamped upon the rocks.

When the wind roars in the distant ravines they groan, and a slight commotion trembles through the lake's abyss. The Eibsee is the hell of Nature—there is something Stygian about its waters.

KLOSTER ETTAL.

Only a few decayed cottages stand on the border of the dark water, and their inhabitants are not less reduced in circumstances than their gloomy abodes. Entangled nets hang about the rocks, and goats climb between the scanty patches of grass, and nibble at the bristly bushes which thrive between the rocks. When visitors come hither in summer, they hire a boatman at these houses to transport them to the numerous groups of islands. Half-naked children run up then with strawberries and Alpine-roses, receiving in return a little present, like the obolus which must be paid in Charon's skiff.

But one of the most renowned spots in the vicinity is Kloster Ettal. High above its roofs stands the Ettaler-Mandl, like a grey-mantled sentinel with weather-beaten features; and many a story written on the ancient and queer-shaped mountain. The convent that lies at its feet was built by Kaiser Louis the Bavarian, who brought home from Italy a miraculous image of the Virgin Mary. Many a monk of noble race dwelt in those lofty halls, pictures by a master's hand adorned the vaults of the ceiling,

and the tone of the organ was famed far and wide in German lands. In the same place was also erected a hostelry for knights and their ladies, where they lived in conjugal fidelity and the fear of God.

But splendour has no duration; for the sons of the great Kaiser confiscated the estates in Ammergau which their father had given to Kloster Ettal. A great fire desolated the remains, which survived centuries afterwards, and even now magnificent capitals of pillars in the Ionic style lie scattered on the roads which ascend the Ettaler-Berg. Only the church, with its broad dome, remains standing, and the little image of the Virgin, which yet occupies its ancient home. Many country folk resort here on feast days as pilgrims; but the solitary traveller, whom accident brings by, will experience a boundless solitude. With profound melancholy the wondrous tones of the organ sweep through the church, when, now and then, an expert mounts the narrow winding staircase and charms forth from the keys their long-entranced magic.

An hour's journey from Ettal lies Oberammergau, renowned for its holy plays, which are performed there every ten years. But it is reported that more than forty works have already appeared on this venerable spot; it will consequently turn to the advantage of some new scribbler, if we refrain here from mixing in the "play."

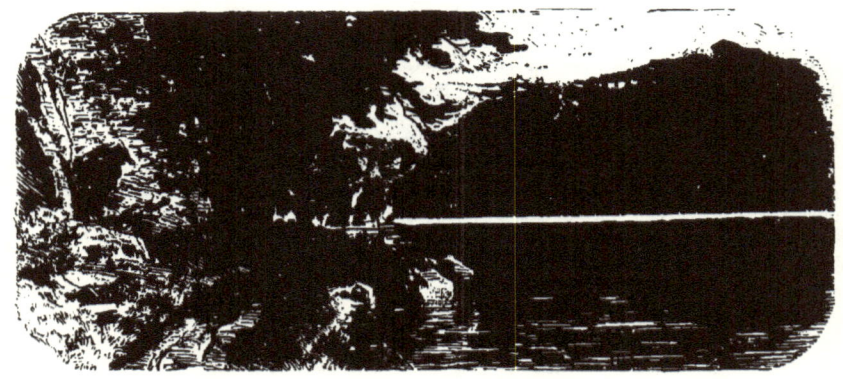

ROAD ON THE WALCHENSEE.

II.
ON THE WALCHENSEE.

URNING our backs on the gigantic and pallid rocks of the Wetterstein, and quitting the course of the Isar, which rolls its light green waves through white boulders, we espy the ancient Wallgau. The road leaves the mountains, dense pine-forests appear, and in the midst of them slumbers the Walchensee, the fair and mournful pearl of the mountains. Its expanse stretches far away, and yet it appears enclosed, contracted. The rays of the sun play upon its surface, and yet it appears dark. And even when its lovely mirror lies in motionless calm, there is a vehemence in its features which affrights the gladsome traveller.

It is on this account, and not alone because the banks are uninhabited, that a wonderful feeling of solitude possesses almost all who visit this silent lake for the first time; for no phenomenon of Nature so much induces to a comparison with mankind, none has such a psychological character as the waves. The waves belong to the tempest, even as our hearts do; to them is ascribed a secret and inscrutable principle of life; and therefore in every lake we involuntarily find a certain human character. The Walchensee is an unhappy Genius. Magnificently situated, with noble outlines and colossal surroundings, it has yet something confined and troubled, one might almost say sterile, about it. Its riches are unblessed. Something enigmatical and mystical remains beyond all its pomp; and the popular mind had a fine instinct in surrounding this lake with numerous myths of the darkest character.

The postal road which leads to Urfeld runs close to the shore. Dark pine-branches hang down into the water, the rotten branches lie a foot thick upon the ground, and only now and then a mass of rock, upon which rests a timid bird, elevates itself above the sombre mirror. Those who saunter along this road on a clear June day, will find few human beings to stop them. They will find time to indulge in the quiet thoughts which the lake will arouse in their bosoms.

The enigmatical character of the Walchensee (also called the Wallersee) is expressed in the earliest legends. They tell of immense fishes which live in its depths, and many would derive its name therefrom. It is more correct to Germanise the word "Walchinsee" as "The Foreigner's Lake," because Celtic or Roman neighbours abode here. As its waters have always been boisterous, all sorts of geognostic explanations have been thought of. The wild mountain-lake was brought into connection with every sheet of water, not excluding the ocean; and the belief was universally spread abroad that the Walchensee was destined for the future annihilation of Bavaria. This accounts for the strange aversion of the people from it; for between the plain and its vast depths stands the Kesselberg alone, like a dam of stone.

It was often apprehended that the latter might be broken through, and as during the earthquake of Lisbon the waves broke furiously against the banks, the terror was boundless. For the "propitiation" of the lake a mass was read daily in Munich, and every year a golden ring was plunged into the inky flood.

Only in rare places is the darksome garland with which the pine-forests border the banks relieved; scarcely twenty houses stand upon the desert strand, although it is miles in circumference. On the southern shore is situated the post-office, a comfortable corner, where one is cheerily welcomed, and in no wise disturbed in one's meditations. Green ivy twines itself around the windows of the lower chamber; a cross-bill pecks away in his cage; and wide antlers, on whose ends the peasant hangs his hat, adorn the walls. Yet another embellishment has been added to the latter; for they appeared so monotonous to a talented young painter who spent his summer here, that he adorned them, for the delectation of himself and others, with charming pictures of the chase. But few guests sit around the green table and interrupt with pleasant conversation the quiet calm of the afternoon.

In the season there is, of course, a brisker traffic, for guests come from the neighbouring baths to the Walchensee at least for a flying visit. The unhorsed carriage, in which parasols and scarlet shawls are left behind, then stands before the house, whilst from the little summer-house which stands by the lake resounds that many-voiced and rapid chatter which announces the presence of townsfolk. Steaming dishes of trout are now brought out of the post-house; and when the trout are eaten, people are fully convinced that they are thoroughly acquainted with the Walchensee. The children, however, who were left dabbling on the bank, are now trumpeted together, the driver drains his tankard, brings out the horses, and, whilst the sun sets in silence, the whole party drives tittering away.

Opposite the post-office a peninsula projects into the lake, and a little ruined convent stands upon it. It is an ancient building of the time when the Walchensee belonged to the Abbey Benediktbeuern, in whose mouldy chronicles the dark *villeggiatura* is often mentioned.

If one of the monks was sick in body or soul, or if the cares of salvation harassed him deeply, he removed hither into this solitude. At that epoch, the iron time of the Franks lay over Germany; the people were barbarous, and the forests were primæval. Many a nobleman wore then the garments of the order, and took refuge with his meditations in a quiet cell. When the evening star arose o'er the magic wilderness, he pulled with quiet hand the bell, and betook himself to the banks of the lake; by his side went the roe, and looked him in the face. Who could say what agitated his haughty breast? The south wind alone rustled in the branches, the waves alone beat on the shore a low song.

"O lost life, love lost for ever,
Incurable is the heart's pang!"

Now the dark convent is turned into a little school, where the bad boys learn their A B C. But as this educational establishment is on the lake, it is often much disturbed by wind and weather; for often, when the hour of study commences, the lake arises with its dark pageant, and wrathfully opposes the spelling of the young inhabitants.

Opposite the lake lies Altlach, where a solitary forester's house looks us in the face. From here the road goes to the Hochkopf and the further Riss, where the royal hunting-boxes stand, for game is very plentiful in these silent districts. Upon those steep ridges feed the chamois; through those lofty beech-woods moves the stag, attentive, with head erect; where there is a clearing in the wood, there comes the doe at eve with her slim progeny. If it is farther on in October, and the full moon sheds her entrancing rays o'er the woods, one hears at times from afar the mighty bellow of the stags in the thicket. Slowly they move out to the glistening shore and swim over to the island; a silver streak shows their track, and only their giant antlers lift themselves above the inky waters.

A HERMIT IN THE WOOD.

On the southern bank one is deeper buried in solitude; but the northern bank is undoubtedly the more lovely, where the inn of Urfeld and two humble fishermen's houses stand. Above the dark waters project the proud forms of the Karwendel range; one sees the Dreithor peak and the lofty Daniel. Here also reigns a deep solitude. Rarely a skiff pushes across its broad surface; only the little post-cart which goes to Mittenwald rolls along the edge of the lake and overtakes the isolated traveller, who salutes it as it passes. I have often sat myself under the broad projecting roof of a house and contemplated the melancholy waters. Bad weather came on, and the mists pressed down ever farther and farther, and the old pines, whose branches it wreathed, became as inky black as if an eclipse was approaching. The shore is flat only for a few paces, the wave plays around the small stones, the little fish feed on their moss, and then the lake sinks suddenly down in horrid depths. It is like an unhappy being who, at every trivial remark, sinks back into the depths of his misery; whom often a playful expression will

A MOONLIGHT NIGHT ON THE WALCHENSEE.

precipitate into the abyss of his dark cares. Still the lake is a noiseless mirror, and the grey gull sweeps over its surface. Each of her motions is full of grace, light and easy, but none are sportive, gay, and aspiring; for she returns ever to the same place, as if she were hopelessly seeking for something lost. The gull is a bird extremely suitable to a melancholy state of mind, and she appears in scarcely any but melancholy songs. She is the type of roving, inconstant desire.

The hues of the Walchensee are deep, but they can sink to a darkness which conjures up night in day-time. At such times there is something terribly imposing about it; a grief lies concealed for which there is no relief but madness. "*Lasciate ogni speranza*" is writ upon the surface of the sultry lake. And, in reality, its storm is a frenzy! When the stormy heavens sink lower and lower, the branches crash, and the snakes flee into their holes—these are its tokens. Then foams up the torrent with a wrathful roar to heaven, and rushes against the fir-trees overhanging the bank as if it would tear them down; each wave is an indistinct utterance, each puff of wind a cry of woe. Then speaks the woe of the engulfed lake, as if it would arraign the Creator—why hast thou enclosed thine enigma within my depths? why is my beauty o'ershadowed by woe, and my happiness by passion?

Those who have experienced a real storm on the Walchensee will never forget the impression caused by this profound commotion. All the more lovely is a moonlight night on those banks. Then the rude genius of the lake relaxes himself in gentle sport; like a fairy-dance is the flow of the waves when they converse with the gnarled roots on the bank or reach up at the slumbering flower. It is as if a dream of joy passed through the entranced soul; in each wave there is a greeting.

Those who love the sombre darkness of the woods will find wonderful footpaths on the steep declivities which surround the lake. The rays of the sun play through the cool branches, and vanish among the trees like golden serpents. Sadness and gaiety alternate with each other in the beaming darkness, and confuse the excited mind of the traveller. Where'er he passes the bramble catches in his clothes, the dog-rose extends its flowers towards him. In the mad orgies of spring, when all throbs with the impetus of life, and in the sultry hours of the glow of summer, I have wandered alone through this green wilderness; many a time have I met in my way the doe, who soon plunged affrighted into the thicket; but the little bird carolled on, and regarded not the unlooked-for disturbance.

LITTLE CONVENT ON THE WALCHENSEE.

PROCESSION OF MARKSMEN.

III.

THROUGH THE JACHENAU TO LANGGRIES.

FROM Sachenbach on the Walchensee the road leads into the Jachenau. It is a long, woody valley, which would be monotonous did not its perfectly mountainous character and the pure, aboriginal type of its inhabitants lend it a charm. Through the latter it has become almost a prototype of the Bavarian highlands. When one speaks of ancient mountain customs, one thinks immediately of these spots; and when Peter Hess or Bürkel painted Bavarian peasants, they were almost always at home in the Jachenau. The costume also has there assumed a peculiar form; it is more complicated, one might almost say more old-fashioned, than in other parts of these mountains. In former times long coats of green material with yellow seams were worn, the hats had broad brims and bauds; and if fashion has now become more frivolous, yet there are still plentiful remains of antiquity. There was something exclusive about the whole valley; scarcely any one left it, because everybody throve there; and scarcely any one settled anew there, because he would have to encounter a closely-arrayed coterie of old settlers. He who wanted a wife found her at home, and so the whole population lived like a single large family. In spite of this, the population did not in any way degenerate, but maintained its

BAGGAGE-HORSE ON THE BENEDICT WAND.

character in unsullied purity and freshness; for here moderation and good morals were more strictly observed than anywhere else.

If we follow the valley which is watered by the Jachen, we shall arrive, perhaps, in the space of an hour, at the first habitations. They cannot be termed a village; for, besides the inn and the church, there are at the most three or four houses, which are surrounded by carved balconies and adorned with pious verses. This is the centre of the spiritual and corporeal joys of this valley. If a marriage is to be celebrated, or a corpse brought for burial, the parish assembles here. On the whole extent of a five or six hours' journey there are not more than perhaps six-and-thirty houses. When people are so shut out from the exterior world, they must become more closely united among themselves, and therefore it is not astonishing if their manners are simple and their hearts faithful. This simplicity, however, never degenerates into coarseness and ignorance; for the couple of recruits who sometimes have to go to Munich can always read and write excellently, and even those who stay at home know much of the world without having seen it.

The second inn, which stands on the side of the valley, is named "Zum Bäcken." If the last stage is completed, it is now not far to Länggries, which lies at the foot of the Benediktenwand and on the banks of the Isar. The latter decides the character of the country; one wanders in a green and blooming valley, over which a larch-covered hill of moderate size elevates itself. Broad and spacious stand the two inns in the village, trim and snug the dwellings of the remainder arrange themselves near at hand. A quarter of an hour from this lies Castle Hohenburg, with its princely rooms and countless rows of windows, round about which spreads itself a magnificent park, —a charming wilderness, with lofty beeches and tangled thickets. We come to deep fish-ponds, upon which graceful swans are floating; we come to a solitary trellis-work door, over which the wild briar stretches its hand towards us full of its roses. The evening sun streams through the glistening foliage, a concealed bird sings, and where the branches leave an opening the mountains look through with their beaming summits. No traveller meets us. It is a magic promenade in these woodland domains, which awake all our desires in turn and again lull them to rest, and which touch in turn all the chords of our inner being.

A BALCONY.

* *
*

Outside, in the village, blows a more bracing air. Formerly Länggries was the head-quarters of rifle-shooting, that sport which grows firmly in the heart of a highlander, and which makes itself apparent in the day of prosperity as in that of adversity. People wore, until recent times, the ancient paternal garments; drummers and fifers marched in front, and the captain of the company assumed all the important air of a general. All this has been abolished, because it seemed contrary to police regulations. But the more they persecuted the legitimate gun, the more zealously was the unlawful use of the same carried on. From marksmen people became poachers, who roamed through the country wide.

The most important occupation of the natives is the timber-trade. Armed with hatchet and rope standing up to the knees in water, these tall figures drive their timber-rafts along on the Isar; some stop at Munich, others float down the Danube to Vienna or Hungary.

Länggries is neither so pastoral nor so virtuous as the Jachenau. Though the exterior build of the inhabitants is herculean, they are less elastic and by far heavier than those of the other parts of the mountain districts.

A DEAD PEASANT.

IV.

A TOUR ROUND THE TEGERNSEE.

MORE than a thousand years have elapsed since the disciples of Saint Benedict erected their house on this shore. Music and poetry flourished there, science and painting were cultivated in the long days of the Middle Ages, and many a monument of vast abilities had its origin in this spot. The most famous name of the convent is Werinher; in it originated the charming "Marienlied," whose lines bring us almost into the circle of the minnesingers:—

> "Thou art mine; I am thine.
> Thou art locked in this heart of mine
> Whereof is lost the little key,
> So there for ever must thou be."

Many pretend that it does not refer to the Holy Virgin, but to a curly-haired child who here concealed her beauty in a quiet cottage.

The abbey, which was elevated to the rank of a principality, possessed a wide renown in German lands. Her disciples went to Bologna and Paris; her prelates had intercourse with King and Kaiser; and among the guests who sojourned in the proud monastery was Walter von der Vogelwaide. That this pomp should lead to destruction was but natural, and so the abbots soon gave in their submission to the Bavarian dukes, who repaid the deed by ample favours. The convent was secularised in 1803; a part of its treasures found their way to Munich, others were squandered in the most unpardonable manner.

One cannot indeed recognise nowadays the Tegernsee of olden times. Walls and battlements are destroyed, and the children of the world dwell with their mundane delights where the disciples of the Spirit once wandered. The church alone is in tolerably good order. Above the portal stands yet the stone image of the two founders, who stare down in blank amaze at the trimly attired ladies who come to mass on Sundays. One thing, however, remains unchanged—the beauty of the landscape; this indeed meets our glance with the eyes of eternal youth, as if the earth had not grown older in the space of a thousand years. Of course we miss those grand features which make the Königssee so melancholy and the Walchensee so full of passion; but its countenance is blessed with endless charms. There lies a harmony and a serenity in those outlines which relieve the heart—a beauty which does not exhaust us, but refreshes and constantly charms, because we can constantly endure it. Around, the eye has a wide field of view, but all is within beneficent limits; the mountains are rocky, not rugged, the people honest, not coarse. Many are prejudiced against the Tegernsee because it holds the mean between two extremes; but the mean does not ever signify mediocrity—it signifies more often perfection. In the village itself the houses are huddled close together; their roofs project far into the street and form that long picturesque street so characteristic of mountain architecture. Slim forms with green hats serve as a set-off to them and give to the whole a life-like freshness which we seek for vainly in the plain. On that side, across the lake, the roads are solitary; the high road winds its tortuous course along the bank, o'ershadowed in places by pines, which dip their branches in the waves. Only scattered moorland habitations, from which proceeds a distant barking, lie here at the foot of the mountains; the woods are more dense, the peasants more rude and sullen on that side. If we follow the streams which storm down to the lake yonder, we come soon to a tangled wilderness; lofty masses of stone, which Nature flung down here (when she was yet in her teens), block the way; damp moss and wild brambles stretch across the narrow way, which is only made to bring wood to the valley. Cool and silent blows the wind, the rush of water is the only sound, and the timid bird who has just flown across yon brook the only wayfarer. When the morning dawns, the weasel peeps with curiosity from between the stones and disports itself in the sunlight streaming through the branches. It is best to visit the western bank in the evening, when the road is shaded and the rays of the setting sun yet illumine the houses of the Tegern See. On the one side is seen the broad lake, on the other is pasture-land, where the foals scamper, and in the evening come into the open. Between the peaks on the Bodenschneid peeps the Brecherspitz; the mountains have such a warm tint of blue and the lake lies there as a mirror to their happiness; in the distance there is the panelled church tower of Egern and the little chapel of Riederstein; a little craft slowly winds its way through the blue.

Two villages, Abwinkel and Wiessee, lie on this bank; they possess the oldest houses in the district, hidden in a dense wreath of cherry-trees. Here is the home of the village idyll, where the old man sits at the door and plays with his roguish grandson; here peeps the foal in at the window, and beneath the gable-end hangs the target with countless shots on its black disc. The daughters of the house are on the common land "in the dark pine forest," the sons are in the mountains cutting wood, a deep calm prevails.

The steep road from Abwinkel leads up to the meadow which lies close to the foot of the Kampen. On account of the charms of the road this has become a favourite spot for travellers, who sip their Mocha in front of the house whilst the woodmen sit by their tankard in the spacious chamber. From here the road goes to Länggries and a quantity of unknown footpaths branch off into the interior of the mountains. If we descend the shortest of these, we move across a slope, covered with magnificent maple trees, and come suddenly on the so-called Ringsee—a small, deep bay, which the Tegernsee forms at the mouth of the Weissach. Here it is calm; the reeds stand motionless on the shore; only a single roof stands hidden behind high tree-tops, and even this was long uninhabited, because it was believed to be haunted. It was called "the dead house."

TEGERNSEE.

AMONGST THE MOUNTAINS.

Following the road which leads along the Ringsee, we come in half an hour to Egern or Rottach, where every charm distinctive of mountain scenery enchains the traveller. Behind the church fragrant meadows extend themselves, stretching up to the foot of the Wallberg. Many an ancient lime stands on the plain, and underneath it a weatherbeaten cross hung with withered garlands. If we penetrate deeper into the mountains we find from six to eight houses bearing their own names, and, after a few paces, we stand in the midst of the charming valley of the Rottach. Here also is many a little community—amongst them the charming ranger's house Oberwinkel. By stopping here during the late autumn, when the woods are yellow, one may become acquainted with the old and simple life of the mountain huntsman. At eve the huntsman's "helps" come home, a spacious wallet across their shoulders, from which protrude the shanks of the slaughtered chamois buck; at one side runs the terrier and announces the prey by his barking. Within, however (according to peasant custom), the stove is already heated, and over it a dozen marten skins are stretched for drying. The hunting boy negligently saunters in and hangs his hat on the points of the antlers. Then comes the evening draught and the story of how it went with the chamois buck. All listeners are expectant, the wife of the ranger walks to and fro, and a pause occurs alone when he lights his pipe at the glowing pine-log.

The last house in the valley is the Enterrottachbauer; it is magnificently situated between the rocks of the Bodenschneid and the waterfalls of the Rottach; a saw-mill and a little inn are also here erected. The latter serves as a rendezvous for the peasants of the neighbourhood when they thirst for their evening draught on Sundays; it is here that affairs, both private and public, are discussed, whilst the stray waggoner passing by with his vehicle stops and joins the boon companions. Mine host, however, is a prudent and experienced man, with whom it is well worth while to have a gossip, and who would read his newspaper daily if only he received it every day in the week. Things went much more cheerily still in this spot when his two lovely daughters were alive, whom he lost at the ages of eighteen and nineteen. A dancing booth was then erected in the open, and every evening the musicians came and played their melodies to the lads and lasses; May-dance and Consecration-dance* were held here, and the passers-by could hear the defiant songs at the distance of a hundred paces.

Approaching the Tegernsee from Enterrottacher, the eastern shore displays a line of charming villas. On the green table before the entrance sit elegant girls with their work, a bowl of fresh strawberries or an open novel before them. They peep out inquisitively as we pass by on the road, which conducts us in a few minutes back into the middle of Tegernsee. The natives call it in summer "the Town." The northern bank will be considered by most the attractive part of the lake; there lies Kaltenbrunn, formerly a farm, now belonging to Prince Charles, over which a "*mascula virgo*," a female Grobian, reigned. Kaltenbrunn is the aristocratic promenade of the summer guests of the Tegernsee; but in spite of that, or on that account, it is the most frequented of all. Gmund, through which the Mangfall urges its green waves, lies to the left. Wonderful beech-woods and mills lie on its banks, and isolated

---

* A festival held on each anniversary of the consecration of the parish church.—*Translator*.

houses are scattered round about. This village is important to the landlord on account of its cattle breeding, and to the traveller because in it stands the last milestone before Tegernsee.

The mountains which border the lake are not higher than five or six thousand feet; but they overlook the plain as far as the Danube, and show the glaciers of the Sentis as far as the Tauren. And if no proud cap of snow adorns their summits, yet the Alpine roses bloom, and there is a gladsome bracing air upon their meadows. Through their woods roams the stag, the chamois feeds among their rocks, their sky is more exhilarating than elsewhere. The Tegernsee inspires the idea that Nature had lavished all on her single favourite.

V.
DORF KREUTH AND WILDBAD.

LONG the road rolls the post-cart which conducts us from the Tegernsee across the frontier. Before this is reached, it halts once at a trim and ancient hamlet, surrounded by the mountains on three sides. Towards the south lies the broad flank of the Planberg, to the left the rocks of the Rosstein subside into valley, whilst opposite towers the Leonhartstein. But on the blue and white sign-board past which we drive, is written "Dorf Kreuth."

The houses also here are wide apart, as often happens in the mountains; their brown roofs, with heavy stones, are seen peeping from the dense foliage of the trees. The inn alone has the place of honour on the road, and is portly and well-conditioned, like its owner. Close behind, the green slope ascends to the hill on which the pretty little church with its pointed tower rests; beyond, the forests of the Black Floor.

The little church is a jewel inspiring a rare sentiment of awe. When a wedding approaches it, or when a religious procession bears its banners through the unmown fields, then we feel the secret charm of the little church! But it is most beautiful in the autumn, when the wind blows sorrowfully, when Nature insensibly becomes speechless, and with every leaf a thought falls at our feet.

As the inhabitants of Kreuth live so deep in the mountains, one would be apt to think that the old intrepid type had here in particular maintained itself, even if the culture of the neighbouring baths had not been entirely without its influence.

Among the peasants of the district is one who may almost be described as the Bavarian Faust, for his grief consists in his experience. His is a rarely-gifted nature—resolution of character united with untrammelled reasoning power. In 1848, when he was a soldier, he was offered the rank of officer; had he obeyed the summons, he would now be wearing the epaulettes and commanding a battalion instead of driving his horse to pasture in shirt sleeves. But his appreciation of the natural limits of his nature was more powerful than his desire for success; he has cleverly avoided every office (even in his parish), and lives as *homo sui juris* in civil pride.

The only dignity he assumes is that of master woodcutter. As in this very spot the woods stand thickest, and as a series of the most rugged valleys extend themselves, the whole business of the woodcutters has involuntarily found a centre in Kreuth. This mode of life gains a certain power over every individual who devotes himself to it; and it becomes so much the more powerful the less points of contact it has with the regular life of the rest of mankind; therefore it is that the woodcutters form almost a caste of their own. Day and night, in storm and sunshine, they abide in the depth of the mountains—their shelter is the pine, and their goblet the brook; their trade is almost a battle. To those who have seen the mighty trunk felled; who know how the green pine wrathfully bows itself, how its golden blood drips from the gaping wounds, it appears as if the assaulted tree were alive in its last hour, as if it resisted and were conscious of what was occurring. Its branches, also, are powerful arms, but they are helpless before the armed hand of man. Groaning sinks the fated stem to earth, but leaves its strength as an inheritance to him who felled it. So comes the mighty tree into the possession of those figures which, with bare breast and resounding axe, move through the forest. Far and wide their blows resound; for the axe is a crier, as the old proverb goes. If there were no woodcutters in the mountains their inhabitants would be much more civilised; it is through this medium that the connexion of the people with the original wild spirit of forest life is kept up. In them lies the anti-civilising principle which stamps a mountain people and guards them from being too easily domesticated.

When the regular work is finished and the numerous workmen separate in every direction, a parting festival, the so-called year-day, is celebrated previously. A union has existed for more than fifty years amongst them, and it is for the members thereof that the festival is principally intended, although other guests also obtain entrance. The festival generally takes place in the first week of November; thick fogs and a cold, piercing air prevail already in the mountains when the stately procession mounts to the little church. Grey, ancient men, who began the bold handicraft fifty years ago, follow in the train, or at least take part in the church ceremony with which the festival opens. In the solemn high mass which the curate sings, their comrades who have perished during the past year are first remembered, and then the survivors pray that a like destiny may not befall them.

The superintendents of forests, who assemble on this day from the environs, preside at the festive meal. Their uniform is a grey jacket, their cap nothing more than the green hat with the chamois beard, a distinction yielded to them at the festival. It cannot be maintained that this official is in general much beloved by the mountaineer, because he manages the wood in too calculating a manner and treats the poachers too absolutely; but amongst the woodcutters, whose immediate superiors the forest departments are, a great veneration of the same is to be expected.

The woodcutters are treated very liberally at their dinners, for it is permitted for each man to bring his better half (and not only the lawful better half) with him. Between each course of the meal comes a dance, and when dinner is ended, come the toasts. And even as every fever augments towards evening, so also does the festive fever, which means that excited and jubilant state of mind which seizes all ordinary natures on extraordinary occasions. The woodcutters are besides fiery souls, and if no oil is poured into the fire, beer and brandy are cast upon it without intermission.

After grace, the press in the little hall becomes closer and closer; a murmur passes along the rows; one feels that an event is forthcoming. In what this consists we shall soon see; for suddenly the atmosphere becomes dark and we perceive on the wall a variegated illuminated transparency, upon which

WOODCUTTERS.

the woodmen return thanks to God and their superiors. One of the assembly commands *silentium* in the Ober-Bavarian dialect, and the silence being as far re-established as it generally is, the same individual delivers an excellent speech, which serves as commentary to the illuminated motto. But the orator is our old friend, Dr. Faust, of Kreuth, and officer *in partibus*.

This original and unique scene of merry-making, working with its own resources and satisfied with its own success, has a peculiar charm. Its power consists in the utter absence of a desire for show, of

RELIGIOUS PROCESSION.

attempt at unnatural ornamentation, or departure from its own sphere. As in the mountains they kindle their fire, so here they burn their self-carved transparency, and as they converse with the cuckoo in the boughs, so here they converse with king and fatherland. They know nothing of *suum cuique*, but they practise it.

After the orator of the woodcutters, the forest ranger takes up the word, and thanks his subordinates for services rendered in so arduous and dangerous a calling. The conciliatory power which is evoked by a superior addressing his men benevolently, does not in this case fail in its effect, for universal applause follows the cordial words. Therewith the official and exclusive character of the festival concludes; both parties take leave, and all now proceed to the dance.

Now come the lads from the neighbourhood with their sweethearts, and the wild noise, without which every dance becomes dreary, sounds through all the rooms of the spacious house.

The animation becomes constantly greater, the hats more and more cocked on one side; girls who at first sat on the long bench now sit on the laps of their lovers and allow themselves to be caressed by their rough hands; the enmity of these would be dangerous, considering the massive striking-rings which guard their little fingers. On the heavy silver bosses are stamped figures of Saint Anthony or Saint Benedict, that their intercession may render whole again the head which the ring has broken. Whether such cruelly pious remedies are ever attended with success has yet to be established, but no one will experience any pleasure in ascertaining this in person; a certain caution is, however, very advisable in any case after nine o'clock in the evening. However interesting a situation may appear, it should be viewed at a distance after this hour, for the idyll often rapidly takes a muscular turn, and the pastoral does not always finish so sentimentally as it is described.

As many Tyrolese are employed in cutting wood, coming to Bavaria from the Zillar Thal, the feast assumes on this account a dangerous international character. They are remarkable forms, those tall, broad-shouldered men, whose curly brown hair grows so low down on the forehead, and those quiet, pretty maidens, with a nascent sensuality in their natures, and yet dropping the eyes as modestly as if they bore the Madonna in their hearts as a model. In both, however, there lurks something humble and patient, which is in painful contrast with their magnificent physique; for it afflicts us to find so much power and so little freedom. The Tyrolese have had sufficient patriotism to face death, but not to allow themselves to be educated; they have a certain passive appearance about them which lies like an unconscious pang on the noblest countenances. But even in this woe we miss that sorrowful twitching appearance, which in Ireland or Poland makes itself apparent on many a face; it is a healthy woe, and afflicts the spectator only, not the sufferer. The Tyrolese are pious, but without passion; strong, but without violence; they are fanatical, but their fanaticism dreams only of quiet endurance.

But 1809 was an exception, and the Bavarians have never got over this exception. From this time dates a certain rancour between the two races, which gives vent to itself at every opportunity; and since the entertainment of the Lapithæ, a festival has ever been the best opportunity for a quarrel. It is difficult to decide which party carries off the palm in fisticuffs when the Bavarian and the Tyrolese woodcutters do battle, for it is a combat between Hector and Diomedes. In the war of song, however, the Tyrolese generally remain masters of the field.

Countless songs of defiance, in which the antagonists chant reciprocal insults at each other, lend to this jealousy an intense emphasis, that admits of no climax but a fight.

This is the proper moment to think of our homeward journey; it is better than to make acquaintance with St. Anthony. If we pass through the open house-door, the dark landscape lies open before our glance, the fog has become dissipated; over the Leonhartstein hangs the silver crescent. All is calm; from within alone we hear the noise and the gay melody, which resounds through the illuminated windows.

"Good night, woodcutter!" cries after us an old peasant, who is trying hard to remember the door which is his home.

. *
*

Half-an-hour from this *prædium rusticum* lies Wildbad Kreuth, abounding in the elegancies of a town. Though visited even in the sixteenth century by consumptive monks, it was first fairly started on its career when King Maximilian I. turned his attention to it. Royal and Imperial Majesties promenaded then on the terraces, carriages-and-six with countless retainers clattered on the gravel, and Kreuth became an aristocratic, nay, almost a regal resort. But when the illustrious guests had departed, the homely, affectionate family life, which was the joy and pride of "old Max," entered into full possession of its rights again, and he associated with almost bourgeois benevolence with strangers, whom he treated exactly as if they were his guests. Then the *élite* of the society of Munich was there assembled; concerts and balls, theatres, and excursions of every description succeeded each other in motley variety. Through the generosity of the King the custom was also introduced of affording to a certain number of indigent strangers a free reception; and even now, Prince Charles, the noble inheritor of this generosity, faithfully follows the custom of his father.

The present appearance of the bath has become naturally as much changed as the times.

Concerning the scenery, it is here much more contracted, it is simply confined. We stand in a small ravine-like valley, which looks as if it had been cultivated and bedded out by a landscape gardener; on the west are the long bath-buildings (something between a castle and a barrack); on the south is the

Plauberg, which hangs over our heads in such a threatening manner, that one almost fears to strike it with the brim of one's straw hat or the point of one's umbrella. Seen through the holes of the latter, the scenery of course appears very gloomy, and much more contracted than it otherwise is; but, nevertheless, this is unavoidably the case, often for weeks together. All its surroundings have something monotonous about them.

Early in the morning we find ourselves in the cool whey-hall, where a series of curiosities is exposed for sale; articles made of carved wood, and productions from the neighbouring marble quarry; books, bound in red, on the Bavarian Highlands, and other objects suitable to the occasion. Even the eternal "gossip glove-maker" from the Tyrol will not be missed by any one.

Whilst breakfast is preparing, perhaps a hundred and fifty persons assemble in the neighbouring

WILDBAD KREUTH.

beech-wood to enjoy the solitude of the forest; here also may we read a book from the virtuous library attached to the bath undisturbedly to the end. In the afternoon, the Königsalpe on the Hohlenstein is ascended; if the ascent is too difficult, asses stand ready, and these are soon gladly joined by an anxious guide.

If we stay at home, we take possession of the terrace, for there we can drink our coffee in the shade and keep an eye on the carriages which arrive during the afternoon. On these terraces vegetates the *beau monde*, like costly plants in separate beds; here sit the noble dames who weary their souls in Kreuth, and level their glasses on the noble dames who weary their souls in Tegernsee, and therefore come to Kreuth. If the season is at its height, in July or August, many Russians and North-Germans are to be found. In the garden-chair under the window is rocking the Viennese banker, clad in snowy white, with double watch-chain and the *Neue Freie Presse*. His wife wears a large emerald bracelet, and the rustling of her silken dress appears much more melodious to her than that of forest or rivulet.

At six in the evening there is music, to hear which all assemble. The ladies change their dresses previously, the well-versed stock-traveller returns home from his excursion, and the visitors float up and down in exact time on the "beautiful blue Danube." At the grating, behind which dwells a captive chamois, stand the children and feed the animal, because it is expressly forbidden to do so. To prevent her from showing ingratitude, her dangerous horns are wrapped in matting.

No one will indeed maintain that these figures (the chamois, perhaps, excepted) arouse especial sympathy; yet one may acquire many a friend in Kreuth. Beside the most frivolous mode of life lures a plenitude of intellectual power which disdains to assert itself; behind the threatening atmosphere of brilliant toilettes we often find the bright sunshine of amiability. Only look at the little Swabian girl yonder, how naïvely she talks, how she enjoys the green fields, as if there were no such thing as an emerald bracelet upon earth!

On the open window-sill of his room leans a powerful man, with noble and strongly-marked features; it is a young professor of music, and the paper he holds in his hands is a proof-sheet of his opera score. Whilst he is buried in calm enjoyment, an incessant tinkling is going on in the drawing-room above; for the young countess is learning a new polka-mazurka.

There are other faces in Kreuth whose aspect sinks deep into the heart—those of the really diseased. The inexorable figures of science have established the percentage of life that is swept off by each disease, and here are those whom destiny has chosen as tribute for the whole, upon whose youth her merciless hand has been laid. A fatality is upon their features, and with justice has a poet of genius said of their greeting, "Morituri te salutant."

WOODEN HUT IN THE FOREST.

VI.

IN THE KAISERKLAUSE.

 N the midst of the wilderness lies an immense ranger's house. Above the door are displayed the gigantic antlers; about the window climbs the ivy with its green loops; around the balcony which runs in front of the walls, stand pinks and geraniums.

If we ascend the stone steps, a slim, yellow hound, who acts as door-porter, springs to meet us. His barking announces us at once to his master and resounds along the long passage, in which we find on all sides the trophies of the chase. In the room we perceive a powerful man with a full beard and broad chest, resting his arm comfortably on the table. He also looks like a Nimrod—guns hang on the wall, and three or four terriers repose in a basket near the fireplace and snap at the gnats which fly past.

The room has not the appearance of a bureau, yet it is one; its occupant is the chief ranger of the Kaiserklause. Of course it is no bureau in a bureaucratic sense, for its chief wears stockings and leather breeches, and the while he enters his documents, the woodcutters are singing their ditties. And in truth the large square chamber which lies close to the house door has an extensive jurisdiction—it is at the same time the writing-room, parlour, and dining-room; a strange mixture of bureaucracy and domesticity lies therein and gives to this wilderness a semi-official character. When the quiet ranger's house was built, two good fairies stood by its cradle—Beauty, who gave it her charms, and Solitude, who gave it her peace. And still these two reign here, and those who would make their acquaintance must come here on a bright May morning when the finch sings in the beech-tree, and the children sport round the steps of the house. Yonder sparkle the pinnacles of the Sonnwendjoch in the clear blue of the morning, and opposite is the Wildbach, across whose depths a narrow wooden bridge is constructed. It pours its white foam roaring against the rocks, and forms cool, emerald-green pools, on which the sun glances, and through which the timid trout darts along.

On the little slope which rises above the house stands a little chapel, plain and without pictures. No priest preaches here, no art has contributed to its decoration, but the whole devotion of Nature hangs over it. It is consecrated by a higher hand than that of man, for hill and vale seem conscious of its sanctity. When the sun sinks in summer, one of the inhabitants mounts the lower steps and tolls the bell for vespers.

Then the Kaiserklause is for an instant mute and still; the labourers who sit near the house raise their hats, children and strong men arise from their seats until the last knell dies away. A day of peace finishes with that sound.

The Kaiserklause (the huntsmen call it Valepp) is a proud and magnificent game park. On all sides it penetrates deep into the dark forests, and the simple, wild mountain life lies almost at the threshold of the house. On the rocks of the Rothe Wand and in the "Kahr" roam herds of chamois; beyond, the Stümpling Dyke deer and the mighty stag appear in turns; and above, in the clearings of the woods, the mountain cock calls to his mate, when the snow is yet on the ground and the day has scarce dawned.

The whole existence of the household is that of the huntsman—the whole day long the rangers or their assistants are in the open air to pursue their costly prey, which is often not brought to the ground until after many hours' chase. The poachers, also, who come over from Bayerisch Zell and Fishbachau, are hard at work, and the park with its dense by-ways is only too propitious for them. Of all the vermin which endangers the young fawns, the fox is slaughtered in the greatest numbers; the otter is also indigenous in the wild mountain streams. Of colossal dimensions are the woodlands surrounding the Kaiserklause, for many thousand cords are yearly cut down in them. To afford shelter to the workmen, a magnificent blockhouse is erected near to the ranger's lodge, which contains, above, the undivided dormitory, and below, the common sitting-room, the "drawing-room" of the woodcutters. The huntsmen's assistants also live here, and if in summer there is an overflow of visitors, they are lodged between these woodmen. In the spring the wood is drifted to the valley; the mighty sluices of the stream are opened, and with a wild cry its heaped-up spoil is hurried away. The last pull at the flood-gates is not unfrequently perilous, and the roaring and crushing of the released stream, which has formed quite a lake before its prison, defies all description. From hence the wood is carried to the Tegernsee, to which it is consigned by the Mangfall for further transit.

Thus the usual society which we find in the ranger's lodge is of a very primitive nature—at the most a charcoal-burner or a peasant comes there, going to Brandenburg to bewail his ailments to the resident quack; now and then a painter, or a surveyor. However, all this is only true for quiet times; in the summer it is quite a different affair; the trim ranger's lodge becomes then a dovecot, in and out of which hundreds of illustrious visitors fly. Several chambers of the upper story are suitably fitted for them and provided with all luxuries that careful provision can obtain. Dignitaries of all sorts have resorted here when they came to chase the deer or the mountain cock, and many of their portraits are to be found in a handsome photographic album which has found its way into this wilderness.

The Kaiserklause is ever beautiful, but it is most beautiful at St. Bartholomew. This is its peculiar feast, for it is the anniversary of the patron saint of the little church. On this day is the Consecration feast, and the guests assemble from far and near. In the morning mass is read in the chapel, the only one in the whole year. Gaily adorned, the little procession winds up the narrow steps, a red flag flutters amongst them, and every one wears his holiday attire. Of course but a few enter the low portal, which is hung with garlands; the rested remain grouped in the open air and listen to the tones of the Agnus Dei or the words of the sermon. When the Host arrives the people fall on their knees. These are calmly joyful moments; the brook itself rolls more gently, the beeches themselves cease their murmurs.

Thus ends the spiritual portion of the affair. But after mass come the pleasures of the world with joyful voice and the insolent strength of youth. The musicians lead the procession, which descends from the little church; the lads pull their hats waggishly on one side and the lasses come down with a lighter step than they went up. All sorts of things are going on below; for the entrance of the house has become a bar; great casks stand ready and are broken open with the hammer; forms of lofty stature, carrying their jackets on their shoulders, watch the operation with satisfaction. And in reality there is no time to be lost for the first draught; the dance may commence at any minute; for the latter

a flooring of planks has been laid down. Only a slight tap on the shoulder and the fair maid follows her lad into the tumult with joyful mien. Between approving glances and aggressive hobnail shoes, she steers skilfully; but when a daring youth snatches at the scarlet flowers she wears in her bodice, she quickly casts down her eyes, and vanishes before he is aware of it.

Handsomer lads and lasses than those of the Kaiserklause cannot be found together. From all the pastures the cow-girls descend, if they are young and pretty; the lads also, who cut wood all the summer in the forests, come at St. Bartholomew to the Kaiserklause. Then may the ranger be proud of his men. In long rows they occupy the improvised benches, each one has his maiden on his lap, his plume in his hat, his song of defiance on his lips. If a good friend arrives, he will engage her for one dance or another, but he makes savage jealous eyes at most, that his predilection for one may be more apparent.

As the borders are not far distant, many Tyrolese, with fair forelock and dark broad hat, attend the consecration. They dance slower and more heavily than the Bavarian Highlanders, and bring almost always their treasure (of a sweetheart) "from the Empire," which is better provided with such treasures than with those of another description.

As Consecration comes but once a year, dancing is kept up pretty late; when the stars begin to pale, then return to home is first mentioned. Most of the girls ascend the same night to the pastures from which they came, and the woodcutters go straight away from the feast to their work at four o'clock in the morning.

In the Kaiserklause it becomes quieter and quieter when once St. Bartholomew is over; the season rapidly declines, soon the leaves fall, by night there is icy frost, and with November falls the first snow. This is nothing uncommon; but here the snow is like ice, for like an impassable bar it divides the quiet Klause from the rest of the world. For a short time only does the sun send its greeting into the deep, solitary prison, from which no one can escape, and which no one can reach; and only when it ceases snowing can one think of cutting a way, upon which the wood can be transported to Schliersee or Tegernsee. If the winter is severe, the famished game approach from all sides the feeding-places erected in the depths

CONSECRATION OF A CHURCH IN THE KAISER KLAUSE.

of the forest, though these prove often unapproachable; only in the early hour of the morning, when the snow is still hard frozen, can it be passed on snow shoes—during the day the whole country is impassable. The winter lasts here seven months, and perchance not a single human being has entered the quiet Klause during this time. How strange must Christmas night appear in this state of isolation! How noisily heaves life in great towns on this evening, and here nought but snow, benumbed pine-trees, and the sparkling stars of a winter night!

THE SPITZINGSEE.

VII.

ON THE SPITZING.

BETWIXT Schliersee and the Kaiserklause runs a narrow mountain-pass called the Spitzing. As the road mounts to the height of almost four thousand feet, we find the lower ranges on either side of the way, and even the wild roses luxuriate close to it; the whole of mountain life, with its diversity and silent charm, descends here almost to the road.

In the midst of this secluded world lies a little lake of melancholy aspect, almost always dark, yet almost always transparent. Its mountains are not savage, its character has nothing of storm and nothing of grandeur; if passion is wanting, we see a grief in its features which our thoughts follow, and which fetters us as a glance from darkly beautiful eyes. We love to dwell on its banks: we might almost exclaim, with the poet—

"Rest on me, thou darksome eye!"

A garland of flowers blooms around the shore, but they adorn the brow of a mourner, who rejoices not in May-time, and exclaims to Spring herself—

"Serious is Spring! . . . ."

No house stands on the shore of the Spitzingsee; only a lowly hut is erected under the pines which clothe the southern edge. There resided until lately an ancient couple, celebrated conversationally by their jargon, and in writing by Meister Steub. As the State placed obstacles to their marriage, they followed the course of circumstances, and lived together unmarried in the lonely mountain-valley. This lasted for years and tens of years, and if they had performed the marriage ceremony, the silver one would have been already long celebrated. Man must, however, make himself useful upon earth. The old people found this out; and, in consideration thereof, their calling in life was to seek roots and make brandy of them. In a secret chamber the mysterious beverage was brewed; peer and peasant sought after it; and when their heads were inflamed with it, the old woman sat before her hut, like a witch, and congratulated herself on the evil deed.

Just as a charcoal-burner is always sooty, so must a liquor-distiller be always drunk. It belongs to the craft; and this pseudo-husband laid especial stress on the fact that he himself was the best customer for his liquor. One could see he was responsible in the matter, his face guaranteed the quality of the stuff. What he left was sold to the wild woodcutters, or to inquisitive gentlemen, who came in great numbers to this romantic spot. So it came to pass that speculation introduced itself into the quiet idyll, and the little hut soon got a name.

The personal element has, of course, changed since the "gaffer" departed this life. He was almost eighty years old, and, as *postillon d'amour*, has gone before us to eternity. Were the world not so ungrateful, she would plant a gentian-flower on his grave. His grey-headed wife has returned to the Ziller Thal to enjoy "well-earned repose."

Nevertheless, the firm which these two have founded in the wilderness yet flourishes in undiminished splendour. In the place of the old woman, two fine young girls appeared, who likewise came from the Ziller Thal, and, under the ægis of a real or nominal mother, carry on the brandy trade. They are true Tyrolese girls, of that pliant disposition which is at the same time so obliging and yet so timid, which evinces such ardent desire and yet seems so modest. When asked what they do the whole day, they reply, "We dig for roots;" and when asked for the bill of fare, they smile seductively. The inhabitants of the Spitzing hut have bought for themselves the right of collecting roots and valuable herbs, which they employ in making spirits. It is evident that the attainment of these is physically very fatiguing. At the first peep of day the maidens arise, and, in order to cover a greater extent of country, each goes her own way, often many leagues apart from the other.

The stores which they take with them from home are not extensive. They consist of a broad basket, a sharp hatchet, which serves both as tool and weapon, and a modest dinner.

So traverse they the broad and darksome State forests, in which many thousand acres have never yet been touched by the axe. So move they along the still, sloping meadows, where the huts hang like nests on the rocks, and the fairest flowers are plucked only by the cattle. Here and there are found pools of water on the heights called "Tümpl," or "Gümpl." They lie in a narrow ravine, and look like craters originated by former volcanic action, which have become filled with water in the lapse of time. On this account they are often of fearful depth. Dense creepers crown the precipitous banks, over whose mirror projects the rock upon which the mountain-bird twitters; on the ground lie rotten and massive pine-trunks; large fish ascend from the depths and disport themselves in the sun; hither comes the stag in the summer-night and quaffs the refreshing cordial.

The flora of the Alps also luxuriates the most voluptuously in such a spot. Many a costly plant blooms on yon brink, but at the peril of life is the hand extended over the calm, deceptive waters. Round the banks of such lakes a wreath of secrets is oft wound, and many a dim saga rests in the cups of these flowers.

Because a *natural* force is concealed in the root, men have been induced to locate a *miraculous* force in it; and many a herb which sprouts from it was accounted a magic herb. The superstition of by-gone times has filled up whole books with such receipts, intended to relieve not only maladies, but desires of every sort. We recommend to those who would consider this subject more closely, the "Krauterbuch von 1687."

It is in truth a solitary, almost engulfed life, this filing day after day through the woods, as these two girls do, only looking at the leaves on the ground. No sound is heard; only the lizard rustles on the sun-lit earth, whilst the squirrel swings in the branches. And yet this calling has its charm, for one approaches the inner life of Nature so near; intercourse with beautiful surroundings acts on the character. Many a trait in the character of the mountaineer is to be thus accounted for; striking delicacies of expression are borrowed from such fine, acute intuitions alone.

Before, when the old couple yet ruled the hut, it was inhabited even in the winter. Now a sort of

season is introduced; for at the end of November the two girls depart together, with their chaperon and a male who is termed the "host." They spend the winter in the Ziller Thal. Hundreds of the natives of this charming valley follow the same custom, leaving home *during* summer to seek for employment; whole families are dissipated in this fashion. Some earn their bread as mechanics or carpenters, others by working on the roads and railways. Why should not the speciality be conceded to them of brewing schnaps on foreign soil?

Some summers the Bavarian Highlands are overflowed with Tyrolese, mostly from the Ziller Thal.

When a country feast is celebrated, they have their own table in the inn, their own "lasses" (for almost more women come than men), and they sing their ditties, each on his own account.

When May comes, the peregrination begins anew; then the root-hut on the Spitzingsee is again peopled. It is true that in May it is not yet spring there, for the lake wears yet a coat of ice a foot thick, even whilst the cowslips are blooming in the valley.

He who has seen only knows what masses of snow are accumulated there in winter. Between Schliersee and the Spitzing hut, at all events, a road is excavated through thousands of fathoms which have been carried down. Between Valepp and Spitzing, on the other hand, the snow stands like an impenetrable wall, from ten to twelve feet high and a league thick.

In the early morning only, when it is hard frozen, dare one travel on snow-shoes; the road lies the depth of two men beneath the traveller. Over the summits of the trees, over the roofs of the huts which border on the way, he glides along. He who sinks is lost.

Thus we experience one of the most remarkable contrasts if we ascend in May from Schliersee to the Spitzingsee. Below us, in the warm valley, the trees are already green, and the air has that mild tone without which we cannot imagine spring. And then the heights. Here the gray

GOAT PASTURE.

and naked rocks stare us in the face; here lies the smooth snow-field and the icy surface of the lake.

No bird sings, no bud is opening here. Then may we know what desire for spring is when winter and spring are placed in such close juxtaposition. No one sings in winter. One longs for a clear human voice; and when the first hurrah sounds above here, it is not only a signal of joy but a token of deliverance. But only men feel this joy; o'er the landscape remains a melancholy shadow. "Serious is Spring."

SCHLIERSEE.

VIII.

THE SCHLIERSEE.

HE road from Spitzing to Schliersee is a steep, tortuous mountain road. To the left stand the ragged rocks of the Brecherspitze, to the right the Jägerkamm, with its dark pine-wood; far below, the valley, overgrown with short Alpine grass, and choked up by mighty boulders. Solitary huts lie there in the basin; we hear the tones of the Alpine bells, we feel the coolness which even in the afternoon is experienced in the dark blue shadow of the Brecherspitze. Its peaks are so close that a gunshot might reach them, and we see with the naked eye the chamois who climb about on them. Still and solitary are the roads here; only the red cross stands on the road, where the huntsman's lad takes off his hat reverentially as he passes by.

At the next bend which the road makes we look down on the Schliersee; its small blue flood lies smiling between woods and meadows. Passing by a shady mill we reach the southern bank, where the little church of Fischhausen and the frontier station "Neuhaus" stands. Here opens out the Leizachthal, and the Wendelstein lies in marvellous blue, with its charming outlines and legendary beauties. These cannot be passed by; you are spell-bound to look closer into the light green valley and the misty pastures which shine down from its summit.

Then we first come upon the narrow road which leads along the lake into the pleasant hamlet. It is one of the most genuinely charming in the Bavarian mountains; but one does not at once perceive that it can claim historical pretensions. Many indications point to that time when the Romans possessed the ancient Rhætia, and in others we find the remains of the ancient German days. For the mouldering walls which peep through the firs were once a stately baronial castle. Above these, in their rocky nest, sat the Counts of Moxelrain and the Lords of Waldeck; the bumpers went round the oaken table, and the fierceness of the times was reflected in the fierce features of those figures. However, the dear, quiet valley was not a fair field for strife, so the knights moved soon against Miesbach, and established there their predatory domicile. Other "lords," who wore, not the coat of mail, but the cowl, settled down by the blue wave; but the residence did not suit them either. They returned to Munich, to the monastery of Our Lady, and were spared the grief of witnessing how the Reformation pressed forward even to the Schliersee. Thus we have here the whole splendid apparatus from which to compose a very respectable representation of the Middle Ages; heretics and monks, robber-knights and helots, yes, even hunger-towers, where faithless spouses were immured.

Long, long after the Middle Ages came the "good old times." We mean by that those innocent and gladsome days when young artists first began to *discover* the mountains, when the brutality of the past had become extinct and the scepticism of modern times had not yet arisen. Not only peace, but a love of peace prevailed, and in this happy epoch fell the rule of "la donna del lago."

The Schliersee is as much entwined with this name as Weimar is with that of Charles Augustus, or Padua with that of Saint Antony; the Schliersee is not to be thought of without "Fisher Betty." Young painters came then in crowds from Munich: Monten and Ott, Gail and Peter Hess, Stieler, and many others. In the homely inn which lay opposite the peninsula they took up their quarters, and painted a magnificent sign-board before it, representing "Fisher Betty" in a slender skiff. Above the signboard was inscribed, "Alla donna del lago." The rule of "Fisher Betty" was very patriarchal for the rest, both by water and land; she levied few contributions, as the guests paid only what seemed good to them; no police regulations disturbed the general enjoyment; no administrative arrangements obstructed the genial individual. And he who would inscribe a verse in the visitor's book enjoyed full liberty of the press.

Thus "Fisher Betty" gradually acquired a name known throughout all Germany, and when she died some years ago, the *Allgemeine Zeitung* considered it necessary to mention the fact to its readers. The period connected with her name was indeed laid in its grave long before herself. The world is now too knowing and too pretentious to bask in the clear sunshine of the village idyll; life is become too complex and artificial for men to devote themselves to the undivided enjoyment of nature; all the force of enjoyment and comprehension is turned upon those objects against which the great stream of time hurls us; no sentiment or thought remains for quiet contemplation. The modern life of visitors who seek their summer outing in Schliersee is not different from elsewhere, only the time is perhaps somewhat more *allegretto*, for the piano in the comfortable eating-room scarcely ever gets a holiday. "Alpensängers" who come from Munich to Schliersee, instead of the reverse, frequently make the country insecure, and the taste for mountain excursions is so much developed that people ascend even the steps at the entrance with great sticks. The *ensemble* of Schliersee must be sought on the northern bank, perhaps on the highest point of the Mierbach road, and if it charm no one by the grandeur of its outlines, yet it displays to us a greater perfection of loveliness than any other corner in the mountains. Particularly charming is the contracted foreground which the hamlet Schliers, the woody prominence of the peninsula, and the slim church of Westenhofen form. Between these and the mountains of the background, which allow a view of the Spitzingstrasse and the distant Sonnwendjoch, lies the little lake full and unconcealed before our eyes.

Not less pleasing appears the landscape if we ascend to the little chapel which lies hard by the post. At our feet lie the roofs of the pretty hamlet, the sound of bells ascends to us, and all the beauty which we survey is so close! Here indeed may we dream away an hour in the clear sunshine, or in the evening, before the light flees beyond the mountains, and if the hoarse puff of the locomotive, which has subdued this quiet valley a year since, do not arouse us, we might unconsciously deem it were the old times with their solitude and calm existence!

In the little church of Fischhausen, which lies at the end of the Schliersee, a feast is celebrated in the autumn which calls to mind times passed by. It is dedicated to Saint Leonhart, who is the patron saint of cattle, and therefore a great authority in the mountains. His portrait hangs in front of each stable door and displays the saint with uplifted crozier; at his feet are, to the right, a foal, and, to the left, a sick ox. For these as patients Saint Leonard is summoned as physician in ordinary; but as

THE "LEONHARTSFAHRT."

nowadays all are specialists, his assistance is not so much required. He has multiplied by himself and is adored in many localities with a different object: here he is specially famed for horses, there for cows, and in other places (as a child-doctor) for calves.

The "Leonhartsfahrt," however, forms his day of honour, and it is in Fischhausen, more than elsewhere, that it is beautifully performed.

It takes place on a Sunday, late in the autumn, when all visitors have long quitted the mountains and the solitary sun shines alone on the fields.

Deeper than before is the blue of the Wendelstein on these days; he is the king among the mountains, and like a golden crown shines the many-tinted wood. The atmosphere is then brilliant and transparently clear, the meadows are mown short, and only the timid gentian discloses its latest buds.

Then it becomes suddenly lively before the little church on the Schliersee. Fine waggons, crowned with plaits of pine-branches and harnessed with powerful horses, approach from all sides. Above their collars waves a red cloth; in the waggon itself sits the master with his mate in Sunday attire. Those who cannot produce a four-in-hand come with a pair or a simple one-horse vehicle, wherein there is room enough for both man and wife. The servant drives neighing horses; others approach mounted, and amicably call upon their stallion not to obstruct the ancient rite. The cattle also, returned from the pastures, are in many parts brought to the Leonhartsfahrt, and the shepherdess in trim bodice who drives them wears an extra bunch of flowers to-day on her pointed hat.

Before the procession is held, there is a solemn mass; the clear voices of children and the full tones of the organ swell from the little church, whilst the crowd stands before the open doors in quiet devotion. The blue and cloudless Brecherspitze looks down, the blue surface of the lake lies yonder, clear as a mirror, and glistens through the branches of the primeval lime which o'ershadows the church.

After divine service the "course" commences; each waggon drives round at a rapid trot three times, and devotion is transformed into curiosity as to whether the abrupt turn will be made by each. Waggons and postilions are mixed up pell-mell, the arches of leaves which are erected over the vehicle and enframe the passenger, shake with the commotion, the variegated peunants which adorn the two sides of the waggon flutter in the breeze, and many a passing word, many a greeting, flies among the motley throng.

The stalls also, which to-day are erected under the lime-tree, filled with spiritual and temporal trifles, are industriously visited; the fair peasant girls purchase here their silken neckerchief and take also a sugar-drop for the *filius naturalis*. At last the chequered crowd disperses. After the Leonhartsfahrt there is a dance in the "Neuhaus;" old and young are here collected, and only an ancient female still sits near the sunny church wall. How mild the air is; how the sunlight delights her weary eyes! The withered leaves fall from the lime like a message sent to her by Autumn.

Yonder resound the fiddles; her grandchildren are there at the dance. She listens; it is the same old melody which once was played to her—which was once her marriage dance; but that was long ago, and those who then led her to the dance are long dead. All, all are gone; only hill and valley remain from those times, also the ancient lime. So thinks the old woman, whilst the faded leaf falls upon her faded hands, and whispers,

"Do but wait, soon
Thou too shalt rest."

THE WENDELSTEIN, SEEN FROM JOSEPH'S THAL.

IX.

FISCHBACHAU AND BAYERISCHZELL.

A NARROW little road, which cannot lead us astray, leads through the valley of the Leizach. Entrusting ourselves to its guidance, we wander along a broad green valley, bordered by marshy meadows and overlooked by the lofty Miesing and the Trondn, the Geitaueraibl and the broad Seeberg. The end of the valley is formed by the craggy Wendelstein, which is not indeed like the Almighty, all-seeing, but is, at any rate, all-seen. Upon the windy plain, extending beyond Munich as far as the Danube, the pointed pyramid of the Wendelstein overlooks the country for miles and miles; but one may hear him from a greater distance than one can see him, for the "Song of the Wendelstein" has an almost world-wide reputation.

It is prudent to walk over this little road in the cool of the evening, because it is very hot at noontide, and seems as long again after sunset. One is tolerably certain not to meet figures to disturb our peace of mind; there comes at the most a party of pilgrims from Birkenstein or a Paterfamilias enjoying his patriarchal summer outing in this valley.

Now and then a peasant, with bare breast and a scythe on his shoulders. He saunters along the valley to the left, for there is the mighty iron hammer of the Oppenrieder, whose distant stroke resounds through the whole valley; no brutalised pair wait there to receive the pious lad.

Only a few villages meet us on the way on this pilgrimage; and as nobody as yet knows anything of Hundham and Ellbach, so it is all the easier for Bayerischzell and Fischbachau to make a name for themselves. Both date back to ancient times and drew their origin from the conscientious scruples of the pious Countess Haziga. When the latter desired to erect a quiet retreat in the wilderness, Fischbach and the Bavarian Zell were looked on as means for "pious objects," and were only then emancipated when later times cleared aside the convent ruins.

Not far from this lies Marbach, a mansion of ancient reminiscences. In modern terminology, however, nothing is left but a simple and solid inn; the race of Hafner, however, which resided there, is now only represented by a single daughter.

No one can dispute the saying that the pure mountain customs are especially indigenous in Fischbachau; parsons and rangers share respectively the highest spiritual and temporal dignities. The taste for music also lies deep in the blood of the people; the greater part of those charming pastoral songs which one hears in the mouths of the people are native in Fischbachau, whose inhabitants call themselves for brevity Fischbäcker (boorish dialect for Fischbacher). Now the Fischbäcker meadows are praised; now the bells and the maidens. How charmingly *naïve* are those lines which bewail the waters of the Leizach,

PASTURE ON THE WENDELSTEIN.

because they depart black from this glorious valley; how insolently gay are those which the poacher sings on the mountains!

Generally speaking, Fischbachau and Bayerischzell are visited by but few strangers, and even these touch only in transit, because the inns are of rather a primitive description. Those who are not to be alarmed by these circumstances may enjoy uncommonly cheap fare there, and for six kreutzers pass a very tolerable night. But in spite of this undisturbed solitude, which is so favourable to the preservation of ancient customs, much here also has undergone a change—even the choir of singers is smaller than it used to be. In such cases people are always ready to cite the gravity of the times; but the phrase is a little too high-sounding to be applied to their roundelays. We must seek the reasons nearer (or deeper if you will); we must see if aught is changed in the mountains—if a murrain, a shower of hail, an epidemic, a parson, or a justice of the peace has intervened or not. And in reality rumour speaks of something of the latter sort. It is said that a clergyman, who was of opinion that in heaven one took pleasure in nought but litanies, and that a hurrah was as distasteful to the Almighty as it was to himself, worked zealously against the pastoral singers, and as the latter thought that he must understand these things best, his wish became a command.

"Les extrêmes se touchent." Quite close to the place which adorns the little church of Birkenstein exists a glorious fisticuff meeting; people not only sing, they thrash each other to music. Forty years ago this was arranged quite according to programme—quite a formal tournament was held; but as my lord priest cut short the delights of music, so my lord magistrate abolished the pleasures of boxing.

GIRL IN THE BALCONY.

But as poison can only be cured by poison and enemies only overcome with their own weapons, he appealed at last to the lictors who disposed of the rods of the county court of Miesbach, and chased the devil by Beelzebub—the cudgels by cudgels. This picture has in the mean time become so immoral, that we must decline a closer description, although many a striking phrase may thereby be lost.

It was impossible to extirpate entirely the ancient custom, for (as the French say) "On revient toujours à ses premiers amours." But the regular old "go" which existed has disappeared, and occurs only in rare instances. Those who desire to assist nowadays at a capital "scuffle" as of old, must have peculiar luck; for the rule has become the exception, and the far-famed expression, "Now for fun ; to-day yet another must be off," is so intimidated by the penal code, that it has almost departed into the regions of fable.

Thus we find in the valley of the Leizach all which lends a charm to existence, if we do not look too closely at it. On the mountains, lovely scenery; in the valleys, lovely maidens; on week-days, a green and elevated field, which is well worth cultivating; and on Sunday, skittles, guitar, and a "row."

What wonder, then, that each native is attached to his home by a thousand ties? And, in fact, no other mountain race loves in an equal measure the globe where he was born: home-sickness for the Wendelstein is often as painful as home-sickness for Dachau.

LANDSCAPE ON THE MANGFALL.

X.

TO MIESBACH.

IF we go from the valley of the Leizach towards the north, the country suddenly loses its rugged and mountainous character; it becomes level and pleasing, and stretches easily towards the blue peaks, which redound to its adornment and not to its misery. The country in which we stand is already termed the Vorland.

Before we visit Market Miesbach, one of the most famous spots in this domain, let us be permitted a rapid glance at its environs. Through the valley which stretches before our eyes, the Mangfall sends its green waves, broad forests on either side; but on the heights towers a castle, with long, uninhabited rows of windows. Thus there is Weyarn, Altenburg, and, above all, the magnificent Castle Valley.

The race which dwelt here belongs to one of the most ancient in Bavaria, for the Counts of Valley are traced in the earliest history of Wittelsbach. At any rate, a family must be of very ancient stock to become extinct (*cum laude*) A.D. 1238.

The aristocratic significance, the historical scope of such castles is naturally lost in the course of time. As the owners cannot be at all castles at the same time, the personal nimbus falls aside, and only the economic side remains. They form now more the centre of great agricultural estates, and have nothing more to do than pay a good rental. A taciturn bailiff dwells in the wide ground-floor; the heavy-laden harvest-waggon rolls through the yard, and the vats of the brew-house simmer audibly when the winter beer is brewing for the landlord of the neighbourhood. No sign of life is discovered of the old lords who once ruled, and the images of whose ancestors stand on high there in the solitary passages, unless when the peasants remark, with a shrug of the shoulders, "They're going their rounds, up there in the castle."

If we enter Miesbach itself, we meet with an unadorned but solid comfort; this prevails in the inn "Beim Waizinger," of ancient fame, in the official and semi-official personages who take their meals there, and even in the abode of the summer visitors, who become yearly more numerous. To sum up, a decided taste for good living, not to be despised by the stranger, exists in Miesbach.

A new and interesting feature has entered into the physiognomy of the Market through the great coal-beds which have been discovered here and at Schliersee. For, sauntering along the road on Sundays,

MIESBACH.

we meet everywhere the slim miners in their picturesque costume, Belgians and French, Silesians and Poles. The Miesbach railway (which has now assaulted Schliersee also) owes its existence to the transport of coal. In summer there are long rows of carriages, but in winter one may with ease experience the pride of being the only passenger. One has then, for one-and-twenty kreutzers, the kingly feeling of having a special train!

The natives of Miesbach naturally belong to the pure old mountain race; yet nowhere more than here have the peculiarities of the same become so smoothed down; the town element becomes constantly superior to the country element, through active trade, and absorbs the costume, the dialect, and the rudeness of the latter. The wearers of knee-breeches in Miesbach are certainly come over from Schliersee or Fischbachau; also in the hat-shops one sees more black hats than green.

Nevertheless, Miesbach serves still as a type of Upper Bavarian manners and customs; indeed, it has lent its name to all which concerns them. Even now the hat with the black-cock's feathers is called a "Miesbäcker hat," and the entire mountain costume "the Miesbäcker dress." That both are gradually disappearing is not the fault of the inhabitants, but lies in the natural development of things, which no reasonable being will impugn. If only the ancient and pure mode of life becomes not extinct, the Miesbäckers are still in a very good way.

FRAUENWÖRTH.

XI.

THE CHIEMSEE.

BEHIND Rosenheim a series of smiling pictures soon open themselves to those who rush along the railway; if they are mere clearings in the woods, glances through the mighty forests, along which the railway embankment is piled up, they suffice to assure one in passing that far below a mighty and extended sheet of water stretches itself, bordered by graceful hills, covered with wood and turf, and over which mighty mountain summits and ridges erect themselves—a prospect as surprising as it is lovely; so lovely, that, ensconced in our carriage and waking from sleep, we might easily light upon the idea that we were rushing past the banks of the Würmsee or Starnberger-see, so famed for their peculiar charms. The deception does not, however, last long; for along with the comparison which involuntarily impresses us the following distinction is apparent:— the Würmsee is resplendent with villages and country-seats, castles and towers, which announce that an active and powerful race have chosen these fair banks and those heights for their home. On the bank of this lake, on the other hand, it is so solitary that not even a footpath leads round it, and that the two human abodes which one perceives at either end of its basin have withdrawn themselves timidly on the cliff; no skiff, no stroke of oar disturbs its majestic mirror; as one passes by a strip of moorland, no other sound is heard but the cry of a bird, no other movement but that of a vulture which slowly flies across. There also is a sort of virgin land, of which we speak. Though it may sound strange, there exists in the centre of Bavaria a not less fine district of land and more adapted for culture and profit, which allures the settler by every charm, and has not been discovered either by landlord, manufacturer, or philosopher. The lake of which we speak, and which is an interpolation in the journey on the Chiemsee, as here in these pages, is called the Simssee, a pearl of landscape beauty yet slumbering in its shell, an unpolished diamond, which will perhaps, at no distant period, find its place in the jewel-casket; for Industry will not long delay to open up the stores and treasures which contented Agriculture here leaves disregarded; she will lay a road along the lake for her behoof, and on this, close behind her, and veiling and compensating for her ruthless footsteps, will well-to-do Comfort make her joyful entrance.

With these meditations we pass by Endorff (so called because for some years it attempted to rival the Passion Plays of Ammergau), and the plains are reached where the blue waters of the Chiemsee extend themselves; this is the largest of the Bavarian lakes, which, although at one time it must have been considerably larger, and have filled for leagues around the neighbouring moors and fens, yet it still has a very respectable extent, for it is four leagues long and three broad, and has a circumference of fourteen leagues. Coming from the road, one gets a comparatively inferior view and impression; even on the railway-station one is scarcely better off, for the hamlet Prien and its houses suddenly starting up, offer no view of the lake; one must undertake a little promenade to arrive at the bank. This is done gladly, for we pass through beautiful landscapes and fair woods; and the departure from Prien does not afflict us, for it has not yet mastered the opposition between town and country, and remains an unrefreshing mediocrity. Formerly, when we travelled on the Salzburg road, we were more fortunate; there is a slope, from which the entire glorious panorama suddenly displays itself: the magnificent foreground of verdant land, where the dark moors form a beneficently darker tint, relieved by the bright towers and castle-walls; behind, the country, gradually swelling into hills, stretches out from the mountain-chain in magnificent extent; from the majestic Stauffen, the Hochgern and Hochfelln, and, above all, the Kampenwand, with its fantastic crooks and peaks, around which the legend loves that her flowers should twine.

It is glorious to sail along the lake; and those who desire a treat in views, ought now to secure this treat, for the islands vie with each other in opportunities.

The friend of comfort finds in a trim steamboat accommodation for this journey; those who love the primitive can be rowed along in one of the fast-disappearing hollow trees. These are skiffs hollowed out of a single great oak, which, of course, appear somewhat narrow and strange to those who are not accustomed to them; but they have this inestimable advantage, that they do not upset in the most violent storm. This is no slight advantage upon waters where the tempest displays a violence which gives it a well-founded claim to be termed a sea. Many fair spots upon the bank hospitably invite those making the tour of the coast to a visit, such as the pleasant Seebruck, at the end of the lake, where the Alz discharges itself; or, farther inland, Grabenstüdt, once situated on the lake; or Kloster Seeon, now transformed into a bath; or one of the numerous strongholds and castles, of which glorious mention is made in their own proper place.

The lake has two islands, named after the abbeys or convents founded by the Duke of Bavaria, Thassilo II., dethroned and imprisoned by Charlemagne on account of his indomitable aspirations for independence. On the larger one, the Lords' Island, stood a monastery, which was even the seat of a bishop, and whither Thassilo had summoned the learned Greek monk Dobda, in order to found a school, a sort of institute for the nobility; on the Ladies' Island a nunnery stood, in which was prepared a spiritual refuge for princesses and other noble ladies. All is long vanished and changed. Upon the Lords' Island stands only a portion of the convent buildings, reconstructed in rococo style; the church,

A HAUL OF FISH.—CHIEMSEE.

which was said to have been very handsome, is transformed into a brewery. The Ladies' Island has, on the contrary, been more fortunate; it has preserved its ancient, strikingly solemn church, with its gloomy vaults and naves, and its peculiar porch; and in the convent (restored by King Louis I.) nuns again reside; they keep an educational establishment, not now for noble families, but for the daughters of the neighbouring opulent citizens, farmers, and officials, who still are of the opinion that girls who are to be wives and mothers are best brought up for this calling by ladies who have quitted the world because, whatever their reasons, they desired not to fulfil their calling, which they consider inferior to pious solitude.

In visiting the Chiemsee one cannot avoid the discussion as to which of the two islands is the

FISHER COTTAGES AT FRAUENWÖRTH.

more lovely. One is dragged into the controversy, which is at times not less violently waged than that as to whether Schiller or Goethe is the greater poet. And the settlement of the dispute is quite as easy as in this case—it needs only the trifle that the question be precisely stated before commencing the argument, and that it be agreed upon in what sense that most ambiguous of all words, "beautiful," be understood. Considered in itself, the Lords' Island can only make good its pretensions thus: it is so large, that it contains in its interior so rich a variety of meadows, gardens, and fields, of woods, hills, and valleys, that one must walk for hours to make its circuit; and that in this promenade through the beauties of meadows and woods, which are scarcely anywhere else found in this condition of entirety, one may completely forget that one is on an island. Herrenwörth is a little isle in itself; the little Ladies' Island, the narrow strip of land which can be gone through in a half-hour, with its pair of lime-trees and fisher cottages, cannot compete with it; it is impossible to take a walk in it. There can be, therefore, only two reasons which formerly caused Frauenwörth to be so much lauded: an ideal and a real. The ideal was this, that the Ladies' Island, lying a little farther back, offered a somewhat more extended circle of view of the mountain ranges; the real was, probably, that here the view lay, as it were, before one's nose; whereas, on the Lords' Island, one had to walk well nigh a league to enjoy the prospect from the Steinwand or Paulsruhe; but this was so much the more lovely, that the position of the spectator was more elevated, and therefore more favourable. This circumstance has certainly had its influence also, that Count Hunoltstein, the proprietor of the Lords' Island, lives in Paris; and though he allows his steward to prepare entertainment, yet he by no means permits an inn for the special purpose; whilst upon the Ladies' Island, in the time of its bloom, a fair couple were hosts, who became soon an attraction and centre for painters in their excursions, and where the latter, physically well looked after, brought forth a world of that wit and genial humour which has been the incentive to much noble vigour, and to which many a fair creation owes its origin. All this is also changed! The handsome pair, Philemon and Baucis, in the shape of hosts, are long ago gone to their rest; the fine, handsome daughters are married to painters, who (as Haushofer) principally owe their fame to pictures of the Chiemsee. The once so merry artists' inn has been sold, but the genius that once furnished cannot be sold with it: it has vanished like the spirit; and in the very insipid and ordinary inn we see the remains, the sign-board, and the pictorial "Rhyme Chronicle," begun by Frederic Lentner. It is fortunate for Genius, that in the moment of composition he suspects not what hands will hereafter finger the work of his fair creative hours, what eyes will gape over it! Had Lentner and his companions seen the verses and drawings which have been tacked by posterity on to these outpourings of their hearts, had they seen the tourists who turn over and criticise the book, the "Chronicle" would never have been written, or would have fallen to the lot of the last survivor, with the injunction to commit it again to the fire, the element from which it sprang.

Nevertheless, it is not to be denied, that if much is changed, and that not advantageously, that in the main it has remained the same, viz., the unapproachable pomp and glory of Nature, the beauty of the lake, as of the surrounding mountain ranges, whose contours unfold new charms with every shade of colouring. The Ladies' Island also, which, on nearing it, looks like a little castle built in the water, offers delights which are incomparable for quiet minds; those who possess an eye and a heart for a pleasant and dreamy existence; who make themselves at home in the picturesque and yet so simple fishermen's houses, and learn to know the yet simpler, frugal, and yet contented life of their inhabitants, may discover the realisation of an idyll, difficult to find elsewhere. An evening under the great lime-tree of the inn, viewing a fine sunset, or a moonlight night, is a jewel worthy to be preserved constantly in the depths of the soul.

A third Wörth in the lake is the Vegetable Island, tolerably equidistant from both the larger islands, for which it is said to have served as a common kitchen-garden. So the legend will have it, which, besides, spins many a yarn regarding the association between the two shores. What we hear related on the Hellespont of Hero and Leander is here repeated of a monk, who nightly swam backwards and forwards from his convent to visit his beloved in the nunnery, till a jealous associate discovered these nocturnal journeys, and extinguished the light in the cell of the bold swimmer which served him as a guiding star, so that, returning, he sank to the cold, deep bottom, and cooled and extinguished his warm heart for ever.

That the lake was once larger has been already mentioned: it once stretched undeniably from Grassau to Seeau, and from Prien to Erlstätt; yet it is intended still farther to reduce its size by deepening the

Alz, which flows out of it; an undertaking which would not only turn the neighbouring fens and marshes into fruitful land, but also lay bare considerable useful tracts of land; this is so much the more to be recommended, that the existing surface of water amounts to 24,000 tagwerks (Bavarian), and consequently can well bear a diminution, and that the beauty of the landscape would not be hereby in the least injured, for the mountains, and the watery foreground in front of them, would still afford space enough to reflect their peaks, forests, and snowy summits.

THE CHIEMSEE.—VIEW OF THE LORDS' ISLAND.

KÖNIGSSEE.

XII.

ON THE KÖNIGSSEE.

TWO roads lead to the Königssee; the shorter, from Salzburg, past the ancient monastery of Berchtesgaden, with its inexhaustible salt-springs; one, somewhat longer, but remarkable for a high degree of beauty, has its exit at Reichenhall, then mounts the roaring Salach to where the road to Unken and Schneitzelreut branches off, and steeply climbs the Lattengebirge to Schwarzbach-Wacht, and on the other side descends into the charming valley of the Ramsau. The peaceable little village, whose houses, lying under the mighty maples round the church above, look like a troup of children pressing round their mother, invites to rest, and offers in the essentially mountain-tavern good and cheerful quarters; unless indeed it happens that the artists of Munich have requisitioned every corner and every bed. There reigns here still the old tone of honest good temper; for the tourist swarms stop not here, and view the country only from the coach. It is, however, a most peculiar little tribe residing here; incredibly simple, and so shut up among themselves, that, a short time ago, no stranger could marry here; and the four districts into which the valley is divided have for a long time kept themselves quite isolated. It is asserted that the Ramsauers are descendants of scattered Romans, who removed hither at the time of the emigration after the destruction of Juvavium. The opinion is supported by the appearance of the natives, who are certainly often dark, thin, and pale. If, however, they do not display the type of the other Germanic mountaineers, they have acquired their temper and manners in many ways; for scarcely in any other

RAMSAU.

valley do we hear so much of the deeds of the poachers and their constant affrays with the keepers as here—of course from those times when the chase was still remunerative and attractive, because it appeared to a certain degree heroic, on account of the natural and legitimate danger with which it was connected.

The Berchtesgadner country deserves also that we rest a moment in it before we continue our journey to our real object, the Königssee. It is one of the oldest of German places of education, and the foundation of the monastery ascends to the first years of the twelfth century. The mountains which surround it, from the Watzmann to the Untersberg, might relate many a tale of the destinies of nations and the careers of men, whom they have seen pass by on the diminutive spot of earth. The lovers of legendary lore may have related to them the story of the hunter who loved a swan-maiden, and received in consolation for his rejected passion the knowledge of those salt-springs which in the events of Berchtesgaden ever form the

BERCHTESGADEN.

recurring red thread; the friend of history may investigate the feuds of the Halleiners and the Berchtesgadners, or the struggles of the peasants, who refused to give up a preacher of the new doctrine, who was carried off a prisoner, but forcibly liberated him; and when they were at last defeated, preferred to emigrate to the north and found a new home. He may hear also of the monastery Schuldenlast, and how Bavaria, having quietly made herself chief creditor, gradually acquired and maintained possession, and constructed the ingenious device by which the salt-spring was brought on to Traunstein, and farther. The present knows of all this little; but the salt-works flourish still, and Berchtesgaden has remained what it was formerly, a quiet corner of the earth, full of peace and beauty, strikingly suitable for Horace's famous lines—

"Ille mihi terrarum præter omnes angulus ridet."

Near the Ache, which rushes from the Hintersee at the foot of the Mühlsturzhörner, one goes between green declivities under magnificent maples, along the Watzmann, here becoming visible for the first time, towards the majestic Hoho-Göll, past the remarkable fly-press of Ilsang, which forces the salt-spring up to the aforesaid huts of Schwarzbach-Wacht, through the solitary glade Engadein, and then, turning to the right, through the broad and extensive valley of Schönau, which, to the left shut in by the Untersberg, to the right o'ershadowed by the lofty Göll, proves by its name that the earliest inhabitants who spoke the German tongue were very susceptible of the charms of the locality.

Arriving on the bank of the Bartholomäus, or Königssee, between woods and overgrown, erratic blocks, one may be disappointed in the first moment, because that which is at first perceived appears merely a small, inconsiderable sheet of water; but all the more overwhelming is the view, when, after a few strokes of the oar, the boat turns a point of rock near the Bründelwand, and the most extraordinary basin that Nature ever created lies before the spectator; it is a dark green flood, in places black and unfathomable, shut in by steep precipices, which reach the height of five thousand feet, and, sloping abruptly into the water, offer nowhere a hand's breadth of firm ground on which one could land and escape the raging flood if thrown there by the storm, which, confined in the rocky vale, rages with redoubled fury. In the background (the lake has a breadth of half a league and a length of two), the sublime picture is completed by the picturesque peaks of the giant Watzmann. To the left alone, where the Königsbach and the Kerselbach roar over a fall well worth seeing, does the bank ascend less ruggedly; but opposite, on the precipice, a mark shows where a whole marriage procession, surprised by the storm, was swallowed up in the lake. However, there is no danger to fear, for the boatmen know the weather, and if it is threatening hardly one of them can be moved to the adventure.

A wonderful solitude reigns here—such a deep quiet that a stroke of the oar will awake an echo; a soft and magical tinkling often descends from the heights; it is the bells of the cattle feeding on the pastures above. Much more striking is the effect of a shot discharged in a spot where the rocks descend abruptly on both sides—the sound roars as if the mountains were going to collapse; they cast it like an elastic ball from one to another, till the uninterrupted thunder rolls for seconds: one might imagine the voice of the Mountain Genius, as if, startled from his slumber, he roared aloud and then slowly stretched himself down again murmuring.

The journey in itself is also uncommonly pleasant, especially if the mid-day sun does not blaze on the rocky basin; but the shade of one or the other side spreads a grateful coolness over the dancing waves, whose crests beautifully vary the dark green water through which the flood cruelly indicates its bottomless depths. Doubly as attractive is it if the old boatman, who with bristly beard and short pipe will be remembered by every one who has visited the lake, steps into the boat also for the journey across; he is the most expert and the boldest of all, and the richest in the treasures which have, years since, been collected in the mountains and on the lake—merry hunting-songs and dangerous adventures on lake and mountain-height. But those who are so lucky as to find a pair of pretty boatwomen in the skiff, in their tight, gold-bordered velvet bodices, and who know how to hit upon a theme which makes them confidential, talkative, and disposed to rest on their oars and sing one of their fresh mountain songs, those may justly be in doubt whether the enjoyment of the eye or that of the ear be greater. If we are also in good company and find in our wallet a well-kept bottle of noble wine, destined to be emptied in this wonderful neighbourhood, then let us bury bottle and glass in the lake, that no other profane hour may desecrate them; such a day will ever be marked red in our calendar—a fairer one we can scarcely experience! But all beauty is evanescent, and who knows whether the chief charm of the Beautiful does not consist in its evanescence!

Slow and short as the strokes of the oar may be, the journey ends at last; the Watzmann constantly

MÜHLSTURZHÖRNER.

approaches and already displays the ravine, where the ice has arched and covered the channel of a stream, so that but little power of imagination is required to speak of it as a chapel of ice.

Around the foot of the mountain giant a garland of forest is thrown, and a turf meadow of so lively and soft green is spread before it, that the enchanted eye is riveted on it from afar, and the traveller, landing near the insignificant chapel of St. Bartholomew, does it with delight, as one treads the firm earth again after a long and painful sea voyage.

ECHO ON THE KÖNIGSSEE.

That a sanctuary, a place of devotion, stood here, dates back to the earliest times of advancing Christianity, and those who desire to have more exact information on the subject may glean in my novel, "St. Bartholomew," what history, legend, and poesy have to say thereon. The present church shows no traces of its great age; it has been rebuilt piecemeal, and points to those times when the canons of Berchtesgaden spent their summers here in concealment. Yet the chapel with its round cupola forms a characteristic object, and is the adorning spot of the whole landscape; thus it is in the highest degree satisfactory that the tasteful King Louis II. has taken on himself the expenses of its preservation, for it had gone to ruin; and whilst the endless strife as to whose duty it was to repair it was proceeding, the decay was increasing. The little building at hand, now inhabited by rangers, betrays by its entire style its monastic origin. Formerly the abbots of Berchtesgaden, and afterwards the Bavarian princes—namely, Max Joseph I., and his grandson, Maximilian II., have lived in the upper story when on their hunting expeditions. The cool vaults of the ground floor are turned into cisterns, for the preservation of the costly fish in which the lake is so rich. Foremost among them stand the red trout, called by the people "Snibling," and when not full grown "Schwarzreuterul"—a dish always a favourite for its reddish-yellow, well-tasting flesh, but which does not fall to the lot of all. In the passages are representations of especially large specimens, which were captured years ago, kept near the antlers of fine stags—for the latter have their true home here. An ancient picture represents the adventurous affray which, a hundred years ago, the ranger of that time and his comrades had with a bear driven into the lake; and old and homely rhymes recount how the bear had already grasped the boat, and would have buried them all in the lake, had they not succeeded in splitting his head open with an axe, at the very nick of time.

BOATMAN OF THE KÖNIGSSEE.

Whilst our meal is preparing, we have plenty of time to visit the Obersee, a proportionally smaller basin, surrounded by immense walls of rock. It was originally connected with the Königssee, but was divided by a landslip, which, in fabulous times came, according to the legend, from Kaunstein above, and formed a dam which separated the lake into two halves.

Scarcely is there a wilder or more lonely lake, except, perhaps, the little "Wildsee," lying high in the Alps—certainly none is more lovely; for the earnestness which rests on the whole picture is the earnestness of a fair, noble, and smiling countenance, but in the smile lies a victorious consciousness of eternity. The savage majesty of the rocky enclosure is toned down by a turfy slope which rises in the middle, and upon which, enclosed by woods, a shepherd's hut lies. Above climb wood and rock, between which a broad silver band rushes downwards, overshadowed by the red peaks of the gloomy Teufelshörner.

"In der Fischunkel" the desolate waste is termed; it was a favourite residence of King Max II., to whom a just posterity will not deny the name of "the wise," and who, many a morning, caused himself to be rowed here, to compose his serious thoughts in this grand solitude, or to read one of his favourite poets. But he was also a stout friend of the chase, and has pursued many a chamois to the highest mountain ridge, which he, in his amiable liberality, made passable, by means of convenient bridle-paths, for such of the sons of men who do not belong to the mountain-climbers either by business or pleasure. Under his ancestor, Max the Good, a more noisy life reigned on these shores; great hunting parties on the lake, illuminations of the mountains, a holding of *wood falls*, when whole trunks were stowed away in the channel of the Königsbach, as in a sluice, and then set free into the lake, into which they arrived, crushed to pieces, with a noise like thunder.

The sumptuous prince delighted to row his guests along in magnificent boats to the sound of noisy hunting music, whilst chamois and stags, driven together from the surrounding mountains and pressed onward to the steep shores, had no escape but to take the stupendous leap into the lake, during which the deadly shot generally reached them.

OBERSEE.

Those who desire to try the strength of their heels and the endurance of their knees may climb up the mountains through the Fischunkel to the deserted Funtensee-Tauern, where the dismal Grünsee sleeps and dreams, and which no living creature inhabits; or, yet further, to the gigantic rocky waste of the "Stony See," which looks just like an ocean petrified by the stroke of a magician during a raging tempest; or he may, returning to St. Bartholomew, mount the Watzmann, to the so-called "Lubel," and the other green oases, in which the shepherds' huts lie imbedded; or to the everywhere visible "Gap," in which the snow never melts. It is, in any case, an expedition upon which one may look back with

CHAPEL IN THE ROCK.

pride, for the Watzmann is 8,578 feet high; and if indeed the road, which is best commenced from Ramsau, and is accomplished in about six hours, is by no means a promenade, yet the prospect which presents itself from above, over the foreground of neighbouring rocks and glaciers as far as the Gross Glockner, Venediger, and Krimler-Tauern, beyond the Salzburg country and whole Bavarian plain, is one of the grandest and loveliest which a mountain tour has to offer. A huntsman can also pass hither over the ridge of Bartlmä and come to the "Hunstod," which, itself an immense pyramid of rock, commands a not less immense waste of rock, through which the Wimbach rushes, cold and clear, to precipitate itself into a deep and narrow ravine, the Wimbach-Klamm, whose stone walls bend so closely

T

THE BAVARIAN MOUNTAINS.

toward each other on high, that only once in the day can the perpendicular sun cast a glance within and cause the streaks of water to twinkle and glitter which ripple down from all sides like fluttering ribbons over moss and entanglement, whilst the stream itself roars to the precipice over many a waterfall. On one side beams for a narrow bridge are driven into the rock, upon which the ravine can be traversed, and you may gaze at the steep above, and the abyss below, almost deafened by the roar of the foaming stream, which drowns every sound—fanned by the chill as of a grave, moistened by the sparkling drops as at a funeral.

We draw a long and joyful breath when we step from the ravine into the open air again—from night into day; there stand the Ramsau Mountains in the most glorious light of a summer evening.

The lofty Göll glows, whilst the sun dwells awhile upon him, as if he would linger on a spectacle than which scarce a fairer greets him in his passage round the world.

WIMBACHKLAMM.

XIII.

FROM SALZBURG.

HE evening was already waning as we sat on the lofty Mönchsberg; amongst its green summits the south wind was rustling. The numerous visitors who at other times frequent these roads appeared to have returned home long ago; around us it was lonely, and the meditations which at such a moment engross the silent traveller had free play. At our feet lay Salzburg, the ancient and renowned city, with its houses rising in terraces, one above the other; their grey stones are still a foundation for history. Before us the mountains, like an immense wall; the towering Göll, which reaches almost to heaven; the Staufen, and the Untersberg, with its imperial legend, which has again been revived. Thus we gazed long into the depths. Dark bridges arched themselves above, whilst the stream pressed roaring beneath them; the cupolas and towers of the broad city, where the last sound of vespers seemed to die away, waxed higher and broader in the twilight; and, listening longer, one could hear through this calm of a mighty nature the innumerable sounds of that motley existence which swelled below in its ordinary and yet so varied routine. Music sounds in the streets; officers in white uniform and with clanking sabre pass by between fair ladies, who only half hide their languishing eyes behind the veil. Yes, a tone of southern, almost Italian, life pervades the streets. This is involuntarily felt in looking at the people, who sit in the evening at the open doors: it has passed into the habits of the people but not into their dispositions; for, despite all, Salzburg is a German city. It seemed marvellous to me, as I reflected thus above. The twilight deepened, and out of it ascended the bygone thousand years of the town's history, and one felt how the darkness invited investigation.

Whilst the merry throng hummed, I glanced back to the times of solitude, to the days whose symbols were the Roman sword and the solitary cell. Will the reader accompany me in these meditations?

The picture we have of the earliest times of Germany is a remarkable contrast. A mythic veil is thrown over Germany, the theatre of so many great contests; it is marked by darksome colours; the tempest which sweeps through the endless forests is heard. Here sacrifices are offered to the dark gods of old; here moves the wolf on his dark track; and the mighty forms which dwell in these forests, they are tall and fair, the skin of the bear covers their naked shoulders, and their blue eyes look towards the south with eager glance.

Thus stands the representation of our ancestors in the books of Tacitus; a secret terror seized the polished Roman when he took the word "Germania" on his lips. Yet we find now and then in the midst of this wilderness, on this chilly, shadowy background, splendid colonies, here and there a smiling idyll; they are the first settlements of the Romans in Germany. The description of the relator becomes brighter, his hard language becomes milder, a ray of sunshine darts here through the darkness of the woods.

'Twas thus that the sumptuous villas of the prætors, with their cool piazzas and classic statues, bordered the Rhine; the transparent flood bathed their marble steps, and Roman purple was spread o'er the couches of the guests.

There were gardens in the midst of the wilderness. They lay along the mighty and broad military roads which the Romans had constructed along the Rhine from Switzerland to Cologne, and thence into Rhætia and Noricum. The roads were connected by powerful fortresses, and under the protection of these the most flourishing towns soon developed themselves.

One of these towns, and the fairest of all, was Salzburg. Who would believe nowadays, looking at that modern frivolous life, that the memories of a thousand years rest on that spot; that it was already blooming in the glory of youth when Germany still lay in legendary darkness?

And yet it was so. At the Pass of Lueg, where the Salzack breaks through the mountains to gain its freedom, is the proper division between mountain and plain. A great and wildly beautiful valley begins here, which constantly increases in breadth till it loses itself in the immense plain of the Danube. The last impressive mountain scenery on this road is Salzburg. The lofty Göll stands on the left, with the Untersberg and the Staufen; to the left is the Geisberg and those under-features which unite it with the Tannengebirg. The walls of these mountains lie there like the propylæum; and if we look at the gigantic gate of stone which they form towards the plain, we must feel how powerful this is as a strategical position.

The Romans constructed here also a fortress and town; Juvavia was its ancient name.

Although it possessed but the rank of a colony, the young settlement nevertheless developed itself splendidly. Juvavia had legates and ædiles, duumvirs and decurions, and a whole legion was stationed there for its protection. The camp in which it was cantoned stood upon the Schlossberg; Roman temples covered the heights, and fine pillars filled the public squares. Even at that time, however, the houses rose in terraces on the slopes of the mountains, and from this point broad roads, studded with gigantic milestones bearing the imperial names of Septimius Severus and Caracalla, radiated into the country.

This we learn from the ruins which have been erected in the course of centuries; it would appear a glorious dream—until the storm caused by the emigrations of the peoples burst in and buried every glory under mounds of rubbish.

When we speak nowadays of Salzburg, most of us do not think of the Roman town, but of the far-famed town of the bishops.

To this also we may devote a few short words, for it represents a scene of culture which endured almost a thousand years. The imperial figures of Germany meet us here, and all the bloom which the

SALZBURG.

Middle Ages could produce grew up on the ruins of the first epoch, and for the second time Salzburg became the centre of the intellectual power of the Rhætian lands.

The Franks were the first who arrived in that desert which was once called Juvavia. Many Roman families still lived scattered in the vicinity, but lived half savages upon hunting and fishing: the earth yet bore the curse which Attila's foot had imprinted on it.

Now, for the first time, began milder manners and benign culture. Rupert, the leader of the second Frankish colonists, erected a convent, which the Bavarian dukes endowed with many possessions; and when the Briton Virgil came to Salzburg in 745, the first resistance of the untamed country was already broken. Pepin, the Marshal of the Frankish Empire, held his powerful hand over his acquisition; a school was erected in Chiemsee, and messengers went into all the districts to proclaim a gentler doctrine. Salzburg ascended to the pinnacle of glory in the Middle Ages, through Charlemagne. He was the personal friend of the Archbishop Arno; he had that commanding eye which dominated all minds and all lands, and which knew better than many how to spread the triumphs of culture.

Now came the long line of archbishops; good and bad days came in rapid alternation. When the Hungarians inundated the country, Salzburg was frightfully devastated, but in a short space recovered again from its wounds. A rich library was collected in the rooms of the convent; the assiduous monk sat before the parchment, whilst, outside, the fields stood high; everywhere was comfort and peace.

In the year 959, the Emperor Otho the Good came to Salzburg, and celebrated Easter there. From this time the possessions of the bishopric increased rapidly; all the emperors endowed the abbey with woods and lakes, with farms and their appurtenances.

This was, however, the turning-point of its interior development. For out of power grew ambition; and the bishops, who had at first grasped the cross, seized now the sword; and the contests which the unhappy Hildebrand conjured up sucked the marrow of all German countries.

Centuries passed away thus, and the times of the Reformation came, with their bitter severity, and the times of Charles V., when the spiritual princes became ever more worldly, and the love of ostentation led to wild extravagance. Salzburg, on whose features was imprinted a stamp sensually fair, was not to be outrun by the other episcopal towns. Her ruler was Primate of all Germany, and generally was a scion of one of the most distinguished families—so the pleasures of the world secured a splendid arena.

But the gaiety of this life paled when the Thirty Years' War burst over Germany. Salzburg was now fortified in hot haste, and the Archbishop Paris von Lodron, who ruled at that time, acquired imperishable fame by his defence of the town. Many another name was conspicuous for humanity after his death; for these were times when humanity was rather an attribute of the noblest characters than a duty for all. The Bishop John Ernest appears greater than his predecessors in this respect. It was he who constructed the great Hospital of St. John out of his own revenues; and when the first tired pilgrim arrived, it was he again who accompanied him and washed his feet. He concealed with care the great expense incurred for this object; and when search was made after his death, the whole of the accounts were found to have been burnt.

Salzburg also suffered heavily from the fearful wars which form the history of this century. At the time of the secularisation of Church property the spiritual power was torn from the archbishops, and when Napoleon I. rent the map of Germany in twain, it fell to the lot of Bavaria for a short time. It was finally united with Austria in the year 1814, and forms since then the fairest jewel in the brilliant yet thorny possessions of the house of Hapsburg.

All this passed by me in slow procession whilst I sat above, yonder, on the dim Mönchsberg—how immeasurably long is the road from those days to when Napoleon and the Emperor Francis met at Salzburg, and when the new German Emperor rested on his journey!

I descended with circumspection the stairs—those endless gradients which finally lead to the suburb of Mülln: and now must the reader again belong entirely to the present—motley Reality embraces us with her hundred arms.

William von Humboldt has already called Salzburg the fairest town in Germany, as we have read in "Letters to a Friend," and his brother Alexander shared this impression when he sojourned there in the year 1797, for the purpose of taking geographical observations. If this beauty rests in the first place on a marvellous natural situation, yet the architectural appearance of the town has its peculiar attraction. Without being beautiful, in the strict sense of the term, it is, at the least, characteristic; and this is what,

FOUNTAIN AT SALZBURG (HOFBRUNNEN).

us a rule, decides the impression made by a town. Even towns have a sort of individuality, whose chief features we measure with a human standard, and as in intercourse with the latter we experience a longing for firm and decided characters and an individual stamp, so the same thing holds good with regard to scenery.

This is, to a great extent, the case at Salzburg; for besides the potency of nature, there are two other moments decidedly apparent in the physiognomy of the town. Let us first call to mind what we have called a touch of southern life. That bright realistic joy in existence, which is especially seen in the temperament of the Austrian race, is very pronounced in Salzburg and evinces itself in motley and brightly-coloured details. The people involuntarily display this, and without being frivolous, there reigns a certain lightness of heart which soon communicates itself to the visitor.

SALZBURG.

Thus much concerning the public life, which naturally has a powerful influence on the whole character of a town. Equally distinct are the peculiarities of the architecture. For though there is no want of handsome and tasteful buildings (reflecting the above-described life), nor of the modern barrack style, yet the structures which positively decide its physiognomy are all erected on an uniform and strict principle. This is the style of the towns of the spiritual magnates, the style of the seventeenth and eighteenth centuries. Of course it is a little stiff and heavy, but the massive scenery relieves it without injury to the general appearance of the whole. The handiest example of the sort is the cathedral, whose construction was commenced about the year 1614, upon the model of St. Peter's in Rome. Its dimensions are enormous. It was to be also a palace of the episcopal mightiness; and that exuberant and pompous self-importance which then animated the spiritual grandees of those times breaks out in the overburdened top-knot style of architecture. The remaining churches of the town, whose number may amount to about twenty, are built in a similar style. In this quantitative representation of godliness also, predominating over all temporal amusements, lurks a principal feature of the cathedral town. The Margaret Chapel, standing in the churchyard of St. Peter, must be considered a small but valuable example of the Gothic style. It was built towards the end of the fifteenth century; likewise the church of Kloster Nonberg, whose history reaches back to the time of the Agilolfingers. Thus we behold everything concentrated which properly constitutes the being of a spiritual town—numerous churches, whose exteriors are laden with stiff splendour, a crowd of convents, and a wonderful Nature, which mollifies the mind; add to this array a little people which attends mass as industriously as it courts pleasure, and has been called into existence more by the gracious condescension of princely bishops than by its own severe labour.

And though indeed the spiritual principalities have now become a thing of the past, and if the inexhaustible stream of visitors in which the town exists has promoted a cosmopolitan temper, yet the latter has not succeeded in destroying the ancient features. They are partially effaced, but look down on us as the traces of youth are marked on the countenance of an experienced man of the world. Another—shall I call it political or dynastic?—element is added to these characteristic indications. It is apparent that Salzburg is the capital of the district in which a crowd of officials is concentrated, and also that it is an important station for the military authorities. Besides this, widowed and retired majesties of the imperial house of Austria reside there, so that all this together gives the town an official air which must not be overlooked if we wish to become acquainted with its characteristics.

If we roam through the simple streets, where one can get friendly information from every one, we shall meet many things, well worth seeing, if we cannot call them remarkable.

Above all, there is the large and ancient Residenz Square with the former archiepiscopal castle; the lofty fountain stands in the middle, with its colossal river-gods and tritons in the foam of the waters—a real prototype of the heavy and ponderous taste existing at the close of the Thirty Years' War.

The statue of Mozart is of modern erection, and yet recalls ancient times. It was erected in the year 1841 and commemorates the great musician, who, as is well known, was born in Salzburg and lived there in the service of Archbishop Hieronymus. The house where he was born is made known by golden letters, and a series of other memorials pointing back to him proclaim how popular his name is still in the fair city.

The colossal aqueducts possessed by Salzburg since the seventeenth century are foremost among the elementary buildings; likewise the situation is enhanced by the fact that we meet with steep rocks on all sides. A combat with rocks—that is the architectural history of the town in which, alas! tragic episodes are not wanting. We remind the reader only of the horrible landslips which took place in the years 1493, 1614, and 1665; but they were all exceeded by the cruel mishap of the 15th July, 1669.

At about ten o'clock at night an enormous mass of stone detached itself from the ridge which we call the Mönchsberg, and fell crashing on to the long row of houses nestling at its foot. The church of St. Mark, the Brothers of Charity, and a crowd of smaller buildings were buried with their inhabitants. The fearful crash and the cry of anguish which rang through the streets awoke the neighbours from their sleep; they hastened to assist, and a thousand hands were busy in clearing the giant grave. The mountains groaned a second time and a mass of rock, larger than the first, was precipitated beneath. More than three hundred of those who had come to help found a dreadful death, and now flight and despair became the password for all. Even the boldest dare approach no more, and the calls and groans of those smothered died away without help. It is only since that time that it was thought expedient to support or cut away the rocks which had crumbled: the workmen entrusted with the task were let over the perpendicular face of the rock on long ropes.

A rocky wonder of a rare description is the so-called New Gate, which leads through the Mönchsberg. We see at the entrance, where creepers bloom in the crevices, the portrait of the constructor (Archbishop Sigismund), and beneath, the colossal inscription: "Te saxa loquuntur." There is an antique grandeur and brevity about this sentence, whose style is extremely suitable to the gigantic undertaking. Admiration of this work may die out in our time, accustomed as we are to tunnels, but in the seventeenth century it was a masterpiece of art. With a breadth of twenty-two feet it has a length of more than four hundred; the heavy waggon moves groaning under it, and the light-footed traveller hears from afar the echo of his hasty footsteps. This breach is an inestimable treasure for the town, for it relieves the latter from the barrier which the steep Mönchsberg laid across her roads.

The princely stables and the two riding-schools, also, are architecturally famed. The former, erected in 1607, accommodates one hundred and thirty horses; a cavalry regiment is now quartered there, and the Hungarian troopers loiter negligently, with clanking spurs, through the lofty halls; here stands a sergeant, with bristly beard and threatening whip, near the manger, and there the officer's servant, whistling, cleans his master's tunic. The mangers were formerly hewn out of white marble, and through the stable runs a branch of the Berchtesgadner stream, which day and night sings its murmuring song as it hastens forward into the open. The riding-school was formerly the theatre of magnificent tourneys, and three galleries, hewn in the rock, with lofty arches, one above the other, accommodated the guests. Now the hussars of Radetzky and Benedek train their horses there.

The picture of Salzburg would be incomplete, were we to consider the town without those charming environs which play such an important part in its general appearance. We name first the castles Hellbrunn and Leopoldskron. The first was the summer residence of the archbishops of Salzburg: the immense park bears yet the traces of that ambitious epoch for which Versailles was the unattained model. We come upon dense avenues with magnificent groups of trees, created by Nature in the course of quiet years, whilst the eager building mania of the princes piled stone on stone. Thus has arisen, on the summit of the rock, the so-called "Month's Castle." It was built by the Archbishop Marcus Sitticus in thirty days, in order to surprise thereby a Duke of Bavaria who visited the princely court in passing through. When the archbishop conducted the latter through the park and came to the steep rock, the duke remarked that this would be a splendid place for a little castle. When he returned, in a month's time, the magic castle stood complete on the very spot.

Leopoldskron is situated nearer to Salzburg; it is built in Italian style and was endowed with rich treasures of art by King Louis I. These treasures have been taken away, but the castle is still in the possession of the Bavarian reigning family. At only one hour's distance from Salzburg lies Aigen. Ernest von Schwarzenberg transformed it from a watering-place into a princely residence. It has this advantage, that its natural charms are disfigured by no art. The road leads from Aigen up the Gaisberg, which, with little expenditure of labour, offers a view which extends from Traunstein up to the Kaiser Gebirg and away over seven lakes.

But the fairest spot of all in the environs of Salzburg, is Maria Plain, a pilgrimage church, lying on a moderate eminence, not far from the town.

Those minds who first invented the idea of a pilgrimage were possessed of wondrous understanding; they endeavoured to give a new and pious object to the spirit of travel. The elevation of spirits which we all strive after can nowhere be so fully attained as in the presence of fair and harmonious Nature, and

therefore it is that almost all churches of pilgrimage stand in a neighbourhood exercising power over the soul.

Thus Maria Plain stands upon a green hill, and round about, all the glory of the earth is extended—the garland of mountains and the shining town, dark woods and luxuriant fields. But before the church is an open space where green lime-trees stand, in whose branches the breezes play, and beneath whose shade the musing pilgrim reclines.

In order to bring a perfect frame of mind to perfect beauty, one must approach in the evening, when the setting sun lingers over this golden world, when his last rays beam down on the two massive towers, and the feeling of separation trembles through the air which we feel on the eve of cloudless days. Thus

x

did I contemplate Maria Plain for the first time; the clang of the clock died away; beneath the lime-trees sat two lovers, conversing in low and reverential whispers, whilst the dog at their feet gazed motionless into vacancy. All was real—yet it was a poem which Heine alone could have equalled in one of his most perfect songs. We gaze on, and pious, half-forgotten tones of our youth awake again within our hearts. Darkness alone separates us from this picture.

The Untersberg is the most remarkable of the mountains which surround Salzburg. Not only the great imperial story, which has been revived in our days, but countless other legends twine themselves around the ancient rock. Indeed, the mass of stone in itself is so wonderfully put together and creviced that something mysterious remains for the traveller. Nearly six German miles must be traversed to make the tour of it, whilst if we ascend higher we meet everywhere trap rocks, wild precipices, and furious waters, which, foaming, cleave their way. The marble quarries on the slope of the mountain are famed; from these are built, not only the most valuable edifices in Salzburg, but also numerous churches and monuments in all Germany. For quarrying the stone there are immense saws and mills standing close to the quarries. In their neighbourhood is a well of ancient fame which is still called the Princes' Well. At the time when the archbishops yet reigned in Salzburg, wonderful potency was ascribed to its waters, and horsemen hastened daily to the well to fetch the morning draught of the princes.

Among the caves and grottoes which the wondrous mountain conceals in its interior, that one is especially remarkable which lies beyond the Mückenbrunnen, near the Mittagscharte. We enter by a natural gate, which is more than double the height of a man, into a hall whose walls and roof are composed of sparkling ice. The light of day peeps timidly in through the crevices; the twilight is cool and silvery; the wondrous shapes which centuries have formed on these walls are motionless. We have been precipitated from the clear light of day into the midst of a legend; we stop perplexed, because the echo of our own steps alarms us. It is no desert here, it is the cool and silvery abode of a nymph; but the timid fairy, the little sprites, whose delicate voices sounded here lately, departed when they heard our footsteps approach. We are yet conscious of their breath; we stand in the midst of their habitation.

The previous lines, through which the kindly reader has accompanied us, are very far from giving a complete picture of Salzburg; but we have, at all events, shown this—that it is not easy to find a town which constitutes so rich a theme for meditation.

Those thousands upon thousands who flock every year thither bear witness to this. For four months together Salzburg belongs almost exclusively to visitors, so we will devote to them our concluding sentences, since they constitute a chief element in the physiognomy of the town. Sauntering through the streets of Salzburg in August, one may hear at one and the same time five or six foreign languages, as if the spirit of Pentecost were descended on all tongues. The North Germans are the most numerous, venting their inspirations in critical tones; then come the English, with red travelling guides, and all the tokens by which the initiated recognise the nation of travellers. America brings her dollars, and the subjects of the Empire their paper; the hotels are full to stifling, and at the railway station crushes a Babylonian crowd. This is the daily history of the summer days, and the good-tempered population of residents is already so much inured to it that they would miss it were it otherwise.

From the plethora of these days and guests we must distinguish two, having historical significance; these are imperial days in the gay uniformity of the town.

We mean the meeting which the ruler of Austria had with Napoleon III. in Salzburg, and also that memorable hour when he welcomed there the Emperor of the German Empire.

The first of these meetings was on the 18th of August, 1867. Looking back, since the day of Sedan has found a place in history, on the halo which then surrounded the Second Empire, on that awe in which it held the minds of men, the sound of bells and cries of joy appear like a stupid, meaningless dream.

PETER'S CHURCHYARD IN SALZBURG.

The reminiscence of those days appears to me as if tens of years had passed by, as if I were to relate a legend, not an experience.

The heaven above Salzburg was cloudless and clear. In all the streets streamed an inconceivable throng of human beings—foreigners from all lands, and countryfolk from the neighbourhood; soldiers in white uniform, and patrols of cavalry, that insolently forced a passage. Shoulder to shoulder stands the crowd in the Residenz Platz, Court equipages, harnessed with four magnificent horses, press through towards the railway-station; all are in holiday attire; the entire road is adorned with tricolors and waving banners. The railway-station itself is decorated more than the other edifices; the halls are hung with silken drapery and transformed into a flower garden, whilst above, the French eagle expands his wings. Out of a group of gigantic ferns arises the life-size statue of the Empress Elizabeth; above is the canopy of velvet, adorned by the arms of all countries. Wherever the eye roams, it lights on the golden crown and the golden N; everywhere on beaming countenances and golden hope. It was the year 1867, and Napoleon was the mightiest ruler on earth. At about five in the evening the Austrian majesties drove to the reception at the station, the Emperor in the uniform of a marshal and the Empress in a light violet-coloured dress and wearing the Hungarian hat. Four slim Arabian browns drew the carriage through the rejoicing throng; then came the taciturn little man with the staid and dubious countenance, and Eugenie, Empress of France. They drove back to the Residence together—behind them a long following of names renowned for gold or glory. There were Grammont and Metternich, Taxis and Hohenlohe, Andrassy and Beust; and when night had spread her mysterious darkness over the imperial show, more than a hundred mountain fires flamed from above. The strangers looked at them with amazement; but none could say, are they a sign of peace or will the torch of war kindle itself at their magnificence? Four years ago—and now all that glory is buried in the tomb!

Another Emperor made his entrance in these days, but the picture was otherwise than before. How much more imposing was his appearance than the bent and crafty form of the French Emperor, yet how much simpler was his whole behaviour. He came in the ordinary four-horse post-carriage as he lately drove past the cheering soldiery in the field on the dusty line of march; at his side sat an officer in Prussian uniform, and on the back seat two couriers.

The journey, by Werfen and Hallein, experienced much delay, so that the Emperor entered Salzburg almost an hour later than was agreed upon. Francis Joseph awaited him before the hotel, "The Archduke Charles;" and there also stood the noble assembly in rank and file who were to welcome the illustrious guest. It saluted with deep respect; the two Emperors, however, shook hands before all the world, and embraced each other with joyful kisses—the one of a fatherly age, the other almost youthful in appearance.

It was a wonderful picture! Was this the same man who lately rode into the midst of the shell fire of Sadowa, who stood in the wintry snow under the walls of Paris, and became German Emperor in the royal palace of Louis XIV.?

Yet another rose high above the crowd. He stood at the end of the guard of honour which saluted the Emperor, his helmet drawn well over his head, his glance displaying that awe-inspiring force which is only given to the chosen few. It was Prince Bismarck, in the uniform of his cuirassier regiment; he also obeyed the word of command which had just pealed forth, and stood as if cast in bronze before the two sovereigns. The leading statesmen of the land were in the long suite of the Austrian Empire—Beust and Andrassy, the Czech hero Count Hohenwart, and the most illustrious dignitaries of the Court. The Emperor William was received with the greatest distinction. This time also brilliant dinners and blazing mountain-fires were given; but nothing of that imperial pomp was seen as when the presence of the French Emperor was celebrated. And this was good. The times have become more earnest, and have given the necessities of the nations a preponderance over dynastic connections. What was agreed upon in Salzburg became known to none to its full extent; but that half information which was made public bore witness that it was a work of peace.

A few days after the imperial meeting at Salzburg, a simple postchaise drove from Salzburg towards Reichenhall. Two men in light summer coats sat inside, conversing easily, whilst the postilion zealously blew his horn, regardless of what they spoke of inside. They were Bismarck and Beust.

Further and farther the light carriage whirled from the ancient cathedral and the ancient town, and with it we also shall take our leave of Salzburg.

NEU THOR.

STORM ON THE LAKE.

XIV.

TRAUNSEE AND ISCHL.

ORE brilliant than all the other lakes in the Salzkammergut, the Traunsee lies at our feet. The portion which we at first perceive in coming from Langbath is dark and motionless; the banks fall precipitously into the depths, whilst rocky hills enclose the scene on all sides. The Sonnstein peak juts from the east into the lake like the form of a giant, and behind this the Traunstein elevates its bare sides, furrowed by blue shadows. The isolation of this picture increases the impression which the spectator experiences; his mind is not divided between changing ideas, he is struck by the unity and precision of the landscape. The skiff rows slowly along the crystal flood; we constantly near the rocky promontory formed by the Sonnstein, when suddenly the scene changes. For scarcely is the point won when a broad and pleasant country lies before us; the gentle wind plays over the waves, whilst other hues and another atmosphere are about us.

On the left bank a point of land projects into the lake, on whose rocky soil Traunkirchen is built. To the right are heaped the broad masses of the Traunstein, and between them both glimmers, at the northern end of the lake, the town Gmunden with its white rows of houses on green, smiling turf. Let us now pause awhile in order to cast a fugitive glance on the rich singularity by which we are surrounded.

Traunkirchen, where our boat stops, is half hidden beneath thick trees. The foundation of the church is traced back to those times when the Hungarians devastated Germany; the Margraves of Steier erected in those times a house of God to commemorate their victory on that spot. The modern name frequently occurs in the course of history. At last the Jesuits became masters of the place, and possessed it until the abolition of their order, when it lapsed to the Austrian government. Further back, almost, it is proved, as far as the times of the Romans, reaches the origin of Gmunden, which was a free market in the time of the old Empire. The impression which this little town makes on us is that of trim, but not exactly unconscious, beauty. Church and town-hall have something doleful about them as well as something sublime; and in the life of the citizens, which we must characterize as bustling, we see prominent that industry which preponderates in so many parts of the Salzkammergut, and which, in fact, is expressed in the very name. This is the business of the salt-works, the entire apparatus of which has been united in a model collection in Gmunden, in order to give an idea of this industry. A fine carved altar in the parish church, of the year 1626, is also worth seeing, for it was chiselled by an artist of the name Schwandaller, in whom later inquiry believes to have discovered an ancestor of the famed Schwanthaler. But, as aforesaid, all the small wonders are far excelled by those which Nature has here built up; and to them must we ever turn our eyes. We have already named above the mountains which dominate the lake to a certain extent; these are the Traunstein and the Sonnstein. Rugged masses of rock, which obstruct the traveller's footsteps, are comprehended in this term; and, in reality, there are few mountains which, with so moderate a height, are so troublesome to ascend. Seen from afar, indeed, the projecting Traunstein plunges into the depths; and he who ascends the narrow foot-path which leads from three points to the summit will in none be able to avoid those dangerous spots where the sharp rocks sink perpendicularly into the lake. What gives the Sonnstein a gloomy appearance is the traces of a frightful wood-fire which raged for five days together about ten years ago. Even now the rocks are blackened from it, and charred stems stick up on the unapproachable heights.

The lake is as rude as the mountains when stormy days unchain its passions. When the north wind roars its wildest, the waves often foam up as high as a house: more perilous still is the south-west, because it rushes suddenly from out the ravines and attacks the craft like an assassin. The road also leading from Ebensee to Traunsee is torn from this violence of the elements, for long strips of it are really hewn in the rock and protected by avalanche galleries from the rage of the mountain. Here also, as on the steep cliffs, past which the bark glides, we find numerous tablets: and the woe to which they testify is constantly attributed to the waves. Here and there, also, we find a tablet in the houses of the villages on the bank, accusing the flood that it once transgressed its limits, and enumerating the human lives which were lost thereby.

If we follow the course of the clear, green, crystal river which gives its name to the lake, we soon come to the falls of the Traun. Its fall is truly not considerable, hardly amounting to more than fifty feet; but the whole neighbourhood is so rich in beauty, that we stand before one of the most charming pictures conceivable. Man has laid his compelling hand on many spots, in order to overcome rapids and abrupt turns in the stream, so the latter is now secure and in a navigable state. As it moves through several lakes, which seem like gigantic reservoirs, the height of water in the river is subject to great variation, but it is thoroughly controlled by immense sluices. The commerce which enlivens the banks receives, through the heavy wood and salt trade, a special character; and the wood-drifting on the Traun is of a stupendous nature. With tempestuous rapidity the rafts rush forward on the waves; here and there a part of the freight is cast ashore, and those who are very courageous attempt themselves the leap. When all the rapids of the course are overcome, it is not easy to experience a misfortune, although it looks dreadful when the edge of a waterfall is approached nearer and nearer. A legend has truly done its best; for it relates that a wedding train was precipitated into the whirlpool, where all were engulfed without exception. The commencement of this water trade reaches back to mythical times; we owe it to a wood ranger in the imperial service, who was occupied longer than two generations in this work.

If we follow the valley of the Traun towards the south, the road is at first narrow; at the back and side masses of rock crowd above, and are in their turn crowded over by others. The Traun flows past us with bright and rapid waves, now rushing through sloping meadows, now winding round giant rocks resting in the midst of the water. Here a burning charcoal-kiln, there a long row of newly-felled piled-up wood, and, above, the cheerful blue of heaven: thus the road leads us along the long valley. The latter opens out at last, and lies before us in its full length on both banks of the little river Ischl.

The situations which surround the spot enhance the first favourable impression without overdoing it.

GMUNDEN.

The Dachstein, with its mighty outlines, looks towards us; lower down lies the ruin Wildenstein and countless villas, charmingly situated and carefully kept. But the imperial one is to be distinguished from the rest; its park and flower-garden bloom in singular richness, beautiful without being pretentious. We find everywhere light tints; the crowded forests and the juicy meadows, the colour of the waves, and even the paint of the houses are toned down to a cheerful, transparent pervading tone, which the eyes see and the senses feel.

However, the company is not entirely in unison with this youthful freshness of scenery. Ischl has the reputation of being "the most fashionable bath in the monarchy," and the shady spots of this fact are not removed even by the most magnificent sun that beams down here. Nobility and moneyed aristocracy vie with each other in ostentation and the desire to obtain consideration; the hurry to shine is sometimes so boisterous that it drowns the wonderful calm which breathes immutable among this scenery. We

willingly allow each man to choose the road that he finds most pleasant; but the contrast in which the guests sometimes stand to the earth which affords them hospitality is still one of the most remarkable. Heine would have said it was vile. For nowhere lies the unrestrained freedom of the spirit so close at hand; never do we feel so inclined to free and delicate self-communion, as when we stand in the midst of the wonders, before the innocence of fair Nature. The man who is really such feels here the soft invitation to muse within his deeper self; and we espy thousands who, with all the means of art, meditate on rendering self more shallow. People will reply that this concerns us not, and we accept the objection with all calmness; but somewhat yet remains which echoes in our ears also without "concerning" us: we cannot but be sensible of a secret grief that the beautiful which we experience is wholly lost for many.

With such thoughts (unless indeed irony gets the upper hand) we pass by the forms which in each

paradise betoken the "season;" and of such forms there are only too many in Ischl. They govern. Their capabilities give the measure of desires in that domain; for these the trombones play; for these the golden rubbish of the shop is stored; but the tuneful murmur of the waves and shining sides of the Dachstein are for others.

The resident inhabitants also are in some measure under the influence of these elements, as is always the case in the fashionable baths of the mountains. They partake not only of the cash, but of the nature of their visitors, and so arises a sorry mixture of rural-manufacturing natures, of summer industry and winter sloth. The phenomenon which we are speaking of is not intended to refer to a single place, but to all where like causes exist; and let us be allowed to say, that on the road from Ischl one is now and then reminded of it.

Next to the visitors, who leave behind vast sums, Ischl owes her career to the salt-works. The salt which is there evaporated is said to amount to more than 200,000 centners yearly. The visit to the works offers much interest to visitors; but they must not compare them with those of Hallein. Regarding the human beasts of burden, who encamp at the foot of the mountain to drag rich fellow-creatures up it, we had rather be silent, that we may spare the reader and ourselves a shock; for gazing at this heaven so blue and on these mountains bathed in sunlight should relieve our souls from what oppresses them, and thus gazing we will take our departure from delightful Ischl.

XV.

ON THE SCHAFBERG.

WE select the road which ascends from St. Gilgen in steep curves. The first resting-place we meet is a soft meadow, around which the upper forest extends. The brook by the lonely shepherd's hut ripples coolly past, the blue shadows of the afternoon lie upon the pines, and only the sky looks down on this island in the wood.

We now follow the narrow foot-path which leads over the slope, and soon we are again shut in by the darkness of the pines. The road ascends over rotten stems and buried roots, now soft moss and now half-sunken stones, till the eye peeps through the clearing which the abyss opens to the right; there the Mondsee extends its dark clear flood, and reflects the height which we have silently reached.

The wood disappears a second time; and now the roofs of many a pasture shine opposite, and all at once the landscape becomes extensive; the masses of the Dachstein tower on high, and even the domain on which we stand assumes that strongly organized character which is the mark of true mountain meadows. Alpine roses and dwarf firs flourish at our feet, until the rocky ascent begins which leads us to our final goal.

Who can describe those wonders which now lie before our eyes? Who has a soul so great that he comprehends all this beauty in a breath? Yes, every heart beats quicker: let it calm itself in the breast, and then only will we gaze into the distance.

The territory which we overlook belongs to nations, so immeasurable is the horizon. We survey with rapid eye mountains which are in Bohemia, Carinthia, and Bavaria; hardly one famous name is wanting in the gigantic panorama. The "Dead Mountain" and Dachstein group elevate their towering cliffs; not far from these the Höllen Gebirge and the Traunstein. Yonder, the colossal mountain-world, with their mythical names, hangs over the Königssee: the "Stony Sea," the Hohe Göll, and the Untersberg. Yes, they are stony and lifeless; but betwixt them the blue wave, now sorrowfully fair, now gaily laughing in the full sunlight, is imprisoned. Its fluid life is poured among the rocks, and even their grey heads show a reflection of the poesy which dwells among the waves. They appear to us very differently with the undulating naiads of the mountain-lake playing at their feet than if they were alone, without waves, only the rugged, inexorable rock.

ST. GILGEN.

From the point on which we stand the eye sweeps over countless lakes. A series of tiny lakes, which lie in the clefts of the mountain, extend almost half the way up. But below lie their mighty brethren, now in dreamy repose, now agitated by the bright play of their waves. Thus is it with the Mondsee, and the Attersee, and that which rests under the guardianship of St. Wolfgang.

Farther away, for miles, through which the eye glances in a second, lie the broad lakes beyond the mountains and the plain, glistening in the morning like a misty blue veil, and in the evening glowing like a glittering mirror on which the departing day looks down. Of these the Chiemsee is the most important; its surface extends for leagues and leagues, is surrounded by solitary banks, where quiet and storm rule in rapid alternation.

Here, on a perpendicular height, the rich composition of the landscape is displayed in all its glory; it is a labyrinth of beautiful outlines, which cross and pursue each other in a thousand directions. They are soon lost, now in the depths of the lake, and now in the impenetrable masses of the rocky chain;

SAINT WOLFGANG, WITH THE SCHAFBERG.

but, nevertheless, the unity of the whole is not destroyed, the sentiment of its wonderful continuity remains.

It was in those sultry days which July brings that I stood on the summit of the mountain. Heavy storm-clouds were massed around; more and more threatening they arose on high, and yet all the circle was breathless.

Most men who view a storm on a high mountain see only the outward violent effects; but the peculiar force, the psychological thraldom of these moments lies not in the outburst, but in the long, mysterious anticipation—that which the soul of Nature endures before she breaks forth in storm and thunder.

Above, yonder, it gives warning. It is quiet around us, yet there moves a secret, almost feverish life in every vein of Nature; her pulse becomes tempestuous long before the storm begins, and her visage trembles with invisible terror, even before a breath of wind has ruffled her features.

APPROACHING TEMPEST.

Looking closer, we see the power that suddenly domineers around; we perceive how the mighty rocks slowly pale before the dark, cloudy shapes which menacingly approach them. How wonderful their outlines; this one with a drawn sword, that like a winged griffin, those like black and riven battlements. Around extend the massive forests, growing ever darker and darker; they resemble an impenetrable shield which the earth opposes to the lightning. Dark green and motionless lies the lake at our feet; her spirits have plunged into the lowest depths; her flood breathlessly awaits the moment when the hurricane shall precipitate itself on her beauty and ruthlessly tear her bosom.

But a sultry grey tint lies over the plain which we survey; the clouds are so dense that it seems as if they would seize the earth in their wings, as if they would drag the very clods with them when they dart along with arrow-like rapidity to another clime.

This is the grand, dark picture of the mountains before a storm; but the tiniest thing about us trembles also at its approach. Each straw waves insecurely, the mountain grass crackles scarcely audibly, and the little bird flutters restlessly by and vanishes into the copse which conceals him. The vulture descends from his height, and we look up at the broad grey pinions which bear him slowly below.

But the same sentiment stirs in the vegetable world, in that world which we call lifeless. No breath of wind disturbs the deathly stillness, yet an immense pine before which we stand bends its head in secret anguish, as if to prove its strength, like a giant who tests his limbs before the combat. He embraces the rock with his roots more firmly than before—the ancient throne on which he grew up, and which he has possessed a century long. Grey and mouldering, yonder lie his fallen brethren. Yes, a mysterious terror imprints itself on the face of Nature; when the tempest approaches, all is armed for the trying moment, which is a battle in the long struggle for existence. Listen; now the first squall of wind roars: the trumpet-call to battle. The clouds cast themselves upon the mountains as once the giants did, grey darkness envelopes us, the rain pours down in torrents. The glaring missiles are now discharged with a rushing sound, and when the thunder strikes the rocks they groan as if struck by a club. We hear cries of joy and grief, songs and yells—storm! storm! resounds from a thousand voices.

A little hospice stands on the top of the mountain dependent on the innkeeper of St. Wolfgang; it fulfils the meritorious task of providing for five or six thousand tourists yearly. Among the plenty of things to be seen here we cannot include an inspection of the building, which is almost unique in Germany; so we beg the Lares of this "high house" to rest satisfied with this brief acknowledgment.

Although the season does not last long, and the place is subject to the severe climate of the higher mountains, still even in winter the hospice is not uninhabited. Two guardians pass the time of the snows here, cut off from all the world and consigned to the freaks of an irresponsible destiny. No mortal foot can traverse the snowdrifts which the north wind amasses, levelling fathom-deep inequalities in the ground. No word, no cry penetrates through the layers of fog into the abode of men, and it was only a few years ago that they hit upon the idea of erecting optical signals. These are exhibited on a stone pillar, which is easily descried from St. Wolfgang with a glass, and below, in the inn, there is a book kept which deciphers the meaning of thirty-two signals. It is true that these can but express the most primitive ideas, and that the fog often enough bars the way, yet the consolation remains that it is a greeting from life to life, and that the eye can reach where the foot cannot follow.

INN ON THE SCHAFBERG.

XVI.

GOSAUSEE.

T is at a smithy that we obtain the first repose on the road which leads us through the Gosau Valley to the lakes. The brook, rolling along over the bare stones, murmurs its wild melodies; the pines stand alone on the edge, whilst overhead the grey rocks tower in vast peaks. Grandly and calmly the landscape meets our gaze, the melody of the waves is monotonous, and we feel that we are in the midst of a desert. Then we hear in the distance the stroke of the hammers, whilst, if we approach nearer, we see shapes blackened by smoke who rake the furnace or cool the hissing iron. Smoke and sparks shoot from the chimney, and the firs reach almost to the threshold of the old house; and all agrees so wonderfully with the cool and lonely background, that it appears to us as if some legend had been revived which we had preserved in our hearts since the days of childhood.

The little room also, with its wooden walls, and the swarthy forms which squat round the table, is an old and primitive mountain picture. There drop those rough but forcible expressions which are the heirloom of this race; the wood and the chase, the charming brook and the smoking charcoal kiln, are the only objects in their lowly life. We sit down near them and partake of their cool drink, until some one of them discreetly rises and gives us the signal of departure. He travels the same road as we, laden with the heavy axe and the long alpenstock, so we are glad to follow him up to the Gosau Lakes.

The first moment is overpowering when the nearest lake suddenly breaks upon us. It does not *lie* there, it *stands* before our eyes, so precipitously tower the rocky masses; it is as if body and soul were enthralled in this instant. And that ice-crowned peak projecting into heaven juts as far down into the depths, for the lake is as clear as a mirror, and those outlines which we follow in the atmosphere return into the abyss of waters. The Dachstein, almost the highest peak among the Chalk Alps, is enthroned as ruler over this wilderness. The boulders lie dark and confused about the lofty banks, rotten trunks of trees and luxuriant green between, and solitary woodland flowers which dream away the brief spring in this spot.

And, verily, there are dreams also in which the mind immerses itself when standing on these banks, indistinct yet mighty thoughts; we are astounded, but find neither words nor ideas. In this consists that inexplicable feeling which overcomes us in the presence of the colossal, and which is a chief component in that heterogeneous emotion which we are used to call admiration.

More forcible, but less harmonious, is the impression afforded by the further Gosau Lake. The grandeur which here lies before our eyes is that of decay; the landscape is shattered into Cyclopean fragments. It becomes dismally confined around us; the basin of the lake is but a small, bottomless reservoir, in whose waters the sides of the Thorstein, palely glancing in the sunshine, reflect themselves. The thousand feet of lofty precipice plunge almost perpendicularly down; in certain clefts alone grows the fir, but the extreme heights have not even this vegetation, everlasting snow alone reigns there.

Traces of human existence are not, however, wholly wanting in the lower regions of the Dachstein. Here are shepherds' huts; and, if we are not misinformed, there must be more than fifty of them, although they are truly more solitary and dangerous than on any of the other mountains. Animal life is also by no means wanting, and appears in its most savage form; vultures who are a match for the chamois are not a rarity, and many a flock has been thinned by them; ten years also have not passed since the last bears were seen here. But it is not the fear of these which lays its horrid spell on those peaks, it is from the invisible power that mankind flees in silent terror.

If one would seek anything similar (and all that is remarkable and unexampled induces comparison) there is really only the Eibsee which presents a like appearance; and yet, nevertheless, we must allow precedence to the Gosausee. Its aspect is more compact and uniform, and the line of its waters has at times something genial about it, which we miss in the former; also the mysterious power which the name of the Dachstein possesses has its influence. Its formation is, without qualification, one of the most interesting which the whole of the Central Alps displays; for, at the height of 7,000 feet, we find rocky plains, and plateaus with boulders, which relate a complete history of their creation. The nucleus which the Dachstein forms in the junction of the Chalk Alps, branches off into numerous arms, of which two embrace the Gosau Valley, and thereby give it its peculiar outline. However wonderful and romantic the outlines are, the names which we meet in the region are equally so. We may instance the "Dead Man," the "Window," &c., &c.

The ascent of the Dachstein, or of the Thorstein, is one of the most difficult that can be undertaken, as the endless boulders and frequent fogs fatigue the most active. Wonders of all sorts encounter the traveller on the road. If he makes for the Thorstein, the path leads past a rocky vault which is named "The Bear Holes;" but on the way to the Karl ice-field lies a mighty cliff called "Tropfwand," and the riven country around bears the appellation "The Menagerie." I see in my mind's eye how the

GOSAUSEE.

Berliner smiles. In the rocky holes perceived here, not only all sorts of game nestle, but also the legends which relate of "dragons and griffins." Here a hunter (of course this is a long time ago) shot a lizard which was five feet long and as strong as a child three years old: it came at him with open jaws; and one person (who is naturally dead also) has even seen its bones. Such a visitor has not, alas! encountered ourselves; and the reader who is inclined to dare the fatiguing journey may consider himself secure on that score. All who mount the Dachstein cannot be a St. George.

THE MOUNTAIN VILLAGE.

SKETCHES OF MOUNTAIN LIFE.

I.

HOUSES AND CUSTOMS.

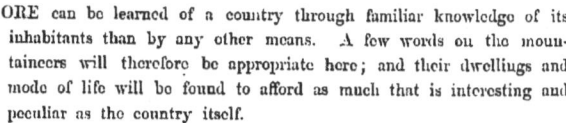

ORE can be learned of a country through familiar knowledge of its inhabitants than by any other means. A few words on the mountaineers will therefore be appropriate here; and their dwellings and mode of life will be found to afford as much that is interesting and peculiar as the country itself.

"A man is known by his company," is an old and well-known proverb: "A man is known by his house" would be equally true. Man imprints his own personality on his home, but it is no less certain that he is in his turn influenced by the character of that home; and a life-like picture will be one in which this constant mutual effect is brought out.

The characteristic peculiarities which distinguish mountaineers from the inhabitants of the plains are seen in these Bavarian Alps, both in the situations chosen and the mode of constructing their dwellings. In the plains, the low stone houses of the country people cluster together in villages, surrounded by the pasture-lands common to all; whilst the highlander, shunning the large towns which have sprung up in the lowlands and on the lesser heights, wherever increase of traffic has added to the importance of the roads, loves to settle down in solitude, and, consequently, most mountain parishes consist of lonely groups of houses, hamlets, and solitary farms, where whole families, engrossed in their work and home interests, and surrounded by their property, live in quiet simplicity throughout the year, without a thought beyond their daily occupations. Their children go backwards and forwards to school, bringing home stray scraps of news, and they go to church on Sundays and fête-days; but beyond this they have scarcely any connection with the outer world. A visit to the annual fair in one of the larger villages, the wedding of a friend, and the church festivals are the most stirring incidents of this idyllic life.

The following are the chief peculiarities of a mountaineer's house:—it is built of wood—that is to say, of hewn beams planked inside, and it generally has an upper story, a sloping gabled roof, and a wooden gallery running round the upper story and called the "Laube" (arbour). In many of these houses, however, the ground-floor is of brick, but the upper part is even then invariably of wood, and stone houses, like those in the towns, are only erected in cases of misfortune: when a village is burnt down, for instance—as was the charming Oberaudorf on the Inn,—or when a peasant has become over rich, and not knowing what to do with his money, feels bound to show off his cultivated taste. The walls of these houses are frequently—in some places, as in Ammergau, universally—painted with figures, chiefly sacred, and the window-frames with chequered patterns or pithy proverbs. The front of the house generally faces east or south, and fruit-trees shut out the view from the windows, however beautiful it may be. Peasants do not care for fine views, they have not time to admire them; and if they do wish to see them, well, they can easily go a little distance from home for the purpose. The decorations extend even to the roof and to the balustrades of the balcony; the former often ends in two animals' heads looking in opposite directions, with a cross between them, and from the top of the roof rises a little wooden belfry, with a bell for summoning the family from their work at meal-times and for raising an alarm in cases of necessity. Few are now able to account for the animals' heads; they are, in fact, an unconscious relic of the old heathen days of Germany, when horses were sacrificed and their heads stuck on the gable as an ornament: the cross between them has converted them. The "Laube" is the prettiest part of the house, and is filled with flowers, principally carnations, in clumsy wooden boxes, and house-leeks, the latter being held in esteem for their medicinal properties. In some neighbourhoods—for instance, in the province of Salzburg and at Berchtesgaden, formerly belonging to Salzburg—a second smaller balcony, or "Laube," is constructed over the first, under the gable, and adds considerably to the beauty of the whole building. When a peasant builds, he is generally his own overseer; carpenter and mason working under him for their board and daily wages, and the whole household energetically assisting. In the district of the Inn it is usual to erect the whole framework of the house and to put on the roof before filling it in with walls and panels. A slightly-raised platform, called the "Gräd" (step), generally runs round the ground-floor, affording a dry and sheltered promenade in all weathers. The entrance-hall opens into the hall, or "Fletz," with the kitchen and entrance to the stable at the end, a sitting-room on one side, a bedroom on the other, and a rude, and sometimes very steep, staircase leading into the upper story. Near the door of the sitting-room, which has generally a wooden ceiling and wainscoted walls, is the large brick stove, with a bench running round it, and in the nook formed between bench and stove a wooden settle, called the "Ofenbruck" (oven-bridge), the refuge of the sick and aged poor, and in the winter of sturdy, frozen-out labourers. A wooden bench runs right round the walls of the room, and in one corner, supported on four clumsy legs, stands the table, polished smooth with scouring, on which the common meals are served. Near to it, on the deep window-seat, lie the only books required by the household, the almanack and the prayer-book, with, perhaps, the children's copy-books. A crucifix—the household altar, decked with a few bunches of artificial flowers,—a cupboard let into the wall, a Black Forest clock, and a few wooden benches complete the furniture. Upstairs are the maid-servants' bedrooms (the men generally sleep in the hay-loft or stable) and the state apartment of the house, where the master and mistress sleep, distinguished by the brightly-painted four-post bedstead and the no less gorgeous coffers in which is preserved the housewife's pride—the linen in goodly piles, adorned with ribbons, flowers, and all manner of ornaments. Here, too, all valuable private possessions are treasured up: plates and dishes, jugs, glasses, cups, or fine fruit and specimens of work of a sacred kind, such as an "Infant Jesus" in wax under glass.

As we have already seen in the cross on the roof and the sacred paintings outside the houses, religious observances are interwoven with the daily life of the mountain-peasant. There are but few circumstances in the narrow circle of his experience which are not associated with religion, although in many cases, as in the gable-heads of animals, this association dates back from pre-Christian times. On the entrance-doors we find the initial letters * of the names of the Three Kings, divided by crosses. This is repeated on every door; and every year on the fête-day of the Three Kings (Epiphany), the houses are incensed and the inscription, to which is ascribed the power of protection from evil, is renewed with consecrated chalk. Beneath these letters, on a paper pasted over with coloured pictures, is printed the "Haussegen" (household blessing), a prayer possessed of similar power. Near the sitting-room door hangs a small vessel of consecrated water, for those who go in and out to sprinkle themselves with. Behind the crucifix of the household altar hangs a bunch composed of palm-buds, branches of the sacred ancestral mistletoe, which grows in trees, and some juniper tied to a hazel-stick, which must be peeled, lest the witches should nestle between the wood and the bark. This bunch is a protection from fire and lightning. In her coffer the peasant's wife carefully preserves a bit of nut-tree wood which has been held in the fire lighted in front of the church on Easter Eve, with a white wax candle and a red wax taper, both of which must have been blessed at Candlemas. If a storm comes on in the day-time a fire is lighted on the hearth and a bit of nut-wood charcoal thrown into it; if it comes on in the night, the candle must be lighted. This ceremony also takes place when any one is dying; and the red wax taper is wound round the hand of a woman in labour. All this is done on account of the evil spirits, who cannot smell wax, especially if it be consecrated, although, in other respects, they are so keen scented as to be able to distinguish the colours in smoke. Quite at the top of the house, in the so-called "Oberhaus" (loft) under the roof, are the all-powerful "Sangen," a bunch of plants picked in the "Frauendreisigst" season,† or the thirty days after the Assumption of the Virgin, at which time the powers of Nature are most favourable to man—poisonous creatures becoming harmless, and salutary plants and herbs attaining their greatest power for good. All these things are but trifles, at which we smile, as at the sports of children; but these apparently insignificant threads spread out like a net-work of nerves over the whole body, and combining in one *commune sensorium*, lead to the explanation of phenomena which would otherwise have remained inexplicable.

The costume of the mountaineer is as singular as his habitation; but we must here remark that any general assertion on this subject will be liable to even more exceptions and qualifications than what we have said about the houses, which cannot readily be altered, and also that the extremes of different styles are often so mixed together as to be scarcely distinguishable. As far as we can judge from solitary instances, or from figures on votive tablets, &c., the costume of the men in the middle of the previous century (1750) consisted of a plain linen smock-frock, a long waistcoat, and full knee-breeches; that of the women generally was a short bodice with a stomacher, the former being made of linen with dark blue sleeves, and the latter of pasteboard covered with coloured stuff, and with a border laid on; a collar of white linen, a black gauze neckerchief, and a silver ornament round the throat, completed the costume. At this time the *Louis Quatorze* mode, somewhat simplified of course, came into fashion. A long coat with a stand-up collar, a red waistcoat, leather knee-breeches with black braces, ribbed stockings, buckled shoes, and the low broad-brimmed hat were more and more generally adopted. The coat, a kind of modification of the *juste au corps*, was the same everywhere, the colour alone being different; in Chiemgau it was brown, in Berchtesgaden blue, in Ramsau black, in Isarwinkel (Länggries, Jachenau) light green, trimmed from top to bottom with real or imitation coins instead of buttons. Little now remains of all this but the pictures of the beginning of this century, and perhaps a few articles of luxury and heirlooms,

---

* These letters are C. M. B., for Caspar, Melchior, and Balthasar.—*Tr.*
† Known in Southern Germany as "Unswer Frauen Würzweihe" (Our Lady's herb-hallow-tide).—*Tr.*

only worn on special occasions, in the processions at the Munich October festival or at masquerades for instance. After this, about 1800, the dress known as the Isar mode came in, and although it had no special beauty to recommend it, it spread rapidly. In this fashion the coat was made with very long tails and a very short waist, with buttons close to the shoulder-blades, a hat of the shape of a shako, a yellow waistcoat, and knee-boots. A thick cloth mantle, falling in heavy folds, was worn over this costume in full dress. This unbecoming fashion spread considerably in the border provinces, but fortunately the people found a remedy for its ugliness by adopting the Tegernsee or Miesbach mode, the principal part of which is the grey "Joppe," or short hunting-jacket, which has become so popular of late that we have been able to rejoice in the general introduction of a new national costume. The "Joppe" itself is of Tyrolese origin, and native to the Duxerthal, where is still worn the old loose

DOWRY-WAGON BEFORE THE BRIDEGROOM'S HOUSE.

collarless shirt without buttons, button-holes, or cuffs, and with a plait at the back. Tyrolese wood-cutters probably introduced it, and at first it was only worn by them and by hunters; but it was soon generally adopted, and has been improved upon so much that it now has green trimmings, cuffs, buttons, and a collar. Many blows, however, were exchanged before the vexed question was decided whether the green collar, the emblem of hope, was to be confined to hunters or allowed to peasants also. Women, too, have a great predilection for this costume, and we meet with the laced bodice, the coloured silk neckerchief, and the high narrow-brimmed hat everywhere; it is only on fête days and in certain neighbourhoods that this head-gear is replaced by the low broad hat with falling ribbons, which is, however, equally becoming. The women are as much influenced by town fashions as the men, as we see by their readiness to distort their figures with huge wadded sleeves and crinolines, which have even reached the

"Almhütten." * Fortunately the unavoidable work to be done is a powerful controlling force, regulating stuff and pattern, and preventing sudden changes. On the whole, it cannot be denied that the increase of traffic, brought about by the railways, exercises a kind of levelling influence on mankind, so that, like short distances and boundaries, national and local differences and peculiarities are effaced. It is, then, scarcely a matter for regret that some old women still case their heads in the ugly old-fashioned black woollen hoods, or that some few beautiful girls still wear the round fur caps pushed back from their fair young foreheads.

Except in remote villages and secluded spots far away from the ordinary routes of travel, the visitor to the mountains will now find only fragmentary relics of the old fashions: a scarlet coat with silver buttons, for instance, like those formerly worn in the Saalach district, or the old "Wagnerkittel" (carter's smock-frock) of Chiemgau, a kind of picturesque shepherd's cloak, consisting of a white woollen cape, with a slit for the head, falling loosely from the throat or pulled in at the waist with a leather belt.

Of the articles of dress worn on special occasions, the bridal girdle and wreath are particularly remarkable; the latter consists of a coronet of silver foil adorned with wire, flowers, pearls, and jewels. At funerals we still sometimes meet with the "Schloar" or "Stauchen," a piece of white linen, the width of which determines the nearness of relationship with the deceased. It is worn round the throat, the throat and chin, or completely covers them and the mouth. The men generally wear short hair, a moustache, and a beard. They are fond of sticking a red flower behind one ear. The girls plait coloured ribbons into their hair and wind it round their heads. In this they follow the primitive fashion of the Boioarii, or ancient Bavarians, distinguishing them from the Swabians or Alemanni, who, as early as the days of Tacitus, had a predilection for brushing their hair flat all round their heads.

The food of the highlanders consists almost entirely of meal, milk, and dripping, with a few vegetables and a little fruit. Meat is not included in their daily diet, but is generally only indulged in on the five great festivals of the year: at the Carnival, Easter, Whitsuntide, Kirmess, or Wake, and Christmas. This has been the established custom of centuries, and is accounted for by the fact that the articles mentioned above are the most plentiful products of agriculture, and an oily diet is as necessary to field labourers as to wood-cutters, who get their muscular power from the quantity of oil they use in cooking—their food literally swims in grease. Breakfast consists everywhere of bread-soup, with milk or greasy water-soup, and a kind of cake called "Koch;" at nine o'clock a second breakfast or lunch is served, varying according to the work to be done; at harvest and thrashing time, bread and milk or boiled preserved fruits; potatoes also, which have slowly made their way as an article of diet, frequently appear, and when times are very good a little small-beer called "Schöps" or "Heinzel" is indulged in. At three o'clock—in some places every day, in others only at harvest time—"vesper bread" is served. Dinner is called "Mittelkost" on the lower hills, and "Bergkost" on the mountains; it consists of maize-cakes, turnips, and sauerkraut, with dumpling and sweet or sour milk; for supper, rye dumplings, called "Schucksen," are in many places indispensable, and are thought so much of that the quantity each man and woman is to have is fixed by rule. Generally they form the Saturday treat, and enough are baked to last for breakfast on Sunday morning; but up on the high mountains, where the greasy "Bergkost" prevails, they must be eaten daily. As already stated, meat is only used on festive occasions. At Christmas a pig, and sometimes an ox as well, are slaughtered, which also supply the grand dinners at Epiphany and the Carnival, part being salted and kept the whole year. Here and there strange tastes are indulged; at Miesbach, for instance, a goat

---

* The same thing as the "Sennhütten;" small wooden huts, in which the door does duty as chimney and window,—the herdsmen's sheds.—*Tr.*

is killed and eaten with relish. The "Kirmess," or wake, and wedding-feasts are the principal opportunities for revelling; then the poorest houses rejoice in cakes and meat, and a popular rhyme says—

> "Ein richtiger Kirta
> Dauert bis zum Irdta
> Und fehlt's nit am Kocha,
> So dauert er die ganz Wocha." *

Then appear all a peasant's culinary triumphs; four dishes are indispensable, namely, soup with meat dumplings and rolls, a sour "Voressen" (a ragout of liver, &c.), beef and vegetables, a "roast," and "wake dumplings" to wind up with. At Christmas the little cakes called "Klotzenbrod," and at Easter the "Eierbrod" (a bread made with eggs and milk), are seldom missing.

It is needless to state that singular usages abound. It would take us too long merely to enumerate them; one thing most of them have in common—eating and drinking form an essential part of them. Town festivities do not in this respect differ from rural. At a child's christening the "Kindmahl" (child's feast) is held, provided by the godfather, who gives his godson all kinds of presents, the "Seelzopf," † for instance, and once at least a complete suit of clothes. If his godchild die first, the godfather also provides the winding-sheet and funeral-wreath. The exit from, like the entrance into life, is celebrated with feasting. After the funeral the company assemble at the inn or home of the deceased, to drink to his repose; before the funeral the neighbours come to watch and pray by the corpse. The coffin is often carried to the grave by friends of the same position in life as the deceased—men by men, maidens by maidens. In the Berchtesgaden district, a bachelor is carried to the grave by old men in light blue cowls, with wreaths of roses on their heads. At one time this parish boasted but one coffin common to all, in which the corpse, sewn up in a linen sheet, was carried to the grave. At Jachenau it was customary to take the corpse to the grave in a white shroud decked with red ribbons, on an open bier, with only a small plank laid across it over the face. From some few places high up in the mountains "Todtenwege" (dead men's paths) lead down, over which none but funeral vehicles are allowed to pass. Here, under old trees, at little chapels, or by wayside crosses, the funeral service—about the length of a paternoster—is performed. The boards on which the corpse has been brought down, with the name and date of the death of the deceased written upon them, are laid upon the ground or stuck up against a neighbouring tree or hedge as a memorial.

But the prettiest and most interesting ceremonies of all take place on the occasion of the most important event between birth and death—that of marriage: the foundation of a new home. Unfortunately its chief charm is gone when we confess that, as in town, so in the country, money, not love, is too often

---

* "The right sort of feast
Takes till Tuesday at least;
And, if the kitchen holds out,
It's the whole week about."

The "Kirmess," or wake, is the most popular feast of the German year. It is the feast of the consecration of the church, and was originally held on the eve or vigil (waking time) of the Saint's day on which the church was consecrated—hence the English name "wake;" but in Germany it is now generally postponed until late in the autumn. In some places the "dying Kirmess" is buried with great solemnity. Young men and maidens repair to a chosen spot near the village, and throw wine, ribbons, and cakes into an open grave, which is then filled in with earth; the mourners return home, accompanied by melancholy strains of music, and finish the evening with a merry dance at the inn.—*Tr.*

† The "Seelzopf" is a cake to which various names are given. It is believed that for each cake of the kind eaten on All Souls' Day a soul is set free from purgatory. The "Seelzopfs" are made of very fine wheat flour, and are given to godchildren by their godparents. Cakes for boys are shaped like hares or horses, and those for girls like hens.—*Tr.*

MARRIAGE PROCESSION.

the attraction between the pair, and that the marriage has been entirely arranged by the "matchmaker." In an affair of this kind a visit of inspection is in the first place made to house, farm, and stable, the last being specially examined; and if all appear suitable, the relations meet as "assistants" or negotiators, and when at last, after many disputes, they are agreed as to the value of every head of cattle and every piece of linen, the suitor himself comes to the bride's house for the final settlement. He gives his future wife an honorarium, which generally consists of a few Bavarian thalers, as earnest-money, and she sets a "Schmarren"* before him, prepared in expectation of his visit, which they eat together as a symbol of their future partnership. When the matter is so far arranged, the bridegroom, wearing ribbons in his hat and flowers in his coat, goes round—sometimes on horseback—to invite all the friends and relatives to the wedding. This is done in all manner of high-flown speeches and rhymes, and is as important as the

SALTING OF THE SOUP.

strictest court etiquette, for a mistake has often laid the foundation of a life-long enmity. On the bridegroom's return from his round of visits, the signing of the documents takes place, all the necessary legal forms are observed, and then comes the "Stuhlfest" or formal betrothal in church before two witnesses and the parish priest, who has previously held the "Brautexamen" (inquiry as to whether the bride has been duly baptised, confirmed, &c.) A small feast is spread for the party, often accompanied by symbolic ceremonies such as the "Krautessen" (eating of vegetables) in the neighbourhood of Tölz. The bridegroom bargains with the barmaid for a spoonful of vegetables, which is a symbol of the bride, and being met with mock refusals, often has to bid pretty highly before he obtains it. On the eve of the wedding the dowry of the bride is tastily arranged in a cart called the "Kuchel," or "Kammerwagen" (kitchen or bedroom wagon), decked out with ribbons, &c., and taken to the bridegroom's house. It contains everything necessary to housekeeping: the large double nuptial bedstead with its furniture, the cradle, the

* A kind of omelette.

spinning-wheel adorned with red ribbons, a distaff, &c. Sometimes the bride sits in the cart, and sometimes she walks beside it, carrying a brightly polished milk-pail. The children of the villages through which she passes, or travelling journeymen, bar her path, and she has to buy them off with cakes or small coins. The "dowry wagon" must be at the bridegroom's door as the clock strikes twelve, and he meets his bride with the beer-pitcher in his hand, whilst she presents him with a pair of shoes, a home-spun shirt made by herself, and the keys of the treasures she has brought with her. Everything is now unpacked, carried into the house, and arranged according to fancy—the bridegroom must himself take in the straw mattress; and when all is done, everything is blessed by the priest. In the evening the bride returns home alone with the empty wagon, escorted only a short distance by the bridegroom; if, however, he marry into *her* house, it is his business to send the "Kammerwagen." The wedding day itself begins with the "Morgensuppe" (a rough breakfast of roast meat, white bread, and sausages), served in both houses, which used to be a very hearty meal. After it a few eloquent words of farewell to the bride on leaving her father's home are pronounced by the "Hochzeitlader,"* after which she is escorted by her "Kranzlherrn" ("wreath attendants," sometimes called "train-bearers") and their friends to the village where the marriage ceremony is to be performed. Music and the firing of guns often accompany their progress. Arrived at the village, the bridal procession to the church is formed, and the rules respecting it are so numerous, and vary so much, that it is impossible to describe them. The musicians always lead the way, followed by the men; the groomsmen, fathers of the bride and bridegroom, the "Hochzeitlader," &c., all wearing bows of white ribbon and sprigs of rosemary—the bridegroom has the latter stuck conspicuously in the dark violet ribbon of his hat. Sometimes another personage, called the "Hennenrupfer" (hen-plucker), also accompanies the procession as a kind of licensed fool or maker of stale jokes. After the men come the women: first the bride with her "train-bearers," then the mothers of bride and bridegroom, with their relations all in order of succession strictly laid down by etiquette, from which not the slightest deviation is permissible. The bridal girdle and wreath are generally indispensable; the bridesmaids wear wreaths, and every guest is provided with a citron and a spray of rosemary. On the way back to the inn after the ceremony, races are often run (the old German bride-race) by boys, colliers, hunters, and others. Girls—the "Sennerins," † for instance—sometimes take part in them, especially if the bride belonged to their class of life. At "gold" and "silver" weddings old men are the competitors, and the first prize of the race—which is evidently symbolic of a contest for the key of the bridal chamber—is a large gilded wooden key, which the winner wears in his hat. Pigs' tails are hung in derision about the persons of the "last in." When the bride enters her new home the cook meets her with a bowl of soup, and asks her to salt it. As a newly-married woman, she is bound to taste some soup and salt it to her liking before she is considered properly installed as mistress of a house of her own. Now comes the real wedding banquet, the style of which is a test of the match being "rich," "mediocre," or "poor." At a "poor" wedding the number of guests will vary from forty to one hundred, according to the prosperity of the place and of the principal persons concerned; at a "mediocre" wedding there will be from seventy to a hundred; and at a "rich" wedding, from one to two hundred guests. Many persons, called "Draufgeher," go to the marriage ceremony who do not partake of the feast. This is often done for the sake of economy, for the guest has to pay for his share of the good things and also to make a suitable present, called "Waisat" or "Weisat," which is put into a dish by the "Hochzeitlader." The dishes

---

* The "Hochzeitlader," literally "wedding presider," answers to the English "best man," but his duties are far more onerous and numerous. He is generally the host of the inn, who exercises a kind of patriarchal authority in his village. He arranges the weddings, &c., settles disputes, and sometimes lays down the law rather arbitrarily.—*Tr.*

† The girls who tend the flocks are called "Sennerins."

provided vary very much, but the food is always good and plentiful; the guests, however, lay aside large portions of it as the share of those left at home. The "bill of fare" always contains three courses, which include numerous important subdivisions. In the Inn district, for instance, the first course consists of maccaroni soup, sausages, sour stew, two or three pieces of beef, bread, dumplings, and "roast meat." In some places boiled millet is the special treat on festive occasions, and is even served at the wedding-feasts of the Dukes of Bavaria. In the afternoon, each guest receives another piece of beef (generally raw) which must weigh exactly one pound and a half; and the entertainment invariably winds up with thick barley-soup. Fish and venison never appear, for they "are for the nobleman's table."

Dancing goes on between each course, and, as we shall presently see, it is often very pretty and

ALM-GIRLS BEFORE THE SENNHUT.

graceful. Towards the end of the day, the "stealing of the bride" is a favourite joke, and the guests give vent to their fun and high spirits by making facetious presents and all manner of jests.

We must now say a few words on the number and condition of the population of the Highlands. In Bavaria generally there are over 2,400 inhabitants to the square mile (German), but in the mountain regions this number is considerably reduced. In the Tegernsee district there are about 874, and in the Partenkirche 650 inhabitants to the square mile. If, as we do not doubt, and are assured by doctors and students of statistics, a tall population is a sure sign of the prosperity of a country, the Highlands must be very prosperous, for the "Landwehr" conscription lists, the recruits for which are measured, show a large proportion of tall men from the mountains; Tegernsee, Traunstein, and Berchtesgaden yielding eighteen, and Tölz as many as twenty-four per cent. The Highlanders are a healthy, powerful, and handsome race; it is indeed quite a pleasure to watch them at their work, which never seems to cost them an effort, however hard it may be, and their genuine, unaffected enjoyment of life on holidays is delightful; nor is this any the less true that we are obliged to admit, on the other hand, that those very neighbourhoods which boast of the tallest and handsomest men also produce the greatest number of idiots or crétins and poor creatures with the "goitre." There may be unexplained local causes for this state of things; but, in any case, it is distressing to hear, that in the most healthy districts one throat in every twenty-five is distorted, and one intellect in every six hundred deranged. The evil is at its height in Berchtesgaden, for there there is one idiot to every hundred and fifty-two inhabitants, and one "goitre" to every twenty-five. The health of the mountaineers is, however, on the whole, perfect. There are no illnesses worth mentioning, and, except in cases of accident, a good old age is generally attained, especially in the mountain-valleys. There are plenty of doctors, but a peasant must be very ill before he sends for one; he generally knows of some homely remedy, or, if not, he confides his case to one of those irregular practitioners, whom it is impossible to exterminate, who knows how to charm away ague, to cool the blood, and to exorcise warts and swellings. Certain regular phlebotomists are also still much trusted. Bathing has, unfortunately, gone out of fashion; but formerly every large place was legally bound to have a public bath-room, which was maintained by the payment of regular rates. It will be some time before the half-religious, half-medical superstitions of the old heathen days of Germany—when doctor and priest were combined in one person—finally disappear.

The mountaineers are a good-tempered, well-disposed race, with heart and head in the right place—not particularly learned, but intelligent and with plenty of common sense, which they retain even if, for the sake of "blessed peace," they sometimes obey their priests against their own better judgment. They are—at least in those places out of the way of the great streams of traffic—disinterested and obliging. They are industrious and sober, but they can't help sometimes letting off some of their superfluous vitality in a friendly boxing-match. Young men and girls mix together pretty freely; and it is a general custom for lovers to talk to their sweethearts at their bedroom windows at night. A young fellow sometimes pays rather dearly for the privilege; as, besides having to travel considerable distances, and to turn out to his work as early as if he had been in bed all night, he runs a great risk of being pelted with sticks and turf, or thrashed by rivals and revellers. Many lives have unfortunately been lost in adventures of this kind, and the evil is at its height on the Alpine pastures. "There is no crime upon the Alps" ("Auf der Alm gibt's keine Sünd"), says the proverb.

Festivals, games, and dances are considered in their place; and a few words on the language of the mountaineers must close this chapter. The Bavarian dialect, a south-eastern branch of that of Central Germany, has a soft and not unpleasing sound, and is distinguished by three peculiarities. The first is the great stress laid on the vowel "a," which often changes or completely obliterates the others; in "Bier," "Stier," &c., not content with the "i," the Highlanders change the mute "e" into "a," producing "Biä," "Stiä." The words "der Pfarrer" (the priest) are converted into "da Pfarr," the "ers" being sounded much too shortly. The second peculiarity is that the so-called soft vowels, or half-consonants (l, n, r), are carelessly pronounced or altered, so that "Geld" is changed to "Goid," and in "schauen," and "stehen," the "n" becomes a kind of nasal tone, and we have "steh̃" and "s-chaü." Lastly, as we have before remarked, the last syllables or letters are positively swallowed, so that, instead of "gleich," "genug," "Sonntag," we hear "glei'," "gnua'," "Sünta'." Many other remarkable peculiarities might be mentioned, such as the broad sound when two vowels come together, as "was dua-r-i'," instead of "was thu ich;" or "I ha's a-r-a'gschaugt," instead of "Ich hab's auch angeschaut."

Nevertheless, the language sounds very well in singing, as is proved by the popularity all over Germany of the ballads of Upper Bavaria, which indeed is so great that many have acquired a kind of recognised art-position. Hard indeed must he be to please who can listen without an amused smile to the Sennerins singing in front of their huts:—

"Auf d' Alm bin i' ganga,
Und hob mi verspat't:
Wie-r-i aba bin kemma,
Hab'n d' Mahder scho' g'maht:

"Da zieg' i mein Janker aus,
Henk' 'n für's G'sicht,
I denk' mir, am Buckel hint
Kennen s' mi' nicht."

"I went to the Alps,
But I got up too late;
And when I came there,
The pastures were bare.

"I tore off my shawl,
And covered my face,
And thought, by my back
They'll not guess who I am."

The Bavarian rhymes are called "Schnaderhüpfel" (*Schnader*, to talk or chat, *huepfen*, to dance about), and as they are written in the mountain dialect, it is extremely difficult to render them in another language. The translator has therefore, in every case retained the original in the text, giving a translation in a note, reproducing as nearly as possible the jingle of the German. The "Schnaderhüpfel" much resemble gypsy songs; they seldom exceed four lines in length, and as the rhyme is considered the principal thing, many words are often added with no reference to the subject. It is amusing to hear several persons singing these "Schnaderhüpfel" in succession, each one replying to the last, or taking up the same idea with an addition. An illustrated volume of "Schnaderhüpfel," with the music to which they are sung, was published by E. Neureuther, at Munich, in 1820.—See also Boner's "Chamois Hunters in Bavaria." (Chapman & Hall.)—*Tr*.

II.

THE SCHUHPLATTLTANZ.

VERY famous have the Highlanders always been for their dancing, and they borrow the ideas for its evolutions from natural phenomena with which their mode of life has rendered them familiar. This is the case with the renowned dance of the Bavarian Highlands, the "Schuhplattltanz."

"There is an element of great sensuality in this dance," said a North-German writer in his description of it; but this sensuality is of the "beautiful;" and where it does not attain to the realm of the beautiful, it is at least healthy, for its basis is strength, and its aim the graceful.

The idea of the "Schuhplattltanz" is taken from hunting-life—from the movements of the moor-cock and wood-grouse. In the early spring, when the ice on the mountains is still unbroken, the hunter is astir betimes, and, creeping stealthily up the hills in the grey morning twilight between the leafless trees, he surprises the big black wood-grouse whirling round the fluttering hen on the smooth surface of the snow, springing backwards and forwards, uttering his peculiar gulping call, and sometimes toppling over in his excited capers. No other word will express his behaviour—he dances.

That the people themselves are aware of this resemblance is seen in their songs:—

"Wenn der Spielhahn d' Henna kleinweis zu ihm bringt,
Wenn er grugelt, wenn er tanzt und springt,
Und dann lern' i's von dem Spielhahn droben halt
Was im Thal herunt die Diendln g'fallt.

"Den die Diendln die san
Ja grad nett, wie die oan
Wer nit tanzt und nit springt
Der bringt's niedersoht zu koan." *

The young hunter proves that he has taken the good example of the wood-grouse to heart when he enters the dancing-room "down in the valley."

In the "Schuhplattltanz" the rôle of the two sexes is simply and naturally divided. The active part is assigned to the man—he is the suitor, the leader. The part of the maiden is to wait. The dance begins quietly enough; and when its merry mazes are at their height, the different couples waltz slowly round several times; suddenly, however, the girls desert their partners. They must not leave them when standing still, that would be a great breach of peasant etiquette; they must steal away from them unawares. The ease with which the girls slip under the uplifted arm of their partners, and the rapidity with which the dancers separate, make this a very pretty figure; but it is succeeded by a scene of wild, almost frantic excitement.

Whilst the girls are modestly dancing together, the men dash roughly amongst them and form an inner circle. The music becomes louder, and the men begin to beat the time on their thighs and feet with their great brown hands. A shrill whistling adds to the uproar. One must have seen these strapping fellows and their thick, nailed shoes to form any idea of the din. The floor rocks, the ceiling trembles, the music is as loud as the trumpets of Jericho, but it can scarcely be heard. We are blinded and deafened. In the midst of the confusion one will "describe a wheel," and set the windows rattling in their panes; whilst another will perform a *pas* in the air, and spring to the ground with a crash. Gradually the music becomes quieter, the trumpeters take breath—*piano*—*pianissimo*—the men return to their partners. Now comes the "wood-grouse figure." Crowing and whistling, each one springs to his chosen mate, whilst the latter flies from him with circling motions. As the bird spreads out his wings so does the peasant his arms, now sinking to the ground before his partner, now springing towards her with wild gestures. At last he "takes the maiden prisoner."

Very intricate are the evolutions connected with this final conquest, and an old ballad says—

"Die richtigen Diend'ln
Dös san halt die kloan
Die wickeln sich gar a so
Umi um oan." †

When the dance is over, the gallant peasant takes his partner to a wooden pitcher and gives her something to drink; this is as indispensable as the silent bow with which a fashionable gentleman thanks

* "When the wood-grouse is courting the hen,
When he screams and dances and springs,
He gives me a lesson how best to begin,
If I too am anxious a maiden to win.

"For the maidens so sweet
Are not easy to greet;
No kisses for him
Who can't dance and spring."

† "The little maids are far the best,
They twirl and twist and whirl about
With never-failing zest."

the lady on his arm. It is never omitted; and no frightened mamma rushes forward to say, "My child, you are overheated!" In the room with the wooden pitcher the old folks sit and gossip whilst the young people are enjoying themselves. There plans are laid for the future, and the present is discussed with many a growl. Fine studies here for a *genre* painter! Many, too, are the queer figures in the orchestra as the night advances. Though his nerves are of iron, the eyes of the weary fiddler close involuntarily, lower yet, and lower, sinks his head upon his beloved violin, the strings of which he still strikes convulsively. The bugle-player has to be woke up for each dance, and in his hurry and confusion he often seizes the tankard instead of his instrument. It is only the young fellows and maidens who do not like to give in until the morning: "He is a good night-bird," says the proverb, " who can dance for six nights running and keep it up all the more merrily on the seventh."

Country-dances, such as that above described, are most general in the mountains; it is only at Kirmess,

when the journeymen join the dancers, that there is any real waltzing. The stable-boys, cooks, and ladies'-maids of some great man's retinue occasionally get up a polka together. The latter class, who disguise their bold manners in showy costumes, have become a scandal to the dancing-rooms since the rage for foreign travel has attracted so many great personages to the mountains, and their example is very dangerous to the simplicity of the peasants.

But, for all this, the dancing-room is a very exclusive place, where lynch law is more powerful than the police. The dancing is by no means free to all. The company form themselves into "schaaren," or sets of eight or ten. In these sets, of which there are some six or seven, friends or fellow-parishioners go together, and the dance is repeated for each "schaar." Here we see the working, even in amusements, of that class feeling which is so deeply rooted in the whole system of German law and education.

It is remarkable, too, how reserved the girls are with strangers. They do not care to dance with "gentlemen," for greater than the honour would be the disgrace to a maiden if her partner should make a mistake in the unfamiliar figures. And a girl soon loses caste amongst the young fellows of her own class if she show favour to a townsman; for, according to country notions, such a connection might easily lead from bad to worse. In affairs of gallantry, the old principle, "that a foreigner has no rights," still holds good.

Coquetry, jealousy, vanity, and rivalry are to be seen even in the mountain dancing-rooms; they exist wherever the human race has settled, and form the reverse side of the pleasant picture of familiar social life. One peculiarity of the intercourse between the sexes especially distinguishes mountain from town society,—the girls are never accompanied by their mothers. Except at weddings, the latter never appear in the dancing-rooms; and a stranger will look in vain for those worthy dames with whom drawing-room parties have made him familiar, who pry into their daughters' future lives, and themselves propose their hands in marriage. In the country there is none of that scheming which poisons society in the great world. The Highlanders love free, unfettered action far too much to indulge in speculations, and education encourages their ruling passion. As soon as they can run alone, boys and girls go their own way. The lad has his "sweetheart," the maiden her "lover," and there is no interference, except in extreme cases. Father and mother look on, and tell each other that they did the same themselves. It is, therefore, not at all surprising that girls are allowed to go to the dancing-rooms alone, and that a free and easy tone prevails there which is seldom wanting in fun.

In the mountains it is alike the duty and privilege of young men to escort their lasses home, and Gretel does not say as Gretchen did to Faust, "Without an escort I can find my way." The road down to the valley, where the lonely houses nestle against the base of the mountain, leads through fields and woods; the moon has risen above the hills and sheds her soft light over the undulating slopes. It is so peaceful—so quiet. The only sounds are the gentle rustling of the trees in the night breeze and the faint footfalls echoing through the stillness. Slowly the two move on; who could hurry at such a time? Shoulder presses against shoulder, and in the fields the path is so narrow that the long damp grass brushes against the lovers' hands.

The maiden's home is hidden in an arbour of green, the window-panes glisten in the silvery light of the moon, the well by the door whispers softly to itself, crimson carnations droop their heads over the dark brown palings. With hushed steps "Gretel" hurries to her room; she opens the sash, and a sweet face, framed in shining braids of hair, peeps shyly into the night. The lovers linger long—there is so much to say to one another—they are so entirely alone—the well ripples on unheeded. . . . . .

The fullest liberty in this and other respects is also enjoyed on the Alpine pastures, for they lie five thousand feet above—the police penal code. There, too, dancing is cultivated, without gloves, it is true, often indeed without shoes, and yet it is intensely delightful!

On the hearth in the Alpine hut sits the herd-boy, with his legs crossed, and his brown knees shining in the firelight; his hat with the black-cock feather is pushed to the back of his head, and he lazily blows his pipe, the little instrument which is so effective in the "Laendler" or "Schuhplattltanz."

And as he sits there so quietly, whilst the crackling sparks fly to and fro, in burst two or three "sennerins," who have come "zum Haingart"* together. How lucky it is that the two hunters who are going to stalk a stag in the night happen to be up here just now; a woodcutter, too, arrived yesterday; and before one knows how it comes about, the three pairs are whirling in *circulus vitiosus*.

---

* "Zum Haingart" or "Heimgart." When the day's work is done, the herdsmen and "sennerins" meet uninvited at each other's houses; they say it is "Haimgart bei Fritz" to-day, that is, Fritz receives to-day, he is "at home."—*Tr.*

The space is certainly small, but what does that matter! all the shriller is the piping, all the merrier the dance!

Up in these peaceful primitive solitudes there is more toleration of the "quality;" and if a stranger pass the night in one of the huts, he is sure to be invited to join the "ball;" and what girl could say no in such a case?

The sound of the first "jodel" has scarcely reached the lower huts, where the "gentry" encamp, before the young ladies in plaid hurry up and peep shyly in at the half-open door. "Come in, come in!" cries the hunter, snapping his fingers; and they comply in nervous haste—Countess Helena, delicate Matilda, and pretty little Marie. Respectfully the hunter takes the little hand in his on which sparkles the diamond ring, and the three noble ladies take part in the next set. Oh, how delightful is a breach of etiquette now and then! Of course it is rather awkward at first—the fair little Marie is particularly intractable! "Wait a bit," whispers the hunter in her ear, "you'll learn to follow fast enough when the right one turns up!"

Outside the hut whispers the wind, and from the distance sound the Alpine bells. One of the girls paces backwards and forwards listening to their music. There too stands the flaxen-haired "Mariechen," pushing back her curls from her heated, child-like face, and softly murmuring to herself, "Yes, when the right one turns up!" As she gazes into the night a falling star sinks from the glittering heaven into the dark valley beneath.

III.

OF "DRIVING INTO THE OAT-FIELD."

IN the pleasant land that lies between the Isar and the Inn, the old custom known by the name of "Haberfeldtreiben" is still maintained.* Here, as in a former chapter, I may say, "hardly anything remains for me to do;" for the whole of the ceremony referred to has been most fully described times without number.

To compensate the respected reader, who may lose anything by my silence, I will venture here on a new expedient.

After one of the greatest ceremonies of the kind that ever took place ("where?" says the Editor, I suppose), I received a long letter from a young peasant who was an eye-witness of the proceedings, and described to me all their details. I give his letter here *verbatim*.

With regard to its style, I must apologise for the writer, who now makes his first appearance in print, and it must be understood that the apology refers to the spelling as well as to the construction.

For myself, I only hope my young friend may never come to know what I am now doing with his letter, lest he should cudgel me for thus introducing him to fame:—

"DEAR KARL AND FRIEND,—

"I know very well that for a peasant, like myself, it is no easy matter to write an account of anything. I should better like to tell it all with my tongue.

"Yesterday we had rare fun here at our 'Haberfeldtreiben.' 'Tis an old custom, coming down from the Revelation [Revolution?] or the time of Karl the Great, and its use is to correct the bad conduct of the upper classes and of some other people who cannot be reached by the ordinary means of the law. As there are more rogues now than there used to be, so we have had, lately, more 'drivings into the oat-field,' and yesterday was a wonderful fine time for it. All the pools and drains

---

* "Haberfeldtreiben" is the name given to an old popular custom, still remaining in Bavaria, but there mostly confined to the peasantry of the rural districts lying between the Isar and the Inn. It consists in a rude, illegal kind of prosecution of certain

had been hard frozen over during the previous night, and the following night was pitch dark, so that you could not know who stood close to you, unless you were told. At eleven o'clock [P.M.] the gens-d'armes had made their 'patrol' [patrouille], when suddenly we heard of a terrific 'Spidagl' [spectacle?] taking place behind the great hill. Elsewhere, all around, all was quiet and still, as it was likely to be in such a dark night, when suddenly a light appeared alongside of the wood, and a loud outcry was heard. The police now ran forwards toward the wood, but an advanced sentinel, whom they had not seen, called out, 'Stand! or I fire.' As the bold constables would not retreat, the sentinel fired at once, and a couple of bullets whistled between their heads. And now, from the place where the light had first appeared, there came forth several hundreds of men, all 'oat-field drivers' (as we call them), and all bearing arms, and in full equipment as masqueraders. When they had taken their position on the great hill, they fired rockets, made a charivari with all their bells, and then recited their denunciations [of transgressors].

"First of all, they denounced the fat landlord of the tavern, because he sells bad beer, and victuals that are no better. Then they railed against another tradesman, and called him a miser, who has plenty of gold, and is making more and more. 'But he has no more brains than a horse,' said they; 'and he cannot help that, for his head is too short to hold them.'

"When all the denunciations were done, the 'Spidagl' [spectacle] was commenced again; a jingle was made with all sorts of old crockery and other clanking things; there was a beating upon the old drum saved from the time of the Russian war (or from some other old times), and, at last, the men fired away all their cartridges, joined in a dance, gathered themselves together in close order, and then ran off into the wood. When they were all gone, the bold gens-d'armes came out again—now in great force—but all the performers had escaped. There was no serious damage done to any one; only, at Hintermaier's farm, the wall of the pig-sty was pushed down, and two of his goats were driven away; but, early next morning, the goats were brought back by a hand unseen, and money was laid down to pay for the damaged sty. The fireworks and the music were very fine. That is all. The news about which you inquire I will send you the next time I write.

"Yesterday we had a dappled calf, and the shoemaker's little boy Johnny is dead.

"I conclude my writing by wishing you health and good luck, and am

"Yours truly,
"EGIDIUS STEINDERGER."

○　　　＊

So far the original letter of my correspondent. It betrays, with great *naïveté*, the fact that the performance he describes is viewed by the peasantry rather as "a spectacle" than as an expression of earnest moral judgment; and any person who may be present at another of these gatherings will, most probably, find confirmed the impression left by the letter. In old feudal times, when there existed only two classes—slaves and their owners—and when the right was too often thought to be on the side of might, there was, no doubt, some justification for a popular tribunal, such as has been described. Most of the old customs—or say almost all the abuses of old customs—still remaining in Old Bavaria, have their sources in local regulations of land-tenure, and this is the case with the "Haberfeldtreiben." It was, at first, instituted as a secret and masked tribunal, to avenge those who had suffered oppression, and to punish those who could not be reached by the usual processes of law. Hence the disguise, the nocturnal offenders, especially misers and usurers, who have been denounced by a supposed secret society. According to the usual process, the party denounced receives, in the first instance, several warning or threatening letters. If these fail to lead to his moral reformation, the ceremony known as "Haberfeldtreiben" takes place. A dark night is chosen for the performance. A crowd of men, masked or otherwise disguised, and carrying fire-arms, with instruments for making a loud and most discordant *charivari* (or "cats' music" as the German people call it), surround the dwelling of the offender and guard all the ways of egress. No damage is inflicted on either his person or his property; but, after the charivari, or in the course of it, a denunciation of the offender's bad practices is brought forward in the shape of a series of doggrel verses, which are sung or loudly recited.

The custom is said to have derived its name, "Haberfeldtreiben" (which means "driving into the oat-field") from a former practice of driving, with rods, certain young offenders into a field of oats and then home again. It has been asserted that the origin of the custom may be traced back as far as to the time of Karl the Great, but this is doubtful. It is, however, certain that the custom (or abuse) has been maintained, more or less, among the Bavarian peasantry since the time of the Thirty Years' War, and, despite the efforts of the police to suppress it, has continued to the present time. During recent years, it has sometimes assumed the character of persecution, often directed against some thriving man, whose prosperity has excited the envy of his neighbours.—*Tr.*

gathering, and the profound secrecy, maintained by virtue of an oath sworn by all members of the tribunal.

Taking this view of the origin of the old custom, we shall be able to predict its future. Its true destination has passed away; hence its forms have degenerated into abuses. They may continue for a time longer, but only as forms that have no real substance, or as a tree vegetates after its roots have been cut through.

It is now more than five years since the last "Haberfeldtreiben" was held in the Bavarian Highlands, and on that occasion the police were not wanting in their efforts to suppress the disorder. It is true they failed to penetrate the mystery in which the tribunal enshrouded itself; but its power was greatly reduced by calling together all the youth of the district who were subject to military law, while a foreign garrison was, moreover, stationed in the parish where the secret society intended to hold a tribunal. These measures, which sufficed for the time, were, however, only temporary and rather punitive than preventive. The true means of resistance against the illegal procedure must be internal, or rooted in popular conviction. The custom must be understood to be now obsolete in its character, and altogether without applicability to our present social condition.

Even the old-fashioned people among the Bavarian peasantry feel convinced that this is the case with their old "Haberfeldtreiben," as with their "Wilderei" (or poaching). When talking of the relics of "the good old times," they will shake their heads with a pensive expression and say, "But these things are quite unsuitable now!"

IV.

THE POACHERS OF THE BAVARIAN HIGHLANDS.

EVEN from the earliest times, love of poaching has characterised the Highlanders of Bavaria. It is well worthy of inquiry whence arises this unconquerable propensity. It has two roots—an aristocratic and a democratic. The former is that feeling so admirably expressed in the "Schützenlied" (hunting song) which Schiller has put into the mouth of Tell's son: the longing for unfettered freedom of movement.

There is something aristocratic in the character of the mountaineer; he feels a sovereign need of liberty, and it is this which more than anything else distinguishes him from the Lowland boor, with his fond clinging to the "clods of the valley."

Freedom is the heirloom of the sons of the Highlands. The bracing air, and the athletic exercise they needs must take, give them their bold and fearless bearing, and develop that chivalrous character which is so charming to strangers. The love of poaching springs from the very same causes; for hunting seems made to satisfy the innate yearning for adventure and roaming. It gives an object to otherwise aimless wanderings, it supplies an element of difficulty and danger. The hunter, with his gun over his shoulder, feels a just pride; he is no longer a mere peasant, a boor—he is a free man.

The other incentive to poaching is democratic—communistic. The struggle for the right of chase has played a political part in almost every state, much to the benefit of the classes who have no landed possessions. Whilst the lawyers were hotly contesting the matter, others came to a rapid conclusion of the controversy, saying simply, "Game is free, game has no owner;" and this idea is still retained, in spite of all game laws or penalties, and is pithily expressed in the sentence one hears constantly, "Game is for the poor: they do not demand freedom of person, but freedom of possession."

And so many of the poor have taken gun in hand, and from hunting of this sort there is but one step to crime. They no longer hunt for mere pleasure, but for profit—they are not hunters, but thieves.

This bad habit has, it is true, always prevailed; but why is it worse than ever at the present day? The immediate cause, conflicting interests, is, of course, always the same; but it would, I think, be a mistake to underrate the influence of that polemical bitterness which has now spread everywhere, even amongst the lowest classes, bringing all parties and opinions into sharper antagonism with each other. The young generation has grown up in such an atmosphere of opposition, that its more turbulent members have learnt to look upon all lawful authorities as belonging to the opposite party—that is to say, as their natural enemies. This is why so many poachers are treated by the forest authorities with a despotic rigour unknown to milder times. The rough life renders the offenders more and more reckless; and the

foresters, enraged at being set at defiance, use every means to make their power felt. And who can wonder if, under the circumstances, a state of things has arisen which, only in diplomatic language, could be described as a "cordial understanding." Poachers and keepers rival each other in hardihood, duplicity, and spite—sometimes only making each other ridiculous, while the courage displayed is amusing; but sometimes, alas! dreadful injuries or death are the results of their encounters. *Exempla sunt odiosa*, but that does not matter!

A few years ago, an active but slight young fellow was scrambling about the rocks of a mountain which many of my readers have probably climbed, and, feeling tired, thought a little afternoon *siesta* would do him good. He carefully crawled through the low bushes to a projecting ledge of rock hanging over a precipice seven fathoms deep. Here he settled himself to rest, with his "Rucksack" (back bag*), containing the unscrewed pieces of his gun, as a pillow; and, although he had certainly not an easy conscience, he was soon fast asleep. A rough awakening was before him. A kick from a heavy boot made him start to his feet in dismay. There stood a gamekeeper to whom he was unknown, with a cocked gun over his shoulder. What was to be done? On one side the keeper, on the other the precipice! To comply with the forester's order to go down with him as his prisoner would be disgrace—disgrace in the eyes of his sweetheart—he should never recover her good graces if he were brought before the court in fetters. The unlucky poacher clutched convulsively at his loose neckcloth—there was little time for consideration. Flight was not to be thought of, for the precipice was seven fathoms deep, and seven times six make forty-two; beneath were huge masses of broken rock and *débris*, and to jump on them from such a height would be to break all one's bones! But then the dear sweetheart! Anything rather than disgrace in her eyes! The poor fellow sidled to the very brink of the abyss and measured its depth with furtive glances. "Jesu, Maria, Joseph, help!" he cried in despairing accents, and took the fatal leap. One moment his body hovered in the air, one hand clutching at a bush—the next the bush swung back—hark!—a muffled crash and it is all over!

The old forester remained rooted to the spot, and muttered under his breath, "Good heavens, the devil has got a hot supper this time! (*diesmal kriegt der Teufel einen warmen Braten*). He must have been killed before he got to the bottom!" The rough man's conscience began to reproach him a little. "I needn't have driven him to despair," he thought to himself. "He deserved his fate, I know; but I might have given him time to repent!" He shrank from looking over the precipice; but as he gazed absently before him, a shout from below startled him, and he became aware of some one scrambling over the *débris*. It was his prisoner!

Being out of the range of shot, the impudent young fellow paused, and, waving his hat, cried, "Good evening, Herr Förster; many thanks for letting me out of your clutches so easily. I've only one further request to make: for your sake, not mine, don't follow me—don't jump over the precipice, I beg of you—it's dreadfully bad for the feet!" and, with another hurrah, he disappeared in the forest. The gamekeeper, mad with rage, forgot his remorse, and heartily cursed the lad he had pitied a moment before. "I'll be even with you yet!" he cried aloud; but meanwhile he couldn't help envying the boy his bones.

Hans-Anderl, the father of this "bone" hero, was just such another incorrigible rogue, only with grey hair. He would steal his own son's powder and shot when his back was turned, and go poaching on his own account. Merrily he trots along in the early morning twilight, his face blackened, his grey eyes twinkling mischievously, and his white hair hidden beneath a black woollen wig. For a man of seventy he climbs pretty nimbly, and doesn't stop to rest until he gets to the brow of the hill, where the deep ravine slopes down towards the east. Hush! he hears a sound. "Here comes one already," thinks the old sinner, sinking devoutly on his knees. A fine dark-coated chamois clatters over the rocks close to Hans. "Ha, ha! he flatters himself old Anderl's done for, or he wouldn't come so near; he thinks he's got a greenhorn to do with!" Another moment, crack goes the gun, and with a cry of agony the fine creature falls to the ground. As the carcass is too heavy to carry home alone, the old man carefully hides it under fir branches, for the "boy" to fetch it at night.

Meanwhile, two gamekeepers happened to hear the report which broke the early morning stillness. They hurried to the top of the pass and looked down into the ravine. "Hush!" whispered one, "some-

---

* A coarse canvas bag, capable of stretching to an incredible extent. Provisions, clothes, game, &c., are packed into it, and it is fastened to the shoulders with straps.—*Tr*.

thing's moving,—do you see? it must be the fellow who fired." The other brought out his field-glass, and with its aid distinctly saw the old reprobate toiling amongst the stones, without a suspicion of the Damocles' sword hanging over his head. It was decided to creep round upon him from the other side; and when they were about three hundred yards distant from him they shouted, "Who goes there?" The nimble old man started up as if struck by lightning, but, instead of replying, he cocked his rifle. Too late! a shot from above made him drop his weapon and fall backwards on the *débris*.

"What's done can't be undone," thought the gamekeepers, and pursued their way without closely examining their victim; he would be sure to be discovered by some one in a few days. "If only we knew who it was," they whispered to each other. "It would be a cursed mishap if it should turn out to be old Hans-Anderl, for no one would be safe from that boy of his. The only thing we can do now is to keep the matter a secret." They decided, however, to confess to the forester, and beg him to keep their counsel; so they hurried stealthily down to his house and knocked at the door.

Their account sounded laconic enough: "Herr Förschtner," they said, "we've done it now: we shot him down."

"Good Heavens! who was it?" thundered the forester. "Was his face blackened? Did you recognise him? Let's hope it wasn't old Hans-Anderl; he's always at his poaching tricks up there; and if anything happened to him there'd be bad blood enough."

"Very likely it was though," replied one of the men gloomily. "Of course we can't be sure; but, anyhow, it was an old fellow."

"Good Heavens!" again growled the perplexed forester; "a fine set-out there'll be when he's missed in the morning!" And the two culprits, looking decidedly crestfallen, sneaked out of the house without another word.

The forester's household had a terrible day of it. The master had lost his appetite, although there were dumplings, his favourite dish, for dinner; the dog got unmerited blows; and the children crouched in the hay-loft, lest the same fate should befall them.

Meanwhile, Hans-Anderl, lying in the ravine, opened his little grey eyes and accepted the situation. It was only small shot after all. He carefully examined his wound; five or six of the fatal little grains had remained embedded in his thigh. In default of surgical instruments, the old practitioner pulled out his eating-knife and commenced operations. One shot after the other he drilled out of the wound; and when they were all removed, he pocketed them, stood up, and went his way. "If only they haven't stolen my chamois!" he thought to himself. But no! thank goodness, the booty was still where he left it.

The next question was, had the men recognised him in spite of his disguise? If so, he would be summoned before the court, and "the court" is to a peasant what Tartarus was to the Hellenes. Now was the time for a masterstroke of diplomacy. The forester's house was about two hours' distance from the spot where he was "shot dead;" how would it do to go there at once and make some trifling inquiry? No one could then possibly imagine him to be the man whom the gamekeepers had left for dead. No sooner thought of than done. A friendly stream served for washing-basin and looking-glass. The blacking on his face removed, he hid his rifle under a stone at the cross way, and for the rest he trusted to his wits. With the merry face of one about to make a joke, he clambered down and knocked at the forester's door. The ghost of Hans-Anderl had haunted the unfortunate man in authority the whole day, and when he saw him standing before him in the body, he could scarcely disguise his pleased surprise.

"You ordered a few loads of wood the other day," began Hans in a respectful tone; "and as I happened to be passing, I just came to ask how soon you want it."

"Well, this is comical enough!" said the forester. "We were talking about you this very morning. You know you are said to be a reckless poacher, and there was a rumour about that you had been shot in the act."

"Come, come, Herr Förster, don't make fun of me," said Hans-Anderl, assuming a half indignant, half amused expression, "don't you see how lame I am? *My* poaching days are over. So they've shot some one, have they?—serves the rascal right!" and, respectfully touching his hat, he hobbled off, calling back, "I'll bring the wood to-morrow."

"Well," said the forester, "if somebody is killed I'm glad it isn't he! And now we see how easy it is to misjudge a man. Fancy that old cripple poaching!"

Incidents such as these reveal the origin of the exquisite humour of the ballads of Upper Bavaria. Nowhere do the sublime and ridiculous touch each other more nearly than in the adventures of a poacher, and the result is that the national songs vary from the most touching elegies to the maddest satires:—

> "Und bal i amal sti'rb,
> Brauch i Weihbrunn koan,
> Denn mein Grab dös wird nass
> Von mien Dirndl sein Woan." *

The second class of ballads often sparkle with genial fun, and there is an arch irony about them which is inexpressibly amusing. We have met with one referring to the searching of a house for the gun of a suspected person. The arrival of the gamekeepers is graphically described; how they poked and sniffed at everything, ripping up the mattresses and overhauling the bedsteads. After a fruitless search, the accused offered them a plate of sauerkraut, of which he had a fresh barrel in the house. The officers thoroughly enjoyed it, and all the time the rifle lay cunningly hid at the bottom of the barrel:—

> "Und nar in's Sauerkraut
> Da haben's nit einig'schaut,
> Das Kraut habn's abig'fressen
> Und d' Bix ham's ganz vergessen." †

Matters do not however always end so satisfactorily. In the Isarthal district there once lived a gamekeeper who was dreaded far and near. He was seven feet high, with a broad chest, piercing eyes, and a fierce moustache. As he strode through the forest he reminded one of Nimrod the mighty hunter. He had already shot nine men, and added one to his list every year. Vengeance had been sworn against him, and he had received letters threatening to burn his house over his head; but the old man knew no fear. At night and on foggy days he prowled about the mountains with his loaded gun over his shoulder, and his boy running at his heels like an eager hound. Both father and son had been fired at, but they always escaped, and were at last considered shot-proof.

One day, however, when old "Nimrod" was on his wanderings alone, he was surrounded and taken prisoner alive by a gang of seven or eight men in masks. He was flung to the ground and bound, and,

---

* "No holy water waste on me
When Death's cold hand doth set me free,
For wet with tears my grave shall be,
The sacred tears of my beloved."

† "To search the cask of sauerkraut
Ne'er came into their mind;
They only eat the cabbage up,—
The gun was left behind."

after rating him soundly, his captors tied him to a tree and left him to starve. Three days and nights he stood with arms extended; he watched the moon rise over the mountains; he saw the stag break through the thicket and dash away in terror at sight of him; he watched the day dawn, and the evening shadows deepen into night. At the end of the third day the men returned, and as he still breathed they spared his life. They unbound him, formed themselves into a line, and made him "run the gauntlet," finally dismissing him with a hope that he would take warning by his sufferings, for the next time any one met death at his hands the "red cock would certainly fly upon his roof." *

A fortnight afterwards he shot down the next; but before the arrival of the "rothe Hahn," the harbinger of death, an order was received removing him from his post. He was sent to a low-lying district a long distance off, and when he left the mountains he wept like a child. He was a true type of the wild mountain character, in which cruelty and tenderness are so strangely combined.

In the course of last summer, I was present at the *post mortem* dissections of several poachers who had been shot. One amongst them had been a bright, merry fellow, scarcely nineteen years old, tall, well-built, and fair. He worked at a saw-mill in the day, but at night, when the wheels were at rest, he was out on the mountains in quest of adventure. He was a general favourite; for he played the "zither," and sang so beautifully sitting outside the mill of an evening, when the young men and maidens met "zum Haingart" † after the day's work.

Two days before, I had heard his joyous "jodel," and it was a terrible shock to enter the death-chamber and see him lying on the trestle in his ordinary dress. There seemed to be something unnatural about the thick nailed shoes, the short pantaloons, and the jaunty "joppe"—it was impossible to associate this picturesque costume with death. The bullet had entered his heart from the back; and as I gazed at the fine young fellow thus laid low, I was involuntarily reminded of Siegfried in the forest and on his bier.‡

The murdered man's clothes were now removed, and when his pockets were emptied, an incident occurred which I shall never forget. A slip of paper was found in his breast-pocket on which were a few freshly-written lines in pencil—the first verse of a poaching song, which the poor boy had evidently scribbled down in the early morning :

"Und sollt ich heut noch müssen
Im wald mein Leben büssen,
Ich bleib halt doch getreu
Bei meiner Wilderei.
Einmal trifft's uns ja Alle . . . ." §

Here the lines broke off—before the second verse was finished the first had been fulfilled.
The appearance of another poacher, killed by the frontier gamekeepers or custom-house officers, ||

* "Dann fliegt der rothe Hahn auf's Dach." German proverb, meaning that the house will be burnt down.
† See note, p. 111.
‡ Siegfried, the hero of the "Nibelungenlied," slew a terrible dragon; and, bathing in its blood, became invulnerable, "except in one spot, between his shoulders, where a stray leaf of the linden-tree had fallen and hung." His treacherous friend Hagen, having persuaded the hero's wife Kriemhild to show him exactly where her husband was vulnerable, ran a spear through his back as he was stooping to drink at a spring in the forest when heated in the chase. When the murderer approached his victim's bier the wound bled afresh.—*Tr.* (See Gostwick and Harrison's "Outlines of German Literature," pp. 16—21.)
§ "And if I know that I must pay
For all my sins with life to-day,
A poacher true I'd still remain,
And Death would find me still the same.
Sooner or later all must die . . . ."
|| Preventive-service men, who wear a costume like that of the English rifle corps.—*Tr.*

between Kreuth and Achenthal, was more repulsive than affecting. He lay on the bier in all the ghastly mockery of his disguise, with false beard, blackened face, and one hand clenched upon his breast. No one knew him; but, from certain peculiarities about his dress, he was supposed to come from Länggries. A couple of peasants from that place, who happened to be in the neighbourhood, were called in to identify him. With mingled curiosity and horror they approached the corpse. The rigid face was washed and the black beard removed, and there he lay, as if asleep.

"That's Long Sepp of Länggries," said one; "he was my neighbour for fourteen years."

"Yes, it's he," muttered the other under his breath; and the two hurried from the room with downcast eyes, as if they felt they had betrayed the dead.

A bit of twisted lead was found in the very centre of the heart of the corpse: death must have been instantaneous.

Late in the afternoon, a gloomy procession of ten or twelve of his neighbours came over the mountains and presented themselves at the court. Their errand was stated in a few respectful words, but their manner was haughty and threatening. They were friends of the murdered man, and came to ask for his body, to bury it at home. It was given up to them; and in the dead of the night they carried away the dismembered corpse in a well-appointed coffin. Some rode on the cart, others walked beside it as a guard of honour; the noise of the wheels drowned their voices, but the muttered whispers sounded like vows of vengeance. Länggries is now, so to speak, the head-quarters of the poachers. Its geographical position is admirably adapted to the sport, and the natives are an extremely hardy race. Then, again, the Isar, which flows down from the Kerwendel Mountains, is ever at hand to speed the despatch of ill-gotten joints of chamois and haunches of venison to the Munich market.

"It was not thus in the good old days;" and so people grumble, as they do about the "Haberfeldtrieben," that poaching is "falling into decay." The young rogues of the present day are too imbued with the spirit of the times—the annexation fever rages too high. Formerly, boys saved up their money for years in order to buy a gun; but now they steal the weapon to begin with, then the chamois, and then the wheelbarrow on which to carry off their booty. Wood and game are alike more recklessly destroyed. Formerly there existed harbours of refuge in the mountains, where the wounded doe and orphan fawn were protected from the gamekeepers by the poachers; but now they shoot down mother and child without pity. So say the old people, and they are not altogether wrong. The poacher who hunts merely for excitement spares the game, because it is dear to him, because he looks upon it as his own property; but the game stealer, feeling that he is acting illegally, destroys what he cannot carry away.

To what this passion for theft may lead when it entirely masters a man will be seen in the following tale, in which I was myself an actor some few years back, and which I cannot remember even now without a shudder.

THE LIFE OF A MOUNTAIN ROBBER.

It was about the end of October, when the hoar-frost had begun to whiten the fields and footsteps to echo from the hard ground. I had been to a woodcutter's hut far up in the mountains, and I did not start for home until nearly midnight. I had about two leagues to walk, and the road led for some distance through the forest, and then skirted round the lake, on the further side of which lay my house. I dawdled carelessly along, for it was a beautiful starlight night, and the moon was at her first quarter. On either side of the path rose gloomy fir-trees, the branches creaked softly as leaf after leaf fell to the ground; the keen night wind blew in my face, and the deepest stillness reigned around. Suddenly I heard steps behind me, but no one was to be seen. I quickened my pace, but whoever it was, gained upon me rapidly, and soon caught me up. In a rough voice he wished me "Good night," and I examined him closely. He wore the ordinary costume of a peasant, but he was more squarely built, and his manner was more gloomy than is usual amongst the boors of the district. The "Rucksuck" hung at his back, and he held a broad axe in his hand. There was certainly something criminal in his appearance, and the darkness did not improve him. "Good night" from him sounded almost ironical, for I at least felt far from comfortable.

Of course we pursued our way side by side, and I could not help feeling that, however unpleasant it might be to be out on the mountains alone at night, it was far worse to have such a companion. I involuntarily associated the sharp edge of his axe with my own neck. "Well," thought I, "we shall see."

What struck me most about him was a certain boastful tone not at all natural to a peasant, who is generally very reserved with strangers, and inclined rather to under than to over-rate himself. Except for this he seemed a sensible fellow enough, and now and then expressed quite refined and chivalrous sentiments. Only once did he let fall a word which threw a faint light on his real character. When we came in sight of the rugged rocks of the Halserspitze he pointed to them and said, "There lies one whom I sent in," at the same time making a gesture in imitation of a marksman taking aim. "Indeed!" I replied, in a faint voice, thinking to myself, "Matters are improving, certainly."

Silently we trudged along, side by side. Every remark he made I at once agreed to—in fact, I was as "amiable" as possible; but when we came to the precipice overhanging the lake, I managed to slip to the other side of my companion. At last we neared our house. Dangerous as it had seemed to be out alone with the man, it seemed still more perilous to try to get rid of him; yet I was unwilling to let him know where I lived, and to turn my back on him to open the door. My heart beat audibly when I at last stopped at the low garden gate. "Ah, that's where you live, is it?" cried my friend; "then you're one of the climbing fellows?" "Yes, I am," I replied; "and now tell me where you live, and who you are, that we may know each other again when next we meet."

"Oh, I'm Franzl!" he replied, with a mysterious smile. "Good night."

He lounged away, but I dashed into the house and banged the door after me, feeling as if "Franzl" had pushed in with me and was following me up-stairs. It was half-past one.

The next morning there was a rumour afloat in the Tegernsee district that "Wiesbauer Franzl" was about again. He had escaped from prison and returned to the mountains by way of Länggries. I shuddered: there could be no doubt that I had had the honour of his company the night before. The descriptions of him and his laugh at parting all pointed to the same conclusion. So my new friend's proper "home" was in prison.

Franzl was the son of a pauper peasant of the Miesbach parish, and had early given proof of his laudable abilities. Constantly in disgrace for poaching, he gradually sank from poetic to prosaic theft, and from petty stealing to highway robbery. Fear is generally unknown to the Bavarian Highlanders, but a kind of mysterious horror became associated with his name. He never remained long in one place; he was here, there, and everywhere. His haunts were known to none, but he was the dread of every one, far and near, and he at last created a positive terrorism. In the middle of the night "Franzl" would appear at some house, knock at the door, and arouse the inmates. The mistress must get up, light the fire, and cook a meal for the intruder, whilst he sat on the hearth and chatted pleasantly to her. He did not steal for the sake of stealing; he merely asked for what he wanted when he required it. His demands were complied with readily enough, for people were intimidated by the boldness of his manner. If he was well received, he behaved like a guest, and made himself at home. He never took from those who could not afford to give; but if rich people showed any hesitation, he would vow, with awful curses, to set fire to their houses and burn down the whole village. He was a genuine freebooter of the old type, generous or revengeful, as it happened to suit him.

After a great deal of trouble, he was at last captured and lodged in the jail of the principal town; but, with desperate courage, he managed to escape, by letting himself down outside the prison from a height of several stories. Once on firm ground he was soon off to the mountains; and again the name of "Weisbauer Franzl" was in every mouth, whilst the old horror returned with redoubled force. It was unfortunate for me that I was now numbered amongst his acquaintances, for I feared that he would avail himself of the privilege to invite himself to supper some fine night.

Very soon, he gave me fresh uneasiness. I was alone at home one evening, sitting at work near the lamp, when my old maid-servant ran in and said in a frightened whisper, "Only think! there's been some one sitting on the doorstep for the last quarter of an hour! I've watched him from the kitchen-window, and I'm afraid it's 'Wiesbauer Franzl!' Jesu, Maria, Joseph," she added, "he's sure to knock presently and want to come in!"

Annoyed and curious, I hurried softly up-stairs in the dark, meaning to open the window softly and reconnoitre my visitor, as it might be only a harmless journeyman availing himself of a convenient resting-place; but, in spite of my caution, the stranger heard me open the window, and looked up without changing his position or uttering a word.

It was "Wiesbauer Franzl." To propitiate him, I spoke first, saying with assumed friendliness, "Do you want anything, Franzl? Are you hungry? shall I bring you some food?" But the rogue replied with a stoical shake of the head, "You needn't trouble to do that, Karl; I've had my supper, and I've got further to go to-night. I'm only resting a bit." Soon afterwards he got up and went his way.

When the first snow fell I left my summer residence and went back to the town, but my friend Franzl remained in the mountains and continued his requisitions. I did not learn his further adventures until my return the next year.

One day, after an afternoon nap, he fell into the hands of the bailiffs. He was triumphantly lodged in the county jail, and every one breathed more freely, although no one felt perfectly safe even then, so indomitable was his bearing.

Fresh alarm was soon created on his account. The very next morning had scarcely dawned before the jailer was at the doctor's door, tugging at the bell like a madman. "Make haste, doctor, make haste!" he cried. "Franzl has hung himself in the night. I was on my rounds, and I've just found him hanging from one of the window-bars. He was stone cold, so I didn't cut him down." The doctor rushed to the prison and found everything exactly as he had been told. In a fit of the wild despair which comes over energetic natures when all escape seems cut off, the bold robber had determined to make an end of himself. The doctor at once cut the linen noose, cold water was thrown into the poor fellow's face; but it was all in vain, he gave no sign of returning animation. The news spread like wildfire from place to place, and people said it was Franzl's first useful action. "If he's really gone!" croaked some; "the devil is not to be trusted until he is actually in his grave!"

Meanwhile, preparations were made for the dissection, and the attendants were about to undress the corpse, when, behold! the eyelids trembled, the muscles quivered, and the dead was restored to life. It was high time, for the dissecting knife lay ready upon the table. And so the vital force of the young criminal had triumphed over his will, and, in spite of all his efforts, he found himself still on this side the grave.

He was restored to consciousness with every care and taken back to his cell, to be forwarded the next day to Munich, as none of the authorities cared to have the responsibility of him; the prison itself seemed unsafe as long as he was in it. He himself was doggedly submissive, and seemed to be in very low spirits. Instead of rejoicing in his restoration to life, he was evidently meditating some other desperate scheme.

The next day a farmer's cart was hired, and Franzl, bound hand and foot, was placed in it. The people stared inquisitively at the notorious prisoner, and the equipage slowly ascended the precipitous road above the lake. Suddenly a slight snap was heard, the fetters were broken, the cart jerked violently, and the culprit was gone! Head foremost he plunged into the lake; for a moment the waves closed over him, the next he was swimming rapidly away. As none of his escort could follow, or rather as all shrank from a hand-to-hand struggle in the water, a boat was got ready for the pursuit.

In spite of the start he had had, the sturdy rowers soon caught up the fugitive. But what then? At first he dived to baffle his enemies, but his breath being soon exhausted, a fearful conflict ensued. As it was impossible to reach him by other means, some of the men struck him on the head with their oars whenever he came to the surface of the water, hoping by this means to stun him. But his iron skull was not to be cracked, and as for seizing him and dragging him into the boat, that was quite out of the question, for he presently flung himself upon it like a maniac and tried to capsize it. The danger was now all on the side of the pursuers. A storm was rising, and it was found advisable to relinquish the pursuit for the time. With considerable difficulty the little boat regained the shore,

K K

whilst the fugitive found a safe place of concealment amongst the tall rushes on the banks of the lake. When it was quite dark he crept out, and decided that it would be good policy to disappear for a time. For weeks nothing further was heard of him, and it was thought by many that he had perished in the storm. But suddenly he reappeared as though he had risen from the ground. He was not improved. Indeed, his hatred of all legal and peaceable occupations seemed to have been intensified by his late adventures. He took up the feud with society with greater ferocity than ever, and he was now always accompanied by a four-footed friend—a huge yellow wolf-hound, who followed close at his heels. He would lick the robber's hand lovingly, and look inquiringly up into his face; but he was as misanthropically disposed towards all the rest of the world as his master. The devotion was mutual: Franzl always gave the first mouthful of the food he "requisitioned" for himself to Wolf, and Wolf showed his teeth, without any sign from his master, if any one hesitated to comply with his demands.

The dog was the only creature for whom the reckless criminal retained any affection, and it was evident that neither of the friends would care to survive the other. Franzl became more and more overbearing and exacting, and the terror amongst the people increased in proportion. One night he again aroused the wife of a peasant, and ordered her to cook him some food. Trembling, she appeared at the window, and refused to comply with the extraordinary request. He was standing below the balcony, and as she spoke he flung his great knife into the house with such force that it went through the wall. "You saw it, did't you?" he shouted in a menacing voice. "Next time it will go through your body;" and with that he turned on his heel, followed by his dog snarling and foaming at the mouth.

All search for him was in vain; in fact, it is but labour lost to endeavour to track a rogue in his own mountains. He had long been an outlaw in public opinion, and at last, as all other means failed, a price was set on his head. There was nothing else left to be done.

At a certain spot where two roads meet stands a large lonely inn, conducted in quite the old style, with oaken tables and earthenware drinking-vessels. On the wall of the public room hang the carriers' notices, beneath the stove snores the watch-dog, and the host is the despotic sovereign whose authority is never questioned.

One evening a few travellers were assembled in this room, wearing their picturesque hats with the jaunty feather pulled forwards. Suddenly the door opened, and a sturdy looking fellow walked in and sat down with the rest. They all knew who it was as well as we do.

It was the very day on which the writ against him had been issued. "Franzl," cried one, "do you know that a price is set upon your head?" "Whoever takes you will get fifty gulden," added another. "I should think you were glad of that, for folks say you're worth nothing!" Everybody laughed. Franzl, however, did not move a muscle; but stood with arms akimbo, and cried scornfully, "Well, here I am, any one with a knife and no money is welcome to me."

Every one remained seated, but the wolf-dog growled from beneath the table as if he understood what was going on. Without another word Franzl resumed his seat, and went on drinking and chatting pleasantly as had been his wont of old. He was, however, rather more subdued than formerly, and in about half an hour he laid a kreutzer on the table and went out into the darkness without a word of farewell, but the dog turned at the door to snarl and show his great fangs.

"He took no pleasure in cards to-day," observed one who had proposed an interdicted game of chance to him. "It isn't likely," replied his neighbour, "that a fellow whose own game is up is likely to care much for any other." And they drew their chairs more closely together, and whispered, "He won't pull through this time." "'Dead or alive,' says the writ," muttered one under his breath.

PURSUIT.

Two days later Franzl once more knocked at the door of a peasant's house. It was in the neighbourhood of Gmunden, on that lofty pass which encircles the mountain like a chain, and stretches from Tegernsee towards Miesbach. When the housewife came to the door she recognised the outlaw at once, but concealing her alarm, she treated him as a poor traveller, and asked him into the house. Meanwhile her husband called in the neighbours to his assistance. Silently they crept through the back door into the stable, and consulted how best to overpower the unfortunate Franzl. No one had courage enough to volunteer, and murmurs arose of "'Dead or alive,' says the writ; how would it do to shoot him down?"

Amongst those assembled was a young soldier, a capital shot, who had left his regiment but a few days before. He judged the case according to martial law, and was of opinion that the reward would be paid for killing, not capturing, the accused. "He's sure to kill some one else if he lives any longer," thought the young warrior to himself, "so I'd better put him out of the way at once."

"My double-barrelled gun hangs behind the stove," whispered the master of the house, and a breathless silence ensued.

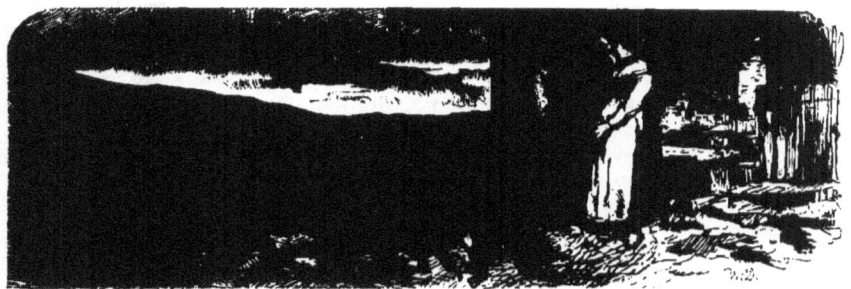

Meanwhile Franzl had finished his dinner, and prepared to take leave. "God bless you!" he exclaimed to his hostess; "and if you are asked who your guest was, you can say it was the 'Wiesbauer rogue!'"

With these words he left the house, but a slight figure slipped in from the other door, wearing the blue soldier's cap. Noiselessly he took down the weapon, and hid it beneath the window-sill. Then the little lattice opened softly and a voice cried, "Not so fast, Franzl; stop, or I fire!"

Franzl turned round with a scornful laugh: "Any one who wants me had better come out to me; I dance attendance upon no one!"

Another step; a whizzing report; and he fell to the ground like a tree smitten by an axe, the blood gushing from his mouth, and his hands tearing up the earth.

"At him, Wolf!" he cried with his last breath; and the poor dog dashed at the open window foaming with rage. Another crack, and the second discharge was lodged in the faithful creature's body. With the death-rattle in his throat, he managed to drag himself to his master's side, and after a few convulsive struggles he expired.

It was a strange coincidence that I happened to pass this spot on my way from the town to the mountains on the very day of this fatal occurrence.

Awaiting legal authority for its removal, the body lay exactly as it had fallen,—nothing had been touched since the tragedy took place.

Very mixed were my feelings as I gazed at the corpse of my old travelling companion of that ever-memorable night in the previous autumn. As all attempts to waylay him had until now been unsuccessful, it was popularly believed that Franzl had been in league with witches and possessed some magic means of making himself invisible; and, sure enough, when his body was searched, a root of mysterious form was found in his pocket. What it signified no one could make out, but, of course, it strengthened the popular superstition. "Wiesbauer Franzl" is still talked of like a ghost in hushed whispers, and the root, which no one dared to touch, is in my cupboard.

One would imagine that there could be no mysteries in the simple, primitive life of peasants, but beneath the quiet surface of country life in the highlands reigns a disguised volunic despotism—a kind of tyrannical class-unionism, the results of which alone are visible: the avenger appears suddenly, as though risen from the ground; the criminal disappears as if the earth had swallowed him up. Every one is in the secret, yet all inquiries are met with professions of ignorance. I will relate a short anecdote in confirmation of these remarks.

To this day I remember a scene in the inn at Kreuth. It was an autumn evening; the moon was at its full, and some custom-house officers and game-keepers were seated round a table close to the window. Suddenly there was a flash, a report; the window was shivered to fragments, and a bullet whizzed between the heads of the two men sitting close to each other, and buried itself in the ceiling. One of them merely passed his hand coolly over his ear, as "Tiras" would his paw; but his companion rushed out of the door. It was the work of an instant, yet not a creature was to be seen. The moon shone brightly; the most perfect stillness reigned around! Every nook and corner was searched in vain.

Legal prosecution is in such cases rarely successful. The identity of the culprit is generally doubtful, and in cases where conviction seems certain means of evading it are found.

Nothing can remedy this state of things but change in the tone of feeling on the subject. It is not the law, as many think, but public opinion which requires improving.

V.

THE BONFIRE OF THE SUMMER SOLSTICE.

DRAWING upon popular tradition, we find that it places the essence of nature in the elements. The common people found the Creator himself in the creative power of flame and wave, and gradually the elements became the centre of worship and legend. Thus was manifested before the dawn of history the innate tendency of the human race to embody the objects of its worship. The Greeks deified the creative power under the name of Neptune or Vulcan, and the early German races —in whose legends the epic and romantic elements are equally powerful—originated the earth and fire-spirits.

It is plain that on the advent of Christianity a turning-point was reached, when the nature-worship of the infancy of nations was supplanted. But the first missionaries of civilisation, with worldly-wise tact, respected the old usages. The long-spun threads of habit were not roughly cut asunder with the sword, but the root from which they sprung was imperceptibly removed, and a new meaning given to the old forms. Wherever it was possible, the same places and mode of worship were acquiesced in, the object alone of reverence being changed. The saints stepped into the place of the heathen gods.

To this we are indebted for retaining so many links with primitive times in our present state of civilisation. Such a link is the solstice bonfire.* Heat is the indispensable vital force most constantly present in the mind of man, and no other element assumes such countless forms. What a chain of associations connects the sacred spark on the hearth of the ancients with the numerous flames of a

---

* Also called the *Beltane* or *Beal* fire; from *tin* or *teine*, fire, and *Beal* or *Beil*, the Celtic Sun-god. Another name is the *Nothfeuer*, English *need-fire*, allied to the Swabian *gnida*, to rub, the fire being obtained by the friction, or "kneading," of two pieces of wood, &c. A light thus obtained was supposed to have special virtues.—*Tr.*

chandelier; how thrilling, how irresistible is the cry of "Fire!" when it rings through a town or when it bursts from the lips of a leader in battle: "Fire!"

Fire-worship, then, became general in the earliest times, and although Christianity has turned it to its own account, it is to those remote days that we must look for the origin of existing customs.

In the Harz Mountains; on the Rhine, and in Westphalia, we find the "Judas fire;" and in Southern Germany—particularly in Upper Bavaria—the "Easter" and "St. John's fires." The former are lighted in the night of Easter Eve, after the Resurrection is over, and are most prevalent in the western angle of the mountains, although we meet with them pretty frequently in the lowlands and Swabia. On the twenty-third of July, St. John's Eve, the Solstice bonfires are lighted. From peak to peak flash the flames, from Alp to Alp echoes the jodel song.

The superstitions and most of the ceremonies connected with the Solstice bonfire are now extinct, but the most important custom of all, the so-called "wheel-driving," is still sometimes practised.*

A round, cut from a wooden water-pipe, or an old cart-wheel, is daubed with pitch and stuck on a long pole. Sometimes an arrow dipped in pitch is used; and when the St. John's fire is lighted, the burning wheel is whirled round and round and flung through the air, describing glowing circles. As it rushes along, the wheel-driver repeats a verse containing the name of the person to whom the wheel is dedicated. Many of these verses are still extant, and in them we find a strange medley of venerated persons. At one time, when the religious element predominated, the fire was blessed by the priest, and the name of the Holy Trinity was pronounced. But at Nauders, in the Tyrol, a wheel was formerly driven in honour of the devil, and the circles it formed in the air were said to be "interminable."

Gradually, however, human interests got the upper hand, and now young fellows generally shout out the names of their sweethearts:

"O du mei liebe Scheib'n
Wohin soll ich dich treib'n?
In die Mittenwalder G'moa,
Der Lisei ganz allein." †

To use a modern expression, we sometimes see at these ceremonies how "exclusive" the peasants are. Many speak diplomatically, that is to say, with reserve, and give their wheel no more definite direction than the following:

"In d' Bayrish Zeller G'moa,
Da weiszt schon, wen ich meine." ‡

Like many other customs, the "Haberfeldtreiben" for instance, this "wheel-driving" provided a means of expressing public censure. The wheels of fallen women were flung in derision, and awkward people were held up to ridicule. A verse has been handed down in which a wheel is dedicated to some one who had led a gosling to the water with a string.

In earlier times solemn preparations were made for the need-fire. Four boys went from house to

---

* The "wheel-driving" originally symbolised the declension of the sun from his solstitial height.—*Tr.*

† "Whither shall I send thee,
Oh, my precious wheel?
To Mittenwald, to Lizzie fair,
The only maid for whom I care."

‡ "Amongst the maids of Zell, I ween,
Thou knowest well the one I mean."

MIDSUMMER DAY'S BONFIRE.

house singing to collect wood for it; all were bound to contribute willingly, and all the saints were invoked:—

> "Heiliger Sankt Veit—Schick uns ein Scheit;
> Heiliger Hans—Ein recht ein lang's;
> Heiliger Sixt—Ein recht ein dick's;
> Heiliger Florian—Zünd unser Haus nit an." *

Another verse closes with a prophetic warning:—

> "Wir kommen vom Sankt Veit—Gebt's uns auch a Scheit,
> Gebt's uns auch a Steuer—Zu unserem Sunnwendfeuer;
> Wer uns keine Steuer will geben—Soll das nächste Jahr nimmer erleben." †

This mode of collection, which formerly prevailed throughout Upper Bavaria, and extended as far as Swabia and Franco, has now fallen into disuse, like the many rites and ceremonies formerly bound up with the St. John's fire.

The earliest records of the need-fire connect with it the burning of witches. These unhappy creatures are mentioned in many of the verses which have been handed down to us, and in many neighbourhoods a straw doll was even recently thrown into the Easter fire. The mug-wort, a magical remedy for all sicknesses, was also flung in, and an old herb-book of 1678 says: "Not only did the old women practise these superstitions, but much higher folks (viel hoher leute), who considered themselves very wise and sensible." Many other mysterious remedies are in the same way connected with the St. John's fire.

It was a general custom to take a charred log from the need-fire and preserve it on the hearth at home or bury it the same day in the flax-field. A special meaning was also assigned to jumping over the fire. The higher a man jumped, the higher his flax would grow that year. Prophecies were made according to the course taken by the wheel. Everywhere, however—but specially in the Bavarian Highlands—the old meaning of the St. John's fire is quite lost, although the custom itself is retained.

The true home of the need-fire is in the district overlooked by the Karwendel Mountains, but it still blazes on the twenty-third of July in Grünwald, Mittenwald, and in the east, from Watzmann to the Benedictenwand. It is a beautiful sight from the valley; and the long rows of illuminated points are visible from an immense distance.

Every one does not admire them, however; for at Starnberg an old lady from the north once said to me quite seriously, "Only look, that must be a torchlight procession on the mountains for the dead students!"

The natives who light the fires generally object to the presence of townspeople: on these special occasions they like to be "private." All manner of "rendezvous" are arranged which strangers might interrupt, and the inn-keepers try to dissuade travellers from mountain excursions on the day of the need-fire.

I myself witnessed a Solstice fire on the Wendelstein, a few leagues from the Schliersee, some years ago. This mountain is famous as the "Hort des bayerischen Almensangs" (Stronghold of Bavarian mountain song).

* "Send us, holy St. Vitus, a large log of wood;
And, holy Hans, a fine one and good;
Holy St. Sixtus, a good one and thick;
Of our house, holy Florian, burn not a stick."

† "We come from St. Vitus, and wood we desire;
Give us too some branches, to help our need-fire.
Who gives us no wood to help our need-fire,
Twelve months shall not pass before he expire."

A merry party of foreign ladies and gentlemen made the ascent with me, and perhaps the reader would like to accompany us to the bonfire.

It was delightful and refreshing to step from the dense wood to the cool Alpine pastures; the sun had set; the grass was already wet with dew, and the cattle, with tinkling bells, were wending their way homewards.

The wood was piled up on a ledge of rock not far from the "Alm," or "Alp" (mountain-pasture). A commanding situation is always chosen. A busy crowd was at work when we arrived, for it is no easy matter to build up such a tower of wood. Look how they drag the logs about; here comes a peasant with half a fir tree behind him, and another with half-a-hundredweight stuck on his "Alpen-stock;" a third hangs over the precipice and hews down branches of the Lats-chen* and mountain-pines, the resin of which burns so well and smells so deliciously.

Twilight is soon over in the mountains; the low Alpine grass waved in the night wind, and the bells of the little church on the Birkenstein were faintly audible from below. The flames now began to crackle and flare, at first gently and fitfully, but gradually increasing into a wild roaring blaze of light. The sparks flew far and near in the clear starlight, and from every height rose rival fires. How huge and black appeared the mountain buttresses, contrasted with the brilliant glow. Presently one of the men came forward, a hardy fellow with a broad chest and lofty forehead; and, waving his plumed hat, he stepped to the edge of the rock. As his first shout rang out, it seemed as if he were making a declaration to the world beneath his feet—a declaration of peace throughout eternity. Above and below pealed forth the echoes of the answering greetings, as though they would extend to the stars twinkling overhead.

Charming groups were soon formed about the fire, and I should have to exchange the pen for the artist's brush to give any idea of the scene. The "Sennerins," who had clambered up from their scattered huts, were laughing and joking with the men close to the blaze. Well they knew that the saints were not the only attraction, and that a fire very different from that of St. John had led up many of the swains. There stood the maidens, with hair flowing loosely from beneath their peaked hats, one hand resting on the hip and the other laid caressingly on the lover's shoulder. Now and then a mischievous rogue would snatch a log from the burning pile and try to stroke his sweetheart with it, and, with a merry laugh, she would rush away from him.

The ladies and gentlemen who had come to see the need-fire took up their position at a little distance. There were some handsome figures amongst them, in every variety of costume. Some of the gentlemen, anxious to get rheumatism, were lounging on the grass; others were leaning on their long "Alpine-stocks," or sitting beside the young ladies, on the low rocks overgrown with Alpine roses which were scattered about. "How I should like to build some huts here!" said one of the elder ladies, who was literally quivering with delight, and whom one recognised for a blue-stocking even in the darkness—"one for myself, one for Moses, and one, of course, I must keep empty, in case I should marry later."

One of the young girls, who leant against a rock apart from the others, seemed to be wrapped in earnest meditation; the green pine-branches swept against the hem of her dress, her hands were folded on her knees, and melancholy thoughts were, perhaps, flitting across her mind. A broad straw hat, with a single red rose at the side, shaded her face and partly hid her pale blond hair. She formed a picture, a faultless picture, such as Riedl delights to paint in Rome, in which day and night, light and darkness, meet in one fair

---

* "Lats-chen" is the *Pinus primulis*, a sort of dwarf pine, which grows on the precipices and in the crevices of the rocks on the mountains. It creeps along for some distance before its stem rises from the ground, and clings so tenaciously to its support, that many a life has been saved by a timely clutch at its branches. The red-deer and chamois feed upon the young shoots of the "Lats-chen."—*Tr.*

countenance. Half the Madonna-like face was in deep shadow, whilst the soft lines of the profile glowed in the red glare. Now and then, as if impelled by some secret yearning, she flung back her head so that her features caught the full light of the fire, and all its glory was reflected back from the magic mirror of her face.

"If only she does not move," I thought to myself in silent admiration; but at that moment the English governess exclaimed in a warning voice, "Jenny, take care!"—Jenny started, and the beautiful picture was gone.

I felt a strong impulse to throw the old lady into the fire to be burnt alive, and she seemed to have some inkling of my thoughts, for I got a basilisk glance through the blue spectacles.

An old doctor of philosophy now proposed leaving, and the country-people were already beginning to disperse for their return to the Alpine huts. For a short distance the merry boors were mixed up with the "gentry," and their rough wit and the mutual misunderstandings were very amusing. The duenna in blue spectacles kept an anxious watch over her beautiful ward, and addressed every peasant as "sir," with a

notion that "*noblesse oblige*." But, in spite of all her care, a bold young fellow suddenly seized the fair "picture" in token of his unbounded admiration. Jenny smiled pleasantly when he tapped her hand with an Alpine rose, and exclaimed, as if he could not help it, "You are the most beautiful woman in the world;" and then, turning to his sweetheart, who was trotting behind them, he added, "You'll never have such a pretty face as that, 'Beside her you look like a goat beside a chamois.'"

"A she-goat's good enough for a he-goat," retorted the girl good-humouredly.

But the governess waiting below for the stragglers cried in a stern voice, "Jenny, take care!"

Soon afterwards the mixed company were resting on the straw in the different huts, and even the owner of the blue spectacles was wrapped in peaceful slumber.

At about two o'clock, I stole cautiously out of my hut and climbed up to the scene of the need-fire. The mountain-world was spread out before me in all its grand immensity. The stars shone more brightly, and the mighty vault of heaven seemed more vast and extensive than before. All nature was shrouded in the silent depths of night—details were lost; but the massive battlements of the everlasting hills, the endless chains of pathless peaks, acquired a new significance as they stood forth wrapped in the black drapery of the darkness. It is this swallowing up of all that is small and petty which gives to the night its awful, its mysterious grandeur; and it is the revelation of little things and its close approach to us in our humanity which makes the day with its bright sunlight so dear to us all.

The conception of the exquisite harmony of the universe in all its parts was borne in upon my soul. I felt that in the full comprehension of this harmony alone lay the solution of the problem of salvation for the individual life—the riddle of the "ego." This is why hours of dedication, solemn transfiguration moments are granted to man, when, in mystic communion with Nature, he catches a glimpse of this harmony, and by faith realises the meaning of the whole.

STONE ALM ON THE KAMPENWAND.

VI.

LIFE ON THE ALPINE PASTURES.

AN "Alp" is one of those fortunate things beloved by all except those who have the gout. Most writers on the Alps have described details: one has taken the scenery; another, the tourists, and so on; but we think the most important fact of mountain life has been overlooked by all. We allude to the intimate connection between the character of the people and the elevated locality in which they have their homes. However "big" a Lowland boor may be, he always retains a certain heaviness and narrowness; indeed, we may almost say a "flatness" of character. He clings to the soil, and the limits of his property become the invisible limits of his ideas. Of course society is more accessible to him than to the Highlander; but, on the other hand, the latter is of a more sociable disposition; and, although his sphere of life is more limited, his views are wider. There is an element of freedom in the very scenery around him. He has a feeling of ownership in the loftiest peaks to which he climbs, and this increases his self-respect. The rocky nature of the soil he tills adds considerably to his toil; and if this be detrimental to his property, it is the reverse to his character, which acquires firmness and steadfastness. It is only in the native land of the mountain firs that tall, stalwart figures, resembling them, grow up; in the Alps alone are the vocal organs fully developed. The Alps, too, are the source of that rhythmical element peculiar—like the regal—to the mountain character, which is manifested in the popular songs and dances.

The "Alm," or "Alp,"* is the connecting link between the mountains and their inhabitants; for it is through the Alm that the peasant acquires his feeling of proprietorship in the lofty peaks.

How fully the people themselves realise this is seen in the repetition in their proverbs, in various forms, of the contrast between the "stay-at-home" and the Alpine vocation. They speak contemptuously of the "Heimkish" (home-cow), who is not active or sturdy enough to climb to the "Alp." A girl who is only fit for house-work is called a "Heimdirndl" (home-girl); and the sense connected with this epithet is seen in the following verse:—

"Für 'n langweil'n Knecht
Is a Heimdirndl recht.
Doch a lustiger Bua
Geht an Almdirndl zua." †

To us, of course, the beautiful scenery of the Alps is their chief charm. The life of large towns is necessarily artificial; all conflict with the elements is avoided. Nature is repressed by education; but out on the mountains her divine energies have free scope now as of yore, and her beauty and cruelty are alike unfettered. The seasons of the year are more distinctly marked, the different periods of a single day are more vividly contrasted; death succeeds life without human interference.

It is only on the mountains that we realise what spring means. Towards the middle of May the sun has chased away the snow, and the primrose peeps forth from every crevice. Green moss springs up beneath the fir-trees, and the young thrushes twitter in their topmost branches. No human voice is as yet heard upon the uplands, no human footfall echoes from the sward. The butterfly flutters to and fro in the sunshine, and the only interruptions of the stillness are the never-ceasing voices of Nature. The full spring gurgles softly, silently open the buds of the Alpine roses—everything is bathed in the joy of re-awakening life. How instinct with youthful vitality is spring! how wonderful is the mere fact of existence! Later come the riper days of summer, when the mountains are of a deeper blue and the tall grass waves in the breeze. Above stretches the cloudless canopy of heaven, far, far beneath lies the glassy lake, and all around cluster the mighty forests steeped in sultry blue vapour. Everything is at its fullest beauty, from the depths of the ravines to the calices of the flowers; all Nature throbs with rapturous joy; for the bashful maiden has grown up to womanhood, and exults in her maternal happiness; every pulse beats with the passionate love of existence. The night wanderer in the forest seems to be accompanied by an elfin throng, and to be followed by magic melodies. Every night is a fairy tale in itself.

But days such as these pass away like a dream; they are but moments of enchantment, of conscious bliss, enjoyed by Nature as she passes through the successive ages of her existence. Presently the air becomes sharper, and the blue of heaven fainter; the quivering beech lets fall its leaves, the faithful fir alone retains its garment of green. Imperceptibly the silver cords of life are loosened: the bird still flutters from branch to branch, but it has become more subdued; the blue flower still blossoms on the sterile ground, but the green slopes have assumed a yellowish hue. Shepherd and flocks are taking their departure; deep silence has once more settled down upon the mountains—they are left solitary—more than solitary—desolate!

* When the word "Alm" or "Alp" is used in the singular, it always means a mountain-pasture.—*Tr.*

† "For a peasant dull and rough,
A 'home-girl' is good enough;
Strong fine fellows, it is said,
Always woo an Alpine maid."

A LUCKLESS CASE ON THE ALM.

Those who gaze at this time of year into the quiet face of Nature will perhaps find her more beautiful than ever; for she has this advantage over humanity—she never grows old or infirm. She does not die like a matron, but like a bride before the benediction is finished, with the smile of life and love still quivering on her lips. She is bewitching to her last hour. Death comes, but not old age,—life, not beauty, fades away.

Each day she opens her eyes more feebly, each day is shorter; and when the last autumn evening closes she is dead. Heavy fogs shroud her form; nothing is wanting but her winding-sheet.

Even the winter is grand in the mountains. The mighty rocks form one huge sarcophagus, and the stillness of the grave reigns over them. The snow is piled up many fathoms high, and the wild wind moans as it sweeps along, tearing the roofs from the huts and breaking stones which have stood a hundred years; but unable to rend open the tomb in which all life lies buried.

Such is mountain-scenery; such are the yearly seasons in the Alps!

Let us now turn to human life on the mountain-pastures.

The huts are generally built in some picturesque spots, in the most sheltered situations on the Alps. From the summit of some steep ascent we look down upon the roofs sparkling in the sunbeams in some green hollow. Several of them generally cluster together, above them rises the weather-beaten cross, and large stones add to the strength of the roofs. All around stretch the pastures strewn with débris. The journey to the Alp is not generally made before St. John's or St. Vitus's day. The procession assumes quite a festive character, for every creature rejoices in the coming freedom from restraint. The oxen triumph in escape from their stalls, and liberty to seek their own food; no longer will their keeper give to each a small portion on a pitchfork! The Sennerin exults, because on the Alp she is undisputed sovereign, and the herd-boy prefers the grass as a seat to the school-bench, and the study of the universe to the multiplication table. It is a fête day to the peasant when his cattle are led to the mountains, for he looks upon them as members of his family; and if Roman law does not recognise them as such, Bavarian usage does. House and stall are under the roof; each cow has her "baptismal name!" Religion, too, protects the four-footed creatures; they have their own patron-saints, their stalls are "blessed," and a sacred proverb is pronounced over them when they are set free.

Of course the scenery looks somewhat prosaic at the time of the pilgrimage; the ground is still soft with the melted snow, the whole procession sinks into it up to the knees. But the Sennerin assumes a *negligé* costume, setting all fashions at defiance, and resembling that of a man from the waist downwards. The "milking hat" is the ordinary coiffure, and any one anxious to find a name for the nondescript appearance presented by a Sennerin might well exclaim, "*Noli me tangere*." Tourists, in fact, grumble at the ugliness of these girls; but, for all that, there are some few who blossom like living Alpine roses; but, to the best of our knowledge, such flowers do not grow by the wayside, and Bädecker has given no "stars" to the Alpine huts.* Beauty, however, is at the best but fleeting, and as other things are more necessary to the Sennerins, we will linger over it no longer. The chief requisites of the character of a good herd are cheerfulness and steadfast courage. Melancholy and timid people are useless in these solitudes, where everything depends on individual exertion. Who is there to lend a hand when misfortunes threaten? The Sennerins are well aware of all this, and there is often something quite touching in the fidelity with which they tend their animals and sacrifice their own comfort to that of their charges. They recognise no difference between night and day, sunshine or storm; at all times and in all weathers they will fetch the strayed calf

---

* In Bädecker's Guide-books stars are put against the names of the best hotels, &c.—*Tr.*

from the deepest ravine and soothe it with the tenderest words. It was indeed a right instinct which assigned the care of the cattle on the mountains to the women of Bavaria, for they have more self-denying affection for the creatures under their care than men would have, and are not inferior to them in physical strength and resolution.

In the Tyrol, where the Alpine pastures are in the hands of men, cattle-breeding is not more successful than in Bavaria. There the bushmen, who are called "Stotzen," are a coarse, uneducated set of men. They are mostly shaggy old fellows, whose clothes are in rags and whose "patois" is absolutely unintelligible. In the frontier districts they sometimes come into collision with the Sennerins, rolling their milk pans down the mountains, or thrashing the cattle in default of their owners.

Strictly speaking, the life of a Sennerin must be somewhat monotonous; but her own bright spirit gives it relish and zest. As soon as the cows begin to low, as early as two o'clock in the morning, she is astir; and when the first faint rays of the grey morning twilight make their way through the cracks in the roof, the cows are milked. At four o'clock a bright fire is blazing on the hearth, and the cattle are set free. Far over the mountains they wander in search of food, and do not return until the evening.

In very hot weather, however, things are reversed; then the herd goes to the pastures at night and remains in the stall all day.

There is plenty for the Sennerin to do between whiles; the big kettle hanging over the hearth must be scoured, saucepan and milk-pail require careful polishing. Generally, too, there are a few patients in the stall—a he-goat who has sprained his foot in some gallant adventure, or a cow which has taken a chill and cannot join the green *table d'hôte*. The latter must have her breakfast taken to her room, and the former requires cold applications on his wounded limb.

As water can only be obtained at some distance from the huts, every pail has to be carried home on the head, which is no easy task in such a rugged neighbourhood. It is only very rarely that the well happens to be near the hut, and then it is generally remarkable for yielding no water!

If we carry our researches a little beyond the actual pastures, we shall find a small enclosed field called the "Haag," or "Alm" garden. On the hedge-stakes we descry various articles of clothing of the simplest description, for here the Sennerins dry their washing. White and red garments flutter in the wind; no master of the house or fastidious critic raises a protest against them, and no robber annexes this "valuable material."

Here alone is the freedom of the herd restricted, the grass which grows here is the forbidden fruit of the quadrupeds. It is cut and carefully preserved, that there may be a little fodder to be had in case of a sudden fall of snow. But the stupid cows, instead of realising the wisdom of this, are always prying about the fence. In this they resemble men. With the fodder around them up to their knees, they remain standing at the edge of the reserved plot and gaze at it with longing eyes. Often when the shepherdess is out of the way and they think themselves safe from the "stocken" (sticking), the only penal code they know, they make a foolhardy attempt and break through. But woe to them when their mistress comes back; like an avenging Megæra, she rushes in amongst them, and, with a *salto mortale*, the uncouth guests dash away. Many, however, are left in the lurch, and do penance for the others, for in criminal cases there is no "limited liability."

In front of the "Almhutte" (Alpine huts) are some rickety palings; and the store of wood, which has been laboriously collected, is piled up outside in picturesque style. Hence the following "Schnaderhüpfel":—

THE MOUNTAIN VILLAGE.

"Schon hoch is in Bergen,
Schon eben im Land,
Und an almerisch Dirndl
Hat Holz bei Wand." *

The immediate neighbourhood of an Alpine pasture is not always exactly pleasant, for it is often frequented by a tyrant with clumsy bones and pointed horns, who acts as *maître de plaisir* on the Alp, deciding in what direction the herd shall make the daily promenade, and confiscating a painter's studies

CHAMOIS HUNTER IN THE SENNHUT.

if he place his camp-stool in the wrong place. He rules his territory with the jealousy of a Turk and the sternness of a policeman: "no admittance" is the inscription over his domain. This tyrant is the bull! Fortunately he is travelling on business to-day, and so we may venture in unmolested, and have a good look at an Alpine residence.

It is a picture of sooty simplicity. The smoke makes its way through the blackened roof; the

* "Very high are the mountains,
And very flat the plains;
But piles of firewood, it is said,
Are owned by every Alpine maid."

Alpenstocks and a small wood chopper rest against the wall. A narrow window in a dark brown frame gives a glimpse of the blue landscape without. The milk-room is underground, and woe betide any one who steps incautiously through the trap-door, which is often left open, for he might easily break his neck. When anything unusual is going on, some of the "live stock" are occasionally sent into the cellar to be out of the way.

The "boudoir" of the Sennerin is in about the centre of the establishment. It is a small but cosy room. In one corner is the little altar, with a prayer-book in large print, a few consecrated palm-branches, and perhaps the image of a saint, with one or two relics. Behind the door hangs the Sunday costume, and near it the little vessel of holy water, in which the shepherdess never fails to dip her hands as she passes out. Here too is her bed, which reaches nearly to the ceiling, and can only be climbed on the unused side with the aid of the Bergstock or Alpenstock. The Bergstock is called "Kreister," and it is obvious how it became the centre of the erotic lyrical poetry. Round the wall runs a wooden bench, and a table with crooked legs completes the furniture. This table serves also as an album or strangers' book, and has been scored all over with names and dates by those who have here shouted and danced, loved and sung. As most of the huts are more than a century old, many famous dates are to be found on these tables. I myself have read 1790, 1802, and July 12th, 1806; so that joyful shouts were resounding in these solitudes whilst the German empire was crumbling to ruins!

The peasants have quite a passion for the "Almbesuch" (visit to the Alpine hut). There is, indeed, a special charm in the open-hearted hospitality of these regions, poor as are the inhabitants. On weekdays none climb up but those whose business brings them; on Sunday evening, however, the "Bua" (peasant) taps at the little window. The wooden bolt which fastens the door is at once slipped back, and with a cheery laugh the sturdy fellow steps in. Carelessly he flings his "Rucksack" into a corner, chooses a safe place for his gun against the wall, and sits down by the primitive hearth. The "Schmarrn" (a kind of omelette) is bubbling in the little saucepan; but the fire will not burn properly, and the shepherdess sings roguishly:—

> "Und die Lieb is a Feuer,
> Da fehlt es sich nit,
> Aber dengerscht kei Brennsuppen
> Wärmt man damit!" *

And if her guest boasts too much of his hunting exploits, she has an appropriate verse ready:—

> "Und a Jager der sieht gut,
> Aber d' Lieb macht ihn blind
> Und da fangt oft den grössten
> A klein's Dirndl g'schwind." †

So sings the maiden, and the hunter's dog flaps his great ears to and fro, as if to say "Bravo!" On Sundays there is company on the Alps. The girls, in their bright bodices and peaked hats, assemble together from the scattered huts, and, choosing some grassy bank as a seat, they laugh and chatter and sing, the indispensable little knitting-baskets beside them.

They are very seldom long alone; some young fellows are pretty sure to join them, and amuse them

---

* "A little fire is love,
It never lacketh heat;
But for all that it warmeth
Neither soup nor meat."

† "A hunter's eyes are strong and keen
Until love's blindness him o'ertakes;
The smallest maiden then, I ween,
The biggest captive often makes."

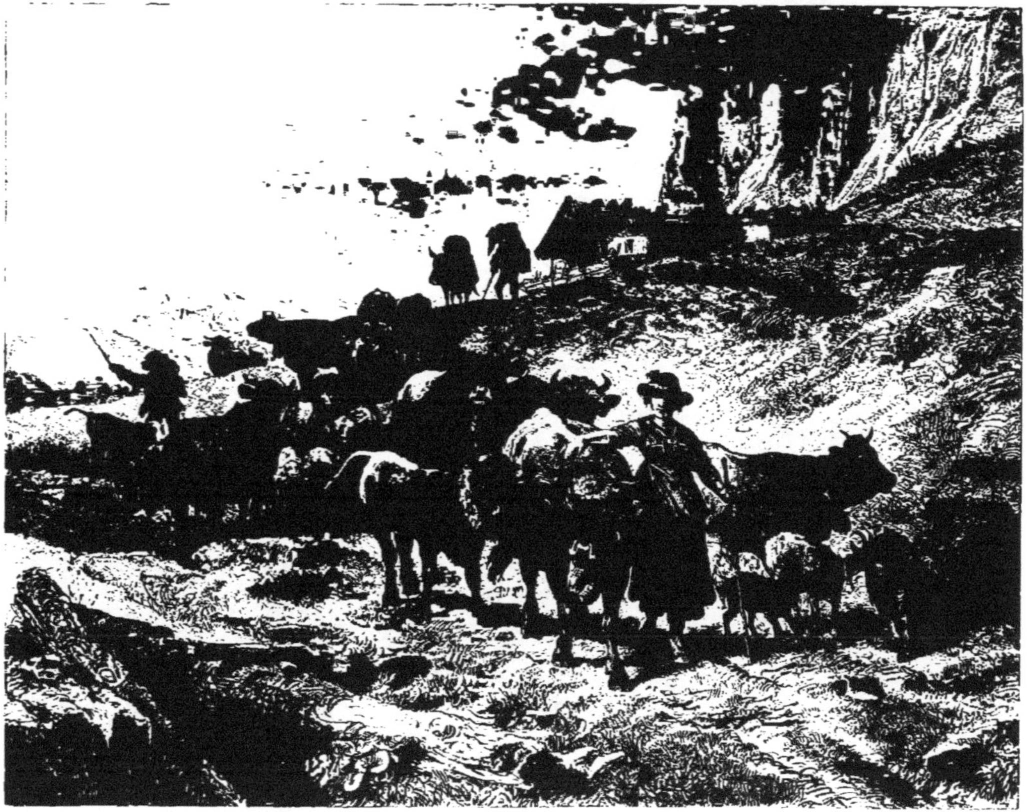

DEPARTURE FROM THE ALM

with jokes and odd scraps of news of every variety. Far and near echoes their merry laughter, for their high spirits are absolutely irrepressible.

This love of fun is reflected in the popular ballads, of which life on the Alp is a favourite subject. According to them, poetry and joy are the exclusive privileges of the mountain-pastures, and public opinion endorses this idea. The comical scenes which are of such frequent occurrence on the Alps are also well represented in the "Schnaderhüpfel;" and never are they more spirited than when they speak of the joyous Alpine life.

When a young peasant is teased about his love affairs, he will answer, laughing:—

"Im Thal ist der Nebel,
Auf der Alm is schön klar,
Und was d' Leut von mir sagen,
Des is auch nit All's wahr." *

And if a hunter is asked questions about his life, he will sing:—

"A Gambsel im G'wänd
Und a Punkt in der Scheiben
Und a Dirndl auf der Alm
Is mei Thun und mei Treiben." †

And so this simple mountain life is full of interest and excitement. The songs generally treat of some lively subject, for comedy is more natural to a peasant than tragedy. Those made fun of are generally foreigners.

* "The mists obscure the valley,
But the Alpine heights are clear;
And of all that people say of me,
Believe just half you hear."

† "An Alpine maid to wish me luck,
In cap a beard * of chamois buck,
One turn of Fortune's wheel to share—
These three make all a hunter's care."

* The beard of a chamois is the long hair growing down the back, and is worn by a successful hunter as a trophy.—*Tr.*

The cattle remain upon the High Alps until the middle of September, when they take possession of the less elevated pastures, called "Niederleger;" staying there until the third Sunday in October, unless a fall of snow should drive them away earlier. The duties of the Sennerin become more and more onerous as the year advances, for the cows require close watching. Fodder being scarce, they wander long distances, and trespass on private property, until they are taught their proper station in life by the keepers.

At last comes the return to the valley. The cattle are decked with green boughs, and the Sennerins wear their Sunday costumes, for the occasion is looked upon as a kind of fête. Not a single calf has been injured; even the wounded goat has recovered his health, and paces proudly along in "conscious worth."

Their owner is waiting outside his house to receive them, and when they arrive he holds a general review. The children shout for joy and clap their hands. Then come the old crib, the old stall, and the short winter days. *Après nous le déluge.* Storms may rage, and winds may blow upon the Alps, but what care we!

In the spacious sitting-room of her home in the valley the Sennerin sits and plies the distaff with busy hands. The fire crackles cheerfully and many a merry Alpine song is sung when the neighbours drop in with their spinning.

MOUNTAIN CASTLES.

AN HISTORICAL RETROSPECT.

MOUNTAIN CASTLES.

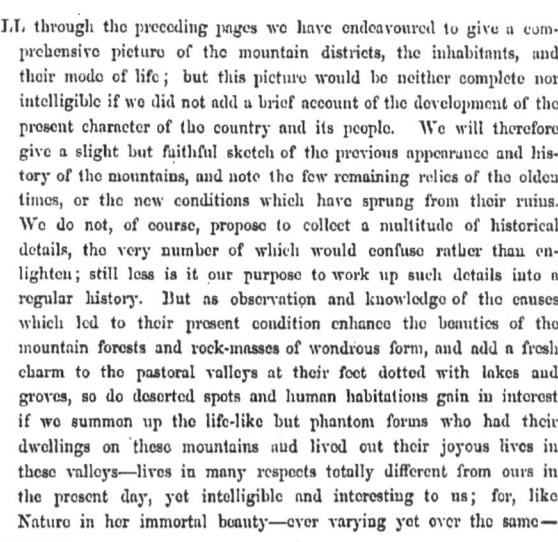

ALL through the preceding pages we have endeavoured to give a comprehensive picture of the mountain districts, the inhabitants, and their mode of life; but this picture would be neither complete nor intelligible if we did not add a brief account of the development of the present character of the country and its people. We will therefore give a slight but faithful sketch of the previous appearance and history of the mountains, and note the few remaining relics of the olden times, or the new conditions which have sprung from their ruins. We do not, of course, propose to collect a multitude of historical details, the very number of which would confuse rather than enlighten; still less is it our purpose to work up such details into a regular history. But as observation and knowledge of the causes which led to their present condition enhance the beauties of the mountain forests and rock-masses of wondrous form, and add a fresh charm to the pastoral valleys at their feet dotted with lakes and groves, so do deserted spots and human habitations gain in interest if we summon up the life-like but phantom forms who had their dwellings on these mountains and lived out their joyous lives in these valleys—lives in many respects totally different from ours in the present day, yet intelligible and interesting to us; for, like Nature in her immortal beauty—ever varying yet over the same— are the hearts and souls of the human race.

The visitor to the mountains will not have far to seek for traces of former days; they have left monuments enough behind them which only await a candid student to examine their silent testimony. He cannot travel many leagues, especially in the outer range of mountains, without seeing some lordly castle frowning down upon him from a lofty peak, or the towers and gables of some strong but hospitable convent or monastery inviting him to enter; and again and again the ruins of one or the other will remind him of the instability of all things here below, and show him that those empires which appear most firmly established, are in reality built up on ever-shifting sand, which is gradually but imperceptibly passing away from beneath them. Castles and convents were formerly the distinctive and most prominent features of mountain scenery and of the surrounding country. Convents were, in a certain sense, merely ecclesiastical castles, sacred strongholds, behind the walls of which the monk found a refuge, as did the knight behind the moats and towers of his secular fortress. Indeed, we may say that ecclesiastical and secular strongholds divided the sceptre of power between them. According to a computation made about a century ago in Upper Bavaria (of which the mountain districts form but a small portion), there were no less than fifty-three convents, and eight hundred and ninety-nine castles, without counting the priories, endowed institutions, &c., amongst the former, or the smaller residences of the nobility amongst the latter. Times are changed now; the monks have left the convents—for the small religious establishments which have sprung up of late years are not to be compared with those of olden times; the French Revolution led to the secularisation of eighteen hundred and three; some of the fine buildings are now empty and deserted, whilst others have been converted into breweries or manufactories. The numerous wars—the ravages of the Swedes, of the Austrians in the Spanish War of Succession, and of the French in later campaigns—reduced many a fine castle to ruins: some have been pulled down to supply materials for a neighbouring building; others were sequestrated on the decay of the families of their original owners; but the greater number—deserted since 1848 by the last remnants of the hereditary nobility—are now places of amusement, or the pretty country residences of wealthy—but not necessarily noble—proprietors.

But before examining them more closely, it will be well to glance back to the remote times when the first seeds of the national history of Germany were sown.

The most cursory examination is sufficient to prove that the mountains and valleys of Upper Bavaria formed one of the earliest civilised provinces. Traces of the Romans abound, and the names alone of many places bear witness to the great influence exercised by them in the old Noricum and the two Rhætias. Remains of the indestructible roads constructed by the masters of the City of the Seven Hills for their legions intersect the mountains and surrounding districts, leading from one settlement to another, protected right and left by numerous strong positions, and overlooked by many a mighty watch-tower. The old military road from Verona to Augsburg—leading past the old stations to Scharnitz, Mittenwald, and Partenkirche, through Ammergau and above Diessen and Andechs—is still in use, and through the pine forests of the uplands round Munich winds the other highway which led from Salzburg to Augsburg, over the Inn; and the traveller on the somewhat deserted road to Rosenheim, which has been supplanted by the railway, probably forgets that a similar branch joins the old Roman road at Aibling. Castles and walled positions are equally numerous; and any one who should pause and look thoughtfully around him, could not fail to perceive that from the mighty bend of the Mangfall Eck to the Aibling hills it would be as easy as possible to command a view of the whole Mangfall plain, and to communicate by signal with the old Aibling castle, lately demolished for the erection of a new court of justice, and blown up with gunpowder, as its strong position was found antagonistic to police rule. A signal from the Mangfall watchman would have been caught up immediately by the castellan of Eigilinga; a few moments later the huge Neubeuer tower would have lit its beacon-fire, and from point to point the fiery tokens would have ascended the Inn to the Falkenstein and Auerberg strongholds, and descended it to the bridge at Pfunzen (*pons Oeni*). Further in the mountains we find other traces of Roman fortresses; such are the few remaining ruins on the Schliersee of the Waldeck castle, in the walls of which we can still make out the bricks with convex swellings, characteristic of Roman architecture. As we have already stated, there is an echo from the Tiber in the names of many places; and we do not think we are mistaken in tracing Valez to the Latin *valles*, Willing to *villa*, and Wieehs to the old *vicus*. The word *Wal* or *Walch*, which occurs in so many names, is equally significant, and points to the same origin; it was applied by the old inhabitants of the country to everything of *walisch, walchisch*, or *wälsch*—that is to say, of Roman origin. Such are the words Walchensee, Walgau, and others; although it must still remain doubtful whether, according to the suppositions of scholars, the inhabitants of certain valleys—those of Partenkirche and Ramsau, for instance—are really the descendants of scattered Romans who fled from the conflict of the nations to remote districts, the inhabitants of which still retain certain characteristics of their appearance and manners. The people themselves remember next to nothing of all this, and any faint traditions which remain are looked upon as mere relics of heathen days, or ascribed, as in other countries, to the devil.

More numerous traces remain of those later days when, the migrations of races having ceased, the nations settled down quietly, like a flood which has spent its force. In the middle of the sixth century the Boii, or Boivarii became domesticated in the mountains under the dominion of the local "Gaugrafen," or counts, and were led to war by kings or dukes of Agilolfinger extraction, to whom five other dynasties were equal in rank and importance. One of these, the Fagani, had their home on the Mangfall, in the so-called Sundergau, where the castle of Vagen still retains their name; another, the Huosii, lived in the adjoining western province, named after them, which included the Anger and Loisach districts. The Walchengau extended over the Partenkirche parish beyond Scharnitz into the Tyrol of the present day. "Ambergoi" formerly occupied the sites of Ettal and Ammergau. There were, of course, other larger or smaller divisions; but we have now only to do with those of the mountain district under consideration. On the other side of the Inn lay Chiemgau, and near it the Salzach province.

As is so common in history, especially in that of Germany, the "Gaugrafen," or district counts, were not long content with their position as petty magistrates; on a smaller scale, they acted as the imperial princes of later days, arrogating to themselves independent power, and gradually assuming the rights of feudal lords, the ducal districts became counties. Such a power arose in the Guelphic lands of Ammergau: the counts of Werdenfels and Eschenloch reigned on the Loisach, those of Wolfrathshausen on the Isar, whilst on the Mangfall and Inn ruled the powerful lords of Falkenstein. Adjoining their domain was that of the Waldeck family, and, stretching in a southerly direction as far as the Chiemsee, the province belonging to the Marquartstein dynasty.

Many are the existing monuments of that remote time, especially of the days of the last Thassilo, when Bavaria lost its independence and became a province of France. To him is due the origin of the once important Polling monastery, the no less famous Wessobrun, where lived the celebrated nun Diemud the transcriber, and of the convents of Herrenwörth and Frauenwörth on the two islands of the Chiemsee. Connections of the Agilolfinger family founded the Benedictbeuer and Tegernsee monasteries. Still further back dates the foundation of the Schliersee convent, endowed by five brothers of the Waldeck race; and of the priory of Schlehdorf, on the Kochelsee, whose abbot was at a council held in Reisdorf as early as the ninth century. The church and convent of St. Zeno, in Reichenhall, are mentioned in the time of Charlemagne; in the tenth century Andechs, and in the eleventh Beuerberg, Wegarn, and Berchtesgaden sprung up. One of the most recent but also most remarkable of the creations of this kind is the marvellous convent of Ettal, founded by the Emperor Ludwig of Bavaria. It was indeed a grand conception to people deserted and all but uninhabited districts with these colonies; for, fertilised by the industry of the monks, the land became fruitful and brought forth abundantly. Towns and villages clustered round the convents; and if the latter assumed authority over the people of the country, it was but in obedience to that natural law which gives the creator power over the created. The inroads of the Huns, it is true, laid waste the land; but, like vigorous roots which have remained uninjured far beneath the surface of the earth, the monastic institutions sprang up afresh and grew apace, until, at last, their shadow positively darkened the land which gave them birth. But the axe was laid at the root of the tree in the unwisely precipitate suppression of monasteries in 1803; the confiscation of property cut off the supply of sap from the roots; and of the many rich convents which gave the name of Pfaffenwinkel (priest's corner) to the lands on the Isar and Loisach, nothing remains but the bare trunks stripped of their branches and leaves. Of the buildings once peopled by the monks, some enjoy a prolonged existence as breweries, like Polling or Ettal; some are empty and deserted, like Schlehdorf; others, such as Benedictbeuern—where Frauenhof the optician made his grand experiments and discoveries—are converted to totally different purposes, as stables or barracks. A few still retain something of a monastic character; for at Beuerberg, Frauenwörth, Dietramszell, &c., nuns have set up schools for girls. Others again, like Bernried, are the country-seats of noblemen; and a few are the resorts of princely leisure, such as the

SCHLOSS HOHENASCHAU.

charming Tegernsee, where Maximilian Joseph, the first King of Bavaria, held his splendid but simple and hospitable court: where Werinher the famous illuminator lived, and Walter von der Vogelweide was entertained as a guest.

The convents had their day and fulfilled their mission; now they have passed away like the secular institutions of the knights, which, however, merit a few words. They were less numerous in the mountain valleys than in the open country and on the banks of the rivers. On the Inn and Mangfall, for instance, they are almost within a stone's throw of each other, and scarcely a village can be met with which did not once boast of a fortress or a nobleman's residence, long since converted into a farmhouse, and only to be recognised for what it once was by the remains of an old moat. At Wolfrathshausen on the Isar, rises the lordly Castle of Eurasburg, the ancient seat of the Irinsburg family, lately restored in the old style. In the secluded Länggries valley the lofty Hohenburg towers above the stream and mountain forests—it too is well kept up; but it has passed into the hands of the present Duke of Nassau, leading us to reflect on the fleeting nature of some things, and the durability of others. In the Partenkirche valley we find the grand ruins of the stronghold of Werdenfels, which is full of painful recollections; for, in the time of the Bishop of Freising, hundreds of poor wretches were confined and executed in its dungeons as witches. Here too dwelt the Bavarian Duke Ferdinand, who married the beautiful Maria Petenbeck, the ward of Haag, and whose descendants long flourished as Counts of Werdenfels, and would probably have succeeded to the Bavarian throne on the extinction of the Ludwig line, had not the last of them unfortunately choked himself with a peach-stone when at the Ettal Academy. In Chiemgau rise the mighty walls of Hohenaschau on the Prien, and those of Marquartstein on the Achen—both extremely old, and tottering to their fall. The former has long belonged to the Preysingers, and the latter was formerly the seat of the Counts of Ortenburg. Both are now, however, little more than picturesque features of the landscape, recalling to our minds the days when they lorded it over the surrounding country. The castles and ruins on the Schlierach, Mangfall and Inn will be best considered together, as they are historically connected, and we now propose giving a

BERG FALKENSTEIN IN THE INNTHAL.

brief sketch of the mode of life of the nobles of the olden times, closing our chapter, by way of contrast, with a description of the internal arrangements of one of the most important of the convents.

On entering the mountains in which the Inn takes its rise, the traveller's attention is at once drawn to the ruins of the fortress of Falkenstein, which form a beautiful and fascinating picture. The mighty outlines of the ruins rise as it were from out of the midst of the houses and orchards clustering around them. Above them all towers the Madronberge, and on one side we descry the wonderful little church of the Petersberg. Any one who should climb the road up to the castle would be richly rewarded for his trouble by the romantic view. Beneath the ruins foams a mountain torrent, which dashes over a huge precipice behind them, forming a cascade which can vie in beauty with many a more famous waterfall. Beautiful indeed are the dreamy solitudes of the ruins, and fair the landscape spread out on every side, extending on the right far over the mountains to the jagged peaks of the Kaiser, and on the left across the swelling and apparently boundless lowlands. But pleasant as it is to gaze on these relics of the days gone by, it is yet more delightful to raise the veil of oblivion which has fallen upon them, and to see the actors in them pass in review before us. At Falkenstein once dwelt the powerful Counts of Falkenstein and Neuburg, lords also of Herrnstein and "protectors" of Aibling, who had many vassals in all the surrounding districts—a race who appear to have combined with their vast possessions, great, though undisciplined, strength of body and mind. Their own hereditary castle of Neuburg on the Mangfall, above Vagen, has all but disappeared from the face of the earth, but Altenburg, which also belonged to them, is in good preservation and can be seen from the railway. A certain Sigbot, of Falkenstein (1130), was guilty, in his ungovernable rage, of a double murder, and was compelled to do public penance, after which he was allowed five years' respite. He seems, however, not to have been softened until his only son died childless, when he converted his huge wine-cellar on the Mangfall into a convent, which was called Wegarn. His skull was found in perfect preservation when his body was disinterred more than six hundred years afterwards, and from its size we are able to see what a giant he must have been. His brother's line, which lasted somewhat longer than his own, was equally famous for unbridled arrogance and lust of power. Sigbot III. made war upon and oppressed the convent over which he held authority as patron, and leagued himself with Count Conrad, of Wasserburg, against Duke Otto, of Bavaria; but he was defeated, and died in prison an excommunicated man: his corpse remained unburied until the urgent prayers of a relative touched the revengeful heart of the Bishop of Freising. His son Sigbot IV. was murdered in his bath by a vassal, who had probably some wrong to avenge. In him the family became extinct, although there is an apocryphal tradition that another Sigbot, calling himself "Von Antwort," retired from the world as a monk. The Falkenstein possessions passed to the Bavarian dukes, and in the first place to Ludwig the Stern. The fortress itself was conferred upon one family after another until it was destroyed by fire in 1784. Part of the property, together with the seigneurial rights over Aibling—of which castle we must now say a few words—passed to the Waldecks of Maxelrain. The appearance of Aibling is, of course, greatly changed; but its four towers, still in good preservation, rise proudly on the height opposite the desolate Falkenstein, and form a prominent feature of the landscape.

The family of the original owners became extinct in the fifteenth century, and it passed to the neighbouring Waldecks, who, having settled down on the Schliersee and at Miesbach, on the Wallenburg, appear in history as early as 760, as the founders of Schliersee and as taking part in the tournaments at Rothenburg in 942. The most famous of all the Waldecks of Maxelrain, to whom Charles V. gave the freedom of the empire and the right to seal with red wax, was certainly Wolf von Maxelrain, who acting in concert with the Freibergs of Hohenaschau, the Ortenburgs, and others, gave a home in the very heart of orthodox Bavaria to the professors of the new religion, which spread rapidly from Schliersee and Miesbach to Rosenheim and the neighbourhood of Aibling, causing no little anxiety to the bigoted dukes, Wilhelm and Albrecht. Lutheran preachers were everywhere welcomed; the people left off going to confession, and demanded the Lord's Supper in both kinds. In those times, however, little ceremony was observed in such matters. Places infected with heresy were cut off from communication with the outer world as if they were plague-stricken. Some heretics were easily convinced of their errors, whilst the refractory were exiled, and about thirty years afterwards it was announced at Court that every one regularly attended the processions and the confessional. The nobles got off more easily: they were summoned to Court, when some were imprisoned, and others humiliated in different ways. Von Maxelrain himself was reprimanded and sent home, after promising on oath never again to protect the heretics. He kept his compulsory vow, but wounded pride and remorse brought him to an early grave. His son was more compliant, and was rewarded by being made a Count of the Empire, which dignity involved the furnishing of a contingency of two men on foot and one on horseback to the imperial army. The race became extinct in 1734 on the death of Joseph von

Maxelrain, the alchemist, who made fruitless efforts to find ore in the Josephsthal, on the Schliersee. The castle of Aibling still exists, and is the seat of a nobleman famous for his success in agriculture, his estates taking rank with those of Upper Bavaria, and distinguished from them only by the stone house and the greater extent of the property.

As an ecclesiastical contrast to this account of life in the old castles, we cannot do better than describe the oft-mentioned Ettal, which has peculiarities all its own. The word "Ettal" is by some supposed to have reference to the deserted (oede), secluded character of the valley, but others derive it from Ethiko, the haughty old Guelph who ruled on the Lechrain and fled from the world to bury himself as a hermit at Ettal in his wrath at his son's submission to the Emperor. However this may be, the still existing deed of foundation proves that Ettal owes its real origin to the Emperor Ludwig of Bavaria, who, finding himself short of money on his journey to Rome, made a religious vow, at which an unknown monk appeared to him from a closed door and presented him with a small stone image of the Virgin Mary. The story goes, that on his return home, the Emperor's horse stumbled three times in ascending the pine-clad slope near Ettal, on the road between Partenkirche and Ammergau, and that the image became so heavy he could carry it no farther. He took this as a divine intimation that his vow was to be fulfilled in this spot. His mode of setting to work was characteristic of the generous romantic temperament for which he was remarkable, and of which he gave such signal proof in his dealings with his rival, the handsome Friedrich. Ludwig was very fond of poetry, especially of the works of Wolfram von Eschenbach, and greatly regretted that the poet's death prevented the completion of his "Titurel" (the Song of the Holy Gral or Grail). Ludwig commissioned Albrecht von Scharfenberg to finish it, but died himself before his orders were carried out. The church at Ettal was built in imitation—on a small scale—of the Gral Temple at Montsalvage, as described in the "Titurel." Like the latter, it is a rotunda of piers with chapels all round it, a bench encircling the wall inside, and a central pier forming the support, keystone, and crown of the whole, and in which is preserved the image of the Virgin Mary, as was the "Gral" at Montsalvage. Nor is the sacred lattice wanting, and tradition says of the image as of the "Gral," that the pure alone can see or move it; to the impure it becomes either invisible or as heavy as a hundredweight; moreover, none can name the wonderful stone of which it is made.* The resemblance to the Gral Temple will be found still greater when we remember that, as a crowd of monks or guardians of the Gral gathered round the Gral King at Montsalvage, so did the knights about the "Master" at Ettal. These knights were allowed to marry, but their wives were obliged to take the vows of the order, and were allowed to remain at Ettal if left widows. To each pair were assigned special duties; they were allowed to ride out, to hunt, and to take part in

---

* According to Wolfram von Eschenbach, the "Holy Grail," or "Graal," was "a vessel made of *lapis Nerilis* (the stone of the Lord). It was filled with the strength of God the Father, God the Son, and God the Holy Ghost, and was in the beginning with God served by angels." When Lucifer and the angels were banished from heaven, the holy vessel was confided to the purest of men. Those who by God's grace were called to guard the "Holy Gral" were called *Templeisen*, a clerical order founded on the model of the Templars. The "Templeisen" formed the "Graal church." No unbaptised heathen can see the Graal, and no Christian can reach it by means of earthly weapons.

Early French accounts state that the "Gral" was the chalice used by our Saviour at the Last Supper, and confided by him to Joseph of Arimathea, who by its means was able to test the sincerity and purity of converts to Christianity, for, as stated in the text, it was invisible to the impure. Joseph brought the chalice to the West before his death, but it was long before any one was found worthy to take charge of it. At last, however, it passed into the hands of King Titurel, who built a temple for it at Montsalvage, and founded an order of "Knights of the Temple of the Holy Gral." Pargival, or Perceval, whose adventures in quest of the Gral are familiar to all, was a descendant of Titurel, but he was brought up in ignorance of his birth and of his high destiny as one of the guardians of the sacred chalice.

For full particulars of the legends of the Holy Grail, see the "Seynt Graal" or "Sank Ryal," edited by F. Furnival, 1861. Wolfram von Eschenbach's poem has been well translated by Simrock.—*Tr.*

knightly exercises; but strong drink, dancing, and card-playing were forbidden. Frugal living was especially enjoined, and the couples sat side by side at meals, which were eaten in common, one of the community reading aloud. They all worshipped together, and were under the authority of the "Master" and "Mistress" (the latter was not necessarily the Master's wife); but they could all vote for their removal. The men were bound " kein ander Barb, zu tragen, dann pla und gra, und die Frauen nur pla " (to wear no other colour than blue and grey, and the women only grey). The children who were born to the knightly pairs remained three years in the "Hofstat" (establishment), but were then sent elsewhere. As Ludwig did not live to see his design carried out, the order was not founded exactly as he had proposed; but the church and residences of the knights were built as he intended, and the original form of the former can still be made out, although it has been injured by fire and was much mutilated by the soldiers of Maurice of Saxony. Subsequent restorations have also considerably altered all the buildings.

A military school for young knights was established later in connection with the Benedictine convent of Ettal, probably with some recollection of the design of the founder. Pilgrims still visit the image of the

Virgin Mary in the brewery to which the monastery is degraded, but the mystery in which it was shrouded has long ago evaporated, for any one can see that it is made of fine white alabaster, and it is supposed to be a work of the school of Niccolo Pisano. It can no longer exercise its miraculous power of testing by its weight the purity of those who lift it, for it has been found desirable to fasten it in its place.

After devoting so much of our space to the monks and knights, the burghers deserve a passing notice, and we will introduce our readers to the good people who lived on the old Roman highway to Verona. This being the only route to Italy in the Middle Ages, the inhabitants of the towns and villages through which it passed, such as Mittenwald, Partenkirche, Ammergau, and others, enjoyed the exclusive right of transport of all property conveyed along it. There were public storehouses in which all wares had to be deposited, none being allowed to remove them but members of the carmen's guild. It will readily be understood that these towns increased rapidly in wealth and importance; but their prosperity as rapidly declined when the flood of traffic subsided. Bad times followed, and it was not until long afterwards that the people rose from indigence by learning different trades: the Mittenwalders became violin-makers, and the inhabitants of Ammergau carvers. But at the present day, when rail and steam are rendering trade in the mineral and timber wealth of the country easy and remunerative, fresh changes are transforming the mountain villages. The coal-mines of the Peissenberg and Penzberg, near Kochel, and in the solitudes round the Schliersee, are already actively worked; at Hohenburg, in Länggries and other places, large saw-mills turn the treasures of the forests to good account; the plentiful supply of peat and timber has led to the success of many speculations, and the vast capabilities of the easily-controlled water-power of the many streams and torrents encourage fresh enterprises, so that the writer who shall undertake some fifty years hence to describe mountain life will have a very different scene before him,—whether it will be more beautiful must be doubtful to all who have felt themselves stirred to the inmost soul by the pathos and mystic charm of the lonely mountains in their unsullied loveliness. But of all this more anon—the aim of the present chapter is accomplished, for we have unfolded to the lover of mountain scenery " the tales the mountain castles have to tell."

TOURISTS IN THE COUNTRY.

I.

SUNNY DAYS.

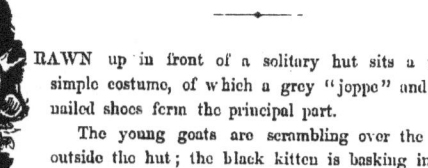

DAWN up in front of a solitary hut sits a man in a very simple costume, of which a grey "joppe" and a pair of thick nailed shoes form the principal part.

The young goats are scrambling over the wood piled up outside the hut; the black kitten is basking in the sun; blue clouds of smoke rise from the roof.

Inside, the fire crackles cheerily, and the Sennerin laughs merrily as she chatters with the guest through the open door. In the country people do not approach each other when they talk, but speak from the position they happen to occupy. It is only in towns that there is a kind of conversational etiquette; and so the Sennerin vigorously pokes her fire, and her visitor retains his lounging attitude, although they are discussing matters of importance.

Who would not like to know what these matters are? Of course stories of marriage come first; but then follow philosophical remarks about virtue, the weather prophets, and other stirring topics. The little goats creep nearer and nearer, and look into the stranger's face with great earnest eyes, as if they understood something about it all. At some very absurd sentence a hearty laugh bursts from the hut, and the Sennerin winds up by saying: "Well, if I had to cry as much as I have laughed in the course of my life, I'd rather die at once!" Is not this a most philosophical way of passing the mid-day hours?

Up here we are indeed in the country.

Things are very different down in the valley, five thousand feet beneath. At about mid-day a vehicle called a "stage-coach" arrives at the inn—the drive in it, shaking every bone and jarring every nerve, is the purgatory through which the traveller passes before he can reach the paradise of the mountains; it is the one instrument of torture retained by modern civilisation.

The coach discharges its contents. "Good gracious! another waggon-load of foreigners," growls the host, whose portly person fills the door of his house. He watches the confusion and tumult with stoical calmness, forming therein a striking contrast to the swarthy waiters who are overwhelming the new arrivals with offers of assistance.

The greatest excitement always prevails on the arrival of the mail and stage-coaches. The people staying in the country for the summer are all eagerness for news, and behave as if a steamer had arrived from Brazil at the very least. The appetite for food and that for news seem to increase in equal proportions. The members of the fashionable world are a truly remarkable set of people. One would imagine that they would be glad to be quit for a time of the whole concern, that the professor would lay aside his wisdom and the merchant his business; but no, there they stand, eyes and ears strained to watch people like themselves descending painfully from their cramped positions in the coach. They have met together to grumble at the arrival of others.

But of course all this is not allowed to appear. On the contrary, the greatest delight must be manifested on recognising some "dear friend." Pretty speeches of every variety must be ready, for at this time of year foreigners of every class and rank are on their travels. We see greetings of all kinds, from the lowest bow to the easiest shake of the hand.

When all have left the stage-coach, the most amusing scenes are witnessed. Great is the consternation of those who cannot get rooms, and the delight of the more fortunate whose night quarters are already secured. Enthusiastic is the reception of paterfamilias come to spend the Sunday with his wife and children. But the most exciting time of all is when the post office is besieged by an eager crowd. With impatient gestures young and old gather outside the little window with its green blind. At last the postman opens the letter-box, and shows his flushed face. "The Journal of Fashions" for the Lady Baroness, the "Law Report" for the justice of the peace, the "People's Journal" for his reverence the priest, &c., &c. With blushing hesitation the maiden advances to receive her lover's letter, whilst packages of every kind are sorted out—a bundle of newspapers for some politician, a packet of private official revelations for "His Excellence," and so on, and so on.

After going through all this before dinner, the company naturally feel that they have earned a hearty meal. At the *table d'hôte* of the newly established hotel, the guests appear in renovated beauty; those who wore yellow yesterday, to-day appear in blue, and *vice versâ*. Of people at their meals, there is of course little to be said, so we will borrow some of their own conversation. The adventures of the morning generally furnish plenty to talk about. The gentlemen have most of them been through experiences which left them with damaged boots and torn trousers, and they own to many mistakes, principally geographical. The ladies have to tell of the raptures they experienced when drinking the "Kräutersaft" (juice of herbs), or gazing at the great waterfall. Sketch-books are produced, and the inscriptions beneath the smudged pages reveal that they represent various aspects of the waterfall. The ladies, too, have their adventures to describe; for whilst one of the youthful artists was sketching, a cow, or perhaps an ox, suddenly appeared in front of her camp-stool, and would certainly have gobbled her up had not a chivalrous charcoal burner, hearing her screams, rushed to her assistance and snatched her from the jaws of death at the risk of his own life. The old professor next to her expresses his sympathy, and takes the opportunity to relate the history of an injury he himself received from a prairie buffalo, for which he has revenged himself by inflicting an account of it on all his acquaintances.

"Look!" whispers the mother of the rescued maiden, "Fräulein Marie always wears the carnation the doctor brings with him of a morning. Do you know what a carnation means? I am convinced the doctor is in love."

Love-making is the chief occupation of tourists. It is just the time of year when a man is disposed to seal his fate, and so young ladies always play an important part during the season.

When the *table d'hôte* is over most of the gentlemen go down to the skittle-ground. Here they are safe from the intrusion of the ladies, and enjoy themselves in their shirt-sleeves. The others remain in the house and arrange their afternoon parties. There is something very amusing in the rage for making up parties. Instead of cultivating the *dolce far niente*, some people must needs rush through their holiday

CITY PEOPLE ON THE ALM. SUNNY DAYS.

at full gallop. They set out at a rapid pace, and do not begin to enjoy themselves until they are quite out of breath with the haste they have made.

"Well, where shall we go this afternoon?" This is no easy matter to decide. "It's too dirty for the 'Hochfeld;' if we go to the Hunting Lodge, we must tie up the dog; Seeau is too far for the children; and if we go to Waldheim we must tell the old professor, for he made us promise; and if we have the professor we must ask the doctor (with the carnation in his button-hole), and if we ask the doctor we shall be thirteen."

Well, where *shall* we go this afternoon?

Some prefer the high road; they enjoy the heat of the sun and like to sit on the convenient seats by the wayside, whilst fine equipages roll by and fill the eyes of the inquisitive with dust. The high road leads to the pleasure-grounds, much frequented in the summer. When you arrive there you will find every place taken. Ladies in thick rustling silks lounge on the wooden benches, and stare into the milking-rooms through their double eye-glasses to see if they can find anything as beautiful as themselves. Scotch-clad children have brought their hoops with them, and spoil the green lawn with the marks they leave. Cavaliers of every rank pour from the door of the farm-house, and peer about as if in search of chairs, but really in the hope of seeing some rustic beauty. Such are the ways of the gentry in their aristocratic mountain haunts, and they look upon other excursionists as the "summer rabble."

Nothing in Nature makes a more vivid and lasting impression upon us than the waves. When the floods lift up their voice they touch a sympathetic chord within us, and exercise an influence, a beneficial influence upon us. We could never gaze upon the mountains in self-forgetful rapture for so long a time as we do upon the lovely lakes which bathe their feet, and the indescribable charm of the Bavarian Highlands consists in the happy combination of the two. The stranger visiting for the first time the solemn Königssee or the sparkling Tegernsee, would find it difficult to explain what it is which so strangely moves him; but it is in fact nothing else than the harmony between land and water—a harmony so intimate that we cannot separate them even in thought.

The delight of those who have travelled far to see the beauties of these mountains is very pleasant to witness, and we can easily understand that their first thought is to hire a boat, and that an early morning cruise is a thing never to be forgotten.

On many lakes we still see the picturesque boats, hewn out of the trunk of an oak, which serve for generation after generation; but they are more used by fishermen than by travellers, and we meet with them more frequently in pictures than in reality.

In some places, alas, commerce has changed the face of the land. The very waves are corrupted, and the boats have lost their simple beauty. They are painted red and white, and carry the flag of Great Britain, or some other naval power, in the stern. In them sit dainty young ladies, splashing the oars into the water and screaming at the slightest movement of the boat. These female sailors (especially when they are fond of singing out of tune) are a veritable nuisance.

Those who like everything on a grand scale are mad to form Alpine parties. No peak is too lofty, no rock too rugged for them, and they know their way everywhere, although they have probably never been in these parts before. Many ladies share these notions, and then of course all argument is useless. A man who joins a mountain party in which ladies are included must resign himself to plenty of inconvenience.

The preparations are as extensive as if for an exodus from Egypt. Plaids, coffee-mills, parasols, and articles of every conceivable kind are carried to the mountains. Terrible scenes ensue when a headstrong mountain brook crosses the path, or a declivity ten or twelve feet deep is reached where Nature has neglected to provide steps. First of all the baggage is all thrown down, and the most courageous leaps upon it, holding out her arms to receive the others, whilst the mothers turn away their heads in horror from the sight of the results to their daughters' costumes—but "necessity has no law."

The Sennerins are not always well disposed towards the fine ladies and gentlemen, especially if they knock at their doors at an inconvenient season. They prefer the heavy tread and lusty shout of their lovers to the soft, plaintive, minor tones of the hungry strangers, who turn everything upside down, soiling the freshly scoured floor with their muddy boots, disturbing a cow with her new-born calf, and expecting the Sennerin to attend to them when she is watching for her lover. At such times we must be thankful if we get so much as a pail of milk to refresh us, and not be surprised if we are treated with scant ceremony.

Sometimes strangers fare still worse, for the oppression under which the peasants so long groaned in the hard times gone by has rendered them rather malicious, so that they take a pleasure in playing tricks on travellers, and often cause them unnecessary and undeserved suffering.

CITY PEOPLE IN THE ALMHUT.

It is quite the fashion nowadays for a peasant who catches a young gentleman stealing to inflict summary punishment upon him; for a guide to hoax his employers about the eggs of the chamois, &c.; or for a host to set roast mutton before his guests as venison à la scholastica. This would not be so bad, for tourists often bring such things on themselves; but sometimes the peasants resort to less excusable means of giving annoyance; as, for instance, near the Spitzingsee a few years ago: It was a fête day, and the peasants had had rather more to drink than was good for them. A number of daintily dressed ladies were seated in one of the huts when several men began to sing "Schnaderhüpfel," not very carefully selected. The mothers hurried to the door in dismay, eager to get their daughters out of reach of the poison. But behold, the door was bolted, and in spite of earnest entreaties, it was not opened until the concert was over.

The possibility of their delicacy of feeling being thus wounded is one of the dangers incurred by

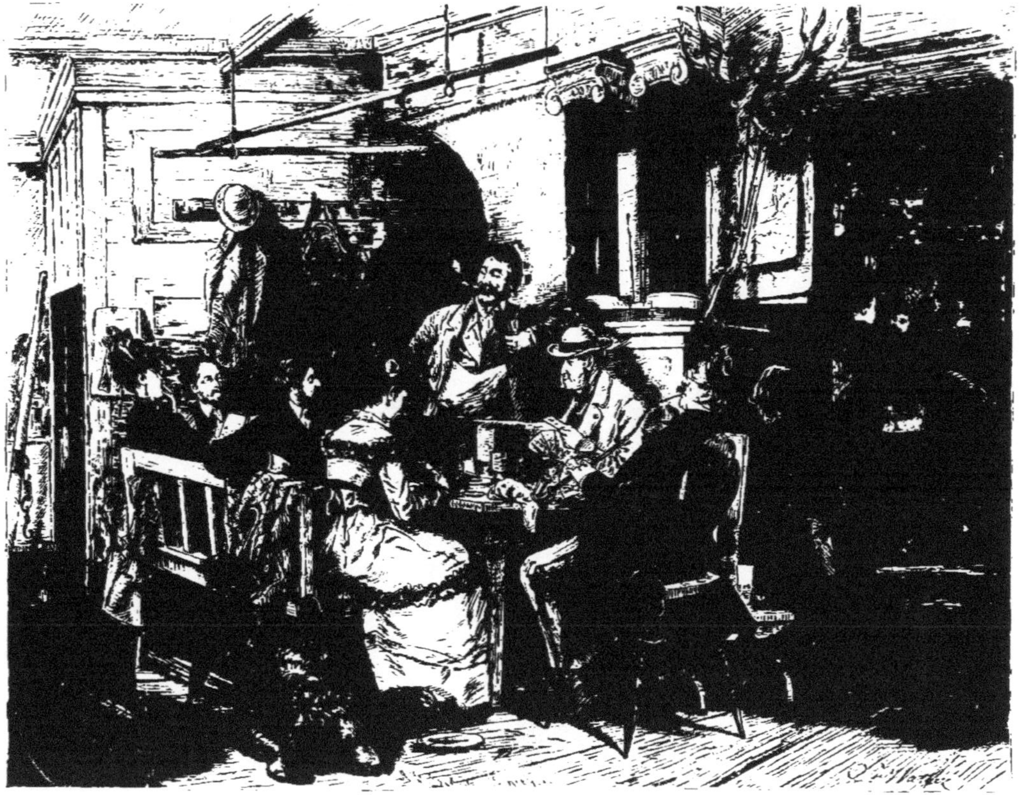

CITY PEOPLE IN THE COUNTRY. RAINED IN

travellers in the mountains. The horned cattle are against them too. Every cow whose family cares are intruded upon protests with prolonged lowing, and woe betide the disturber of her peace, with his red books and red handkerchiefs, if her horned cavalier happen to be within hearing. The oxen in the mountains have their own ideas about the "liberty of the subject," and will never be taught to look at the matter from a legal point of view. But in spite of all this the mountains have an irresistible attraction for townspeople, and they never regret the labour their journey costs them. Look, a procession of them is even now painfully climbing up through the forest. An old, heavily laden gentleman, with three ladies to look after, besides himself. They are steering their course towards the Alpine hut, panting for breath.

In front of the hut sits a man in a very simple costume, of which a grey "joppe" and thick nailed shoes form the principal part. The Sennerin is gone, the hut locked, and so the luckless travellers must climb to the next.

"Oh, if we had but brought a guide!" sighs the poor old gentleman. "It's lucky, though, that there is a peasant here to carry our things. Holloa, my good fellow, will you oblige us by guiding us to the next hut?"

"No objection, if you pay me well," is the answer in Low German.

The packages are handed over to him, and the old gentleman breathes more freely. The path now leads through a shady wood, and the party, forgetting their troubles, chat pleasantly with their guide about all kinds of things—of mowing and thrashing, of poachers and "Sennerins." The man in the grey "joppe" is ready enough with information on every subject, and the old gentleman whispers to the ladies in French, "An intelligent fellow; the peasants here are certainly not so stupid as they are supposed to be."

When the second hut comes in sight the man touches his hat and says, "I must go back now; you can't mistake your way."

"Well, what is there to pay?" inquires the old gentleman.

"Nothing," replies the guide carelessly.

"Eh, what?" says the other. "You'd better stay and carry our things down again, then; you shall have a gulden to get something to drink."

"You'd better not let such an opportunity slip by you," says one of the ladies. "What have you got to do this evening?"

"To write a leading article for the Augsburg *Allgemeine Zeitung* (the Augsburg *News of the World*), which must be in print to-morrow," replies the supposed peasant in High German; "and therefore I regret that I can enjoy your society no longer. I wish you a very good evening." With these words he turns away.

Horror and dismay are depicted on every countenance.

"Good gracious! You are not a peasant, after all! Pray, pray excuse us! No peasant! And your name—might we ask? What is it?"

Dr. Jur. Carl Stieler.

II.

WET DAYS IN THE MOUNTAINS.

"THIS dreadful weather, will it never change?" growls the "Kommerzienrath" (Counsellor of Commerce) meeting the "Regierungsrath" (Counsellor to the Government), as he takes his constitutional under his umbrella.

"Good evening, Amelia," says a voice from the second floor, "are you going out in this weather? Oh dear! when will it stop raining? all our children have got colds!"

There are whole days in the mountains when nothing is heard but this melancholy strain of complaint. Double-soled boots and good temper can't last for ever, and a perfect deluge is testing to the powers of human endurance to the utmost. It has lasted a whole fortnight. Every one is afflicted with colds, headaches and "ennui." Is it any wonder that the whole party is low-spirited and irritable? What do people do with themselves on such days? It is our present task to answer this question; and the fair "Muse" sitting beside us, instead of raising her wing, puts up an umbrella. What would we not now have given for a stout waterproof? But such a thing is not to be had for love or money.

These wet days upset all our plans, and many are the good intentions dissolved in water. Who can tell what aims inspired the crowds assembled here? The "athletes" want to take exercise, the captain to fish, the children to catch butterflies, and the mothers to marry their daughters. All this is, of course, at a standstill on wet days, for neither fishes nor men will bite when the sun does not shine. Most of the families lodge in farm-houses, where comfort is but little understood. All manner of contrivances are resorted to: a trunk does duty as a chair, and the candle is stuck in the empty inkstand of the master of the house. It is a case of making the best of a bad job.

Wet mornings can only be got through by having plenty of occupation, so the mother writes the

BOATING.

long-delayed letter (for who ever writes until they are obliged?), whilst the old gentleman reads his paper in the next room, and stamps his foot angrily to enforce silence when the children become too noisy. The elder daughter, who is already addressed as Fräulein, stitches diligently away at her work; and the children, puzzling over a sum set them by their tutor, are leaning on the table with their legs twisted round their chairs in the cramped attitude always assumed when a problem has to be worked out. All this to be done in one room without making a noise! The rain patters against the windows, and nothing breaks the monotony but the heavy tread of the postman. Hurrah! a letter for us!—but it's only a bill from the linendraper at home.

At eleven o'clock the gentlemen go to take their morning dram. However it may pour, this is never neglected; it is in fact a matter of conscience, quite a moral obligation. There are plenty of pleasant spots all over Bavaria where a "petit verre" may be enjoyed, but the best are certainly those on the shores of the Tegernsee. Any one anxious to meet a friend in that paradise between 11 A.M. and 1, is sure to find him in the "Bräustübl" (little room at the brewery). This praiseworthy custom, now observed in every castle, was originated by the retainers of the nobles; but a reformation spreading from the lower to the upper classes, rapidly increased the circle of readers of the "brown books in glass covers." A small smoky room is the favourite resort. An old mountain hat, suspended from the ceiling by trailing ivy branches, serves as chandelier; the portrait of the late King ("God bless him!"), and a few saints in frames, adorn the walls. Close at hand is a stone porch, a kind of "chapel of ease." Here people lounge on rough benches and all manner of extemporised seats, whilst the barmaid in her smart bodice bustles backwards and forwards, and, near at hand, the huge boilers hiss and splutter, and the sturdy brewers shout over their work.

In this porch and the little adjoining room meet the thirsty, the witty, and the beautiful. A few years ago a number of great actors were assembled here. Many first tenors cleared their glorious voices here and sung the "Evening Star" on their way home.

Another year it is the professors' turn, and the porch becomes a miniature debating hall; celebrities of every faculty, from Berlin and Heidelberg, Munich and Göttingen, argue together here, and some strict ecclesiastic may find himself by the side of a ballet-dancer. "Aurions nous, par hasard, une fois la même idée?"

The bells ring for *table d'hôte* at about one o'clock in all the old Bavarian inns. From every side the guests hurry in, feeling that they have once more a pleasant duty to perform. Well-known tourists, who walk straight to their places; dripping excursionists, who gather nervously round the well-spread table and vacant chairs; pretty girls cowering beneath the wings of their governesses;—a swarm of children, a confusion of greetings and compliments, and all take their places.

Now begins a clatter which makes conversation impossible. The soup is hot, and a wail of pain bursts from the lips of those who have been too hasty, whilst others, wiser, wait until it cools, and watch their neighbours with criticising eyes.

"Do you see that stout man at the end of the table?" says the "Superintendent" to the "Frau Direktorin;" "Do you know who he is?"

"I am glad to say I don't," she replies in a piping tone; "but if his thoughts are as limited as his 'joppe,' I shouldn't care to be the subject of them."

"Don't be so malicious, madam, I beg of you," says the doctor on the left, "we all have our weak sides. I understand that you are fond of music."

"So I am, but not as produced by our deaf neighbour the Baron. People say he has ordered a piano, for he is fond of duets . . . ," but before the sentence is finished the doctor interrupts: "Well, one must be fond of something, and he seems an honest man enough . . ."

"An honest man!" cries the Professor from the other side: "God help Germany!—honest men would long ago have been her ruin had not Count Bismarck . . ."

The appearance of some half-sodden beef, rousing to the utmost the righteous indignation of all, puts an end to the discussion; but the passion for argument is only in temporary abeyance, and bursts forth afresh when the roast mutton and cool salad are served.

After the *table d'hôte* individual peculiarities become yet more apparent. The devourer of newspapers rushes upon the latest sheets, and devours the contents of the Augsburg evening paper before the afternoon is over. The banker retires to his own room, and settles himself to study the news in his easy-chair; and the young ladies bring out their fancy work, and are complimented on their industry.

The proper thing to do on a wet afternoon in the country is to play a game at cards called "tarot." As etiquette is not so binding in the country as in town, the most heterogeneous groups are formed of "high-born," "well-born," and "low-born." The fair sex are sometimes called to take part in the game, when there are not enough gentlemen, and there are some who are positive "tarot amazons."

Such a mountain party forms quite a Highland "genre" picture. At the table a group of three or four eager players, beneath it the long-legged farm-house curs, whose snoring mingles strangely with the fall of the cards, the rattling of the coins, and the sighs of the losers. The sky without is grey with heavy clouds, the atmosphere within is blue with the fumes of tobacco. Every face expresses that combination of weariness and eagerness which is the peculiar result of a gloomy day.

Any one who has taken part in a game of tarot cannot fail to vote it a most innocent afternoon amusement; it is exciting and interesting. Far more hazardous is the attempt to escape "ennui" on "the wings of song." Nowadays there is a wreck of a piano in every inn in the Bavarian Highlands, and bad weather is of course an opportunity for excruciating practising. Oh, the horror of the duets on the battered, discordant two-legged instrument! Oh, the fearful trios!—verily they are a scourge of God to the unwilling listeners! Quite early in the morning the lieutenant comes and plays a march, sitting astride on the stool, making the notes keep step, as if on parade. At mid-day an odour of beefsteaks floats from the room above.

As soon as dinner is over, a piping simpleton, fresh from school, begins to sing; and as misfortunes never come singly, she is soon joined by a friend, and the whole afternoon is made hideous with vocal and instrumental duets. One, two, three—four, five, six—four, five, six—over and over and over again!

The gentlemen—not those who are playing tarot—are charmed, and their applause acts like oil upon the flames. One of them goes so far as to whisper to his neighbour: "Might I ask you to introduce me to Miss Croaker when this song is over?"

The songs chosen, too, are admirably appropriate to the occasion; the first is, "O sunshine! O sunshine!"—"Listen how it pours!" pipes the old aunt. "I would that my Love could silently flow!" squeaks the cousin.

And so the afternoon, enlivened by these trials of skill, drags slowly on. Well, we ought to take an interest in our fellow-creatures. This is why we discuss so earnestly what they had for dinner at the President's to-day, and whether the dreamy "Referendarius" (a Government title) is in love with the elder or younger daughter.

It is very pleasant too to sit in a dry balcony and watch the arrival of one's dripping fellow-creatures. Some come on foot, some in stuffy carriages, and all alike are worsted in the pursuit of pleasure. The procession looks as if it were told off to perform the seven works of mercy; but, alas! in these degenerate days there is no such thing as mercy!

It generally clears up a little in the evening, and people employ this brief respite in making a promenade. Men and women march along behind one another as if they were just leaving Noah's Ark. Young ladies step daintily over the puddles, but the children follow the maxim of Horace, *ire in medias res*, and jump into the middle. Whole caravans of people meet each other in the twilight hours, and the burden of every one's remarks is: Let's hope it will be finer to-morrow. The host shares this general desire, and has bought himself a broken barometer, which always points to fair weather. Hence its name, the barometer of comfort.

And now the evening has to be got through. For those who remain at home the mysteries of preparing for bed begin at half-past seven. The entire family partake of a simple meal in the farm-house they have hired. The tin plates belonging to the master of the house are pressed into the service, so are the drinking vessels painted with roses and forget-me-nots. The cups of a country-house are almost always decorated with flowers, the language of which is well understood. As eight o'clock strikes, the youngest child is bundled off to bed in a commodious wardrobe or a big trunk. Then papa smokes his "pipe of peace," and mamma brings out her knitting.

It is very different for those who "go out" of an evening. They are sitting shoulder to shoulder at the long table in the public room of the inn.

Sometimes there's dancing of an evening. It's easier to laugh and talk and flirt moving about, and so the tables are unceremoniously pushed out of the way, and as no one likes to begin, because some are too old and others too young, they all set off together. The sleepers on the floor beneath start up in horror at this social revolution. They hear shouts of: Parisienne! Polka-Mazurka! Vis-à-vis! Cotillon! and the last word is their death-blow. Meanwhile the conservatives sit at the indispensable corner table, and look on with astonishment at the lawless doings of the townsfolk.

At eleven o'clock the mothers commence the well-known dumb show to get their daughters to come home; but as parents are more long-suffering in the country than at home, these gestures are not noticed until twelve o'clock, when the father becomes peremptory, the mother sleepy, and the girls disposed to listen to reason.

A general wrapping up ensues, a hunt for red hoods, blue hoods, loud warnings not to catch cold, waterproofs, overshoes, umbrellas!

Every one at last reluctantly sets off home, after shrinking back at the sight of the rain dashing in beneath the door.

Struggling groups toil along against the wind and rain through the narrow village streets and between the treacherous prickly hedges. The little lantern goes out when they are about half way home, and the "admirer" escorting the ladies makes the bad weather an excuse for offering his arm to Dulcinea.

At last the creaking house-door opens, and the damp figures disappear behind it. "Good night! Good night!" and all hurry off to bed.

"Only listen how it pours!" says the mother to the father, and he replies with an emphatic shake of the head, "I hate the country!"

"Only listen how it pours!" says the elder to the younger sister, and she nods her head and says, "Yes, but it's great fun in the country!"

— — Parisienne! Cotillon! Vis-à-vis! — — —

III.

LAKE PICTURES.

COASTING.

A SMALL white vessel rocks upon the waves, from which proceed the sounds of merry laughter. The maiden at the helm has taken off her broad-brimmed hat and is playing with the red flowers in it; her bright hair falls over her shoulders in golden ringlets. Her escort looks grave; his hair is dark, and lines of thought are stamped upon his brow. He plays carelessly with the oars, and the boat is at a standstill. The two gaze down through the clear water, many fathoms deep, at the pebbles at the bottom, and at the little fishes with their glistening eyes and supple bodies.

When the east wind begins to blow, the little boat steers for the creek where the mountain rises abruptly from the shore. A wild rose-bush, covered with buds, hangs over the rocks, and the fair girl stretches out her hands towards it with a cry of delight. The boat rocks as she catches at a branch, but she holds it fast, and her companion breaks off a long spray, and twines it in her shining hair without a word.

How pretty she is as she turns and looks him full in the face, laughing with childish glee. But he has no answering smile for her.

"Are you angry with me?" she asks softly. Silently he seizes the oar, and rows rapidly over the blue waters, he feels as if he had set a crown of thorns upon her head.

IN THE STORM.

"How still and oppressive it is by the lake before the storm breaks! Come, let us row out a little way." So speaks the young girl, springing lightly into the boat. Not a breath of air ruffles the surface of the water; the heavens all around are black with clouds; the reeds yield slowly with a cracking sound as the skiff cuts through them; only the sea-gull flaps its wings and flies to and fro in a rapid, uncertain manner.

"I like to hear the storm rage," says the maiden; "this peaceful quiet has lasted too long."

"Yet it is over sooner than we think for," replies her companion. And as she looks in his face, a faint blush tinges her cheek. Silently she plunges her hand into the waves, and plays with the water-lilies floating on their smooth broad leaves.

Suddenly comes the first gust of wind; the boat tosses up and down, and white spray bathes its flanks.

"Hold the rudder firmly!" says her companion. "The storm has heard you."

But the fair child is quite unnerved. She pulls her flapping hat low over her face and clasps her little hand round the clumsy oar. She seems now for the first time to understand the storm. Slowly she bends forward and listens, as though she could hear the echo of the beating of her own heart in the waves. "Hold the rudder firmly!" she whispers softly to herself.

* * *

MORNING HOURS.

The sun shines upon the mountains, the lake is as smooth as glass; but in the stillness the creative power of Nature is silently at work. The strokes of the oar are the only sounds that break the stillness; not a word is spoken by the two in the boat. The maiden's hands rest upon her knees, the dragon-fly flutters playfully about the flowers in her hat. Suddenly she clutches at its wings, and as suddenly dashes her hand into the water. Is her heart burning? Does she long to let the cool waves break over it?

"Your eyes are wet with tears," says her companion; "the shadow of the terrors of the night still hangs over them. Look out into the morning, and see how full of joy everything is."

But the little one bends down her head, large tears fall upon her hands, and a sad smile flits across her pale face.

Then she folds her hands, and the little bark speeds further over the blue waters.

"Are you sad?" inquires her escort; "my poor child, are you ill?"

Slowly she bends her head in acquiescence; she could not put into words what is weighing upon her heart. But her friend knows well enough what it is, and says, "You have lost yourself because you love another."

Then the child bursts into a fit of weeping, and the boat rocks to and fro, so deeply is she moved.

"Yes, yes—it is you!" she sobs almost inaudibly, and hides her face upon his breast, to raise it the next moment and start back affrighted as if the waves could understand her secret, as if a golden crown had sunk beneath the water.

The morning sun shines over the mountains and the waters are at rest, yet the creative power of Nature is silently at work in the stillness.

* * *

AUTUMN FOGS.

Strangers have long since left the country, the mountains are wrapped in fogs—autumn is already far advanced.

Down on the beach is a lonely fisherman's hut, with children playing about the door. Beneath the linden tree now shedding its withered leaves once stood a fair, bright-faced girl; but now it is deserted, and the little empty boat rests upon the strand.

A tall man with dark hair and a broad white forehead comes down the mountain path and looks silently around him; silently, like a fugitive, he steps into the little white boat. The oars glide into the water, the dying evening light struggles with the fog. Pale stars twinkle in the grey clouds, but the stranger clasps his hands together in silent misery. He seems to see a shadowy figure sitting in the stern of the boat, in a soft white dress and a broad hat with red flowers. Soft words and stifled sobs seem once more to break upon his ear, and on his lips quiver the words, "It is you!" Ever deeper grow the shadows, ever darker is the night; the oars hang uselessly in the water, as the stranger gazes absently into space. A light breeze drives the boat before it, he lets it drive on; the waves lash its sides with a never-ceasing monotonous moan, like the endlessly repeated cry of his own heart, "It is you—it is you!"

There are hours in the life of a man, fleeting and precious hours, when he can lay aside and forget the suffering of years; but such hours cannot be enjoyed at will, and are lost to those who strive to clutch them.

He is alone! Dreary sounds the slow splash of the oars in the water, and the distant church bells, muffled by the fog, strike like a knell upon his ear. He is alone!

ON THE ANIMAL AND VEGETABLE WORLD.

CHAMOIS.

ON THE

ANIMAL AND VEGETABLE WORLD.

WONDERFUL and striking as may be the appearance of the mountains to the distant spectator, he cannot fail to be yet more deeply moved by their mighty, mysterious charm when he examines them closely; for the wealth of diverse details revealed by a close inspection is as marvellous and significant as the grandeur of the whole.

No one can for the first time climb one of the Alps without a certain feeling of awe such as he experiences when he draws near to some sacred spot or approaches the solution of a great secret. An early summer morning is the best time for a first visit to the mountains. The land is still under the hushed influence of the closing dream of night; the mountains rise dark and solemn in the twilight. Nothing is as yet stirring in the villages, for it is too soon even for the mowers. In the fields it is equally still; the hare crouches undisturbed in the vegetable garden; partridge and wild dove have their heads tucked under their wings; and it is only when we brush against the way-side willows, sloes, hazel, or barberry bushes, that the chirping and fluttering amongst the leaves reminds us of our entrance into the kingdom of singing-birds of every variety, from the hedge-sparrow and alpine-warbler to the thrush and blackbird, although the queen of song, the nightingale, is but an occasional passing visitor. Unfortunately, in the Tyrol it is the barbarous custom to catch everything in the shape of a bird at the end of the autumn and to cook and eat it without distinction of species.

It now begins to get a little lighter; the dawn is breaking in the east as we near the damp plains which almost everywhere precede the actual ascent, and are the result of the accumulation of water flowing down from the mountains. They are called moors or bogs, and are the haunts of wild ducks and snipes and the hunting grounds of the heron and the stork. Here it is as well to keep carefully to the path marked out by stones and beams; a false step would not be without danger, for many of the bright green and apparently firm patches, so tempting to the sportsman, afford no footing whatever, and the rash traveller who ventures upon them will sink at once, and unless he catches quickly at some shrub or at the tree trunk laid transversely across the swamp, he may be drowned or suffocated in the mud. The rapid growth of the moss under the water and its subsequent carbonisation, leads to a vast accumulation of peat, which makes so firm a foundation that dry heaths are eventually formed, and there are certain species of plants, the reindeer lichen for instance, which will grow on no other soil, and their presence therefore proves the existence of stagnant water. Here, between low mountain-pines, grows the stunted mountain-birch, amongst which the treacherous peasant surprises the black cock and the grey hen, and cuts short their life in all the excitement of their courtship. By the wayside we pass boards, with black crosses and letters painted on them, on which corpses have been carried to the grave, stuck up in remembrance of the deceased, that the passer-by may mutter a word of prayer for the repose of their souls. At last we come to the borders of the actual forest, hedged round with a fence of branches piled one above the other to keep the game from the pastures and the cattle from the preserves. Before entering the sacred precincts of the wood itself, a so-called "Stiegel," a flight of stone or wooden steps, must be climbed, which serves also as a resting-place and rendezvous to the Sennerins coming down from the Alp, and the wood-cutters or hunters who stop at the Stiegel for a pleasant chat. The road now winds through a clearing by a gurgling forest brook, and we pass a miserable little chapel, which invites the lonely wanderer to breathe a murmured prayer. Looking up the stream we see a lonely dark-coloured house, a sooty smithy, in which burns a huge fire, rivalling the brightness of the morning sun. Then blows of the hammer on the anvil ring out distinctly, whilst from an invisible church-tower a silvery bell announces the beginning of another day.

We enter the actual forest!

The woods are very extensive in the Bavarian Highlands, far more so than in the Tyrol, where timber has been recklessly cut down, or than in Allgäu, only one-fifth part of which was forest land some forty years ago, whereas half of the Bavarian Highlands was then covered with timber, more than three-quarters of the Berchtesgaden district alone being densely wooded. The avarice and recklessness of late years has, of course, considerably changed this state of things, but the forest-clad slopes of the Bavarian Highlands are still an imposing sight. In the preserves about Tegernsee there yet remain patches of the primeval forests undisturbed by the hand of man, where the monarchs of the forest, with giant stems, rise from the ashes of their forefathers, and where the decaying bodies of fir-trees which have succumbed to old age remain undisturbed as they fell, until they are clothed with grass, moss, and ferns. Except where cultivation has interfered, the trees of the mountain forests grow together in picturesque confusion; *needle-trees* alternate with *leaf-trees*, producing the beautiful gradations of form and colour which are the chief charm of the scenery at all seasons of the year.* Almost every variety of these two great classes are met with: the two Lindens, the *parvifolia* and the *grandifolia* (*Tiliaceæ*), the Ash, the Rowan or Mountain Ash (*Sorbus aucuparia*), the Common Oak (*Quercus pedunculata*), &c. Most noticeable, however, are the Beech and Maple; the former grow most luxuriantly on the calcareous

---

* *Needle-trees* and *leaf-trees*. As most of the *Coniferæ*, or cone-bearing trees, have narrow, veinless leaves, the Germans call them needle-trees (*Nadelbäume*), to distinguish them from other European trees, which they call leaf-trees (*Laubhölzer*).

soil of the Bavarian Alps, and scarcely anywhere are finer or more numerous specimens of the latter to be found than in these mountains, although there are no forests composed entirely of them. We allude especially to the neighbourhood of Tegernsee, Miesbach, and, above all, to the Ramsau valley, near Berchtesgaden. The Birch and Black Alder (*Alnus glutinosa*) are also abundant; the latter often greatly improves the soil by binding together loose stones with its roots.

Of *Needle-trees* or *Coniferæ*, the Pine and Fir are the most abundant, forming large forests; but the Larch and the Siberian Stone Pine are not wanting, and manage to exist in the most elevated regions.

The so-called "Shelter-firs" (*Schirmtanne*) form a beautiful and curious feature of forest scenery.

SMITHY IN THE FOREST.

They are large full-grown trees, and are carefully preserved and cultivated, as their thick branches, reaching almost to the ground and extending several feet beyond the stem, form a roof which neither rain nor snow can penetrate, and beneath which herd-boy and cattle, hunter and game, alike find shelter in storms and in the mid-day heat.

There are on these Highlands about thirty-two different species of trees and forty-one of shrubs, the varieties differing according to the elevation, &c., of the forests; and no less than one hundred and ninety different herbaceous plants which grow nowhere but in woods, some of them having very distinctly marked peculiarities. At Rothenbuch, on the Ammer, not far from Ammergau, grows a kind of reed-grass

(*Carex Ohmülleriana*), which up to the present day has been found in no other spot in the world, and by the lakes the Oriental *Calamus* (*Arundo donax*) grows wild; but, strange to say, it bears no fruit.

The elevation of the Bavarian Lowlands is estimated at from 1,800 to 2,000 feet, and the mountain regions, commencing where the valleys end, are divided into upper and lower. At 2,000 feet the oak no longer appears, and at 4,300 feet the beech, whilst fourteen new species of plants supply their place; 1,000 feet higher the true Alpine regions begin, where spring does not commence until the end of July and winter sets in at the end of September. Here the *Alpenrosen* (Wild Rhododendrons) and Gentian are indigenous, and the true Pine gives place to the *Latsche* or Dwarf-pine (*Pinus pumilio*), with its knotty creeping stem, which attains only to a very low height; but beneath which, as a kind of compensation, flourishes the most beautiful moss, with delicate buds, and many another thriving Alpine plant, such as the Monk's-hood (*Aconitum lycoctonum*), the Yellow Gentian (*Gentiana lutea*), and the beautiful Heath plants or *Ericaceæ*.

The upper division of the Alpine regions, commencing at an elevation of 6,100 feet, attains to a height of 7,100, and consists entirely of rocks and pastures, where the Sennerin reigns supreme, and where cattle grazing on the true Alp, Alpine hospitality, and Alpine dairies may be seen in their greatest perfection. The actual pastures commence before the upper mountain region is reached, at 4,500 feet, and do not extend beyond 6,200 feet. The zone included between these two elevations is the true home of the plants of the Alpine meadows. Here we must look for the *Speik* (*Valeriana Celtica*); here too grows the hunter's flower, the sweet-scented, delicate, *Edelweiss* (*Gnaphalium leontopodium*),* the queen of mountain flowers. Up to an elevation of 6,800 feet we find different kinds of flowering Saxifrage; and beyond this height we reach the snow regions, also divided into upper and lower. In the latter, small varieties of Saxifrage are met with, which are often remarkable for their large and beautiful coloured flowers, and we come to occasional clumps of Willow Herbs. It is a pleasant surprise, like meeting an old acquaintance in a foreign land, to see scattered specimens of the plants native to the valleys: the Clover (*Trifolium montanum*), or the Alpine Poppy, the "*Benediktenwurz*" (*Cnicus benedictus*), &c., on these lofty peaks. In the upper snow-regions, commencing at an elevation of 8,000 feet, vegetation almost entirely disappears; except for "*Gamskresse*" (*Dosronicum*) and saxifrage, we find nothing but cryptogamic plants, creepers which cleave tenaciously to the rocks, or mosses which clothe them with a soft green cushion. Beyond this we come to those spots, not very numerous in the Bavarian Highlands, where the snow does not melt even at midsummer, and where the ice forms small glaciers. The cold mountain air fans the brow of the pilgrim, and he realises how near he is to heaven, whilst his eyes wander unrestrained over the plains spread out beneath his feet, like children's toys, or he gazes up at the Alps, still towering above the height he has gained, feeling his own insignificance as compared with these stupendous works of God, yet glorying in the intellect which raises him above them.

The woods through which we are passing are the homes of many living creatures besides those already mentioned. In the true forest the noble Stag or Red Deer (*Cervus Elaphus*) and the smaller Deer (*Cervus capreolus*) are still numerous, although gradually becoming scarcer; the Badger and Fox take refuge in the mountain caves, and the sportsman is sometimes fortunate enough to meet with a Lynx. The mountains and ravines round Ammergau and Berchtesgaden are still rich in game, having been jealously preserved by order of King Maximilian. Here peaceful travellers, who would rather

---

* This plant has white, glistening, downy leaves and small brownish flowers. It often grows in almost or quite inaccessible places. Lovers risk their lives to obtain it for their sweethearts; and more than once some fine young fellow who has gone to gather "Edelweiss" has never returned.—*Tr.*

HORSES UNDER THE UMBRELLA PINE

bear of than share the hair-breadth escapes of stag stalkers, can watch the noble creature roving about in unrestrained freedom. Lynxes are now rare, and are generally only stray visitors from the Tyrol; but that they used to be very numerous is proved by the rows of their heads, fifteen or twenty together, nailed up as trophies in the foresters' houses. At the little watering-place of Kreuth, there were no less than sixty in one hunting lodge!

Wolves and Bears, formerly the terror of travellers, are now only passing guests. The last wolf seems to have been shot at Tegernsee in 1837; the last bear was tracked to the Planberg, near Kreuth, in 1828, but managed to get off. How numerous both these beasts of prey once were is proved by the

PRIMEVAL FOREST.

fact that a charm against wolves was formerly said over the cattle in the Alps, and in the year (1667) eighty-six wolves were shot and sent to Munich, whilst in about eighty years there were no less than thirty bears killed near the Tegernsee convent. The visitor to St. Bartholomä, on the Königssee will be forcibly reminded of the dangers of conflicts with bears by the picture shown him of a fisherman struggling with a bear in the water, which is at least strikingly characteristic. A few years ago the skeleton of a bear with an arrow in its back was found in a cave near Unter-Ammergau. The Emperor Ludwig of Bavaria was fond of hunting in this neighbourhood, and may possibly have fired the fatal shot. The most remarkable of the game still native to the mountains since the disappearance of the Steinbock (*Capra ibex*), formerly found on the Wetterhorn, is the Chamois, which haunts the highest and steepest rocks, so that hunting it is a most perilous pastime; but for this very reason most fascinating to a true hunter, who is never satisfied unless he has dangers and difficulties to contend with. Last century the chamois and ibexes were under legal protection in the Tyrol, but in the Bavarian Highlands they became scarcer and scarcer and, strange to say, of less value. Indeed the old regulations for the chase (1481) in Garmisch and Werdenfels, classed the chamois with the squirrel as animals which any one might hunt.

The Electors of Bavaria, it is true, sometimes hunted the chamois in the Allgäu mountains (which are, however, not in the district under consideration), and in the Kaingarten district, especially near Tegernsee and Berchtesgaden. King Maximilian, who was devoted to the mountain chase, extended his protection to the chamois, which still congregate in considerable numbers about the Tegernsee, Schliersee, and Königssee, and in the mountains round Ammergau. They increase rapidly, as they can always

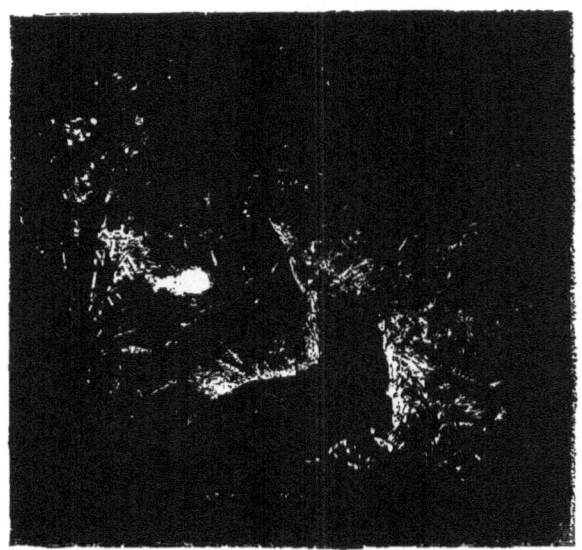

find enough food to sustain life in the clefts of the rocks after the fall of the avalanches, or under the Shelter-firs (*Schirmtanne*), where the snow never penetrates; whilst the stag, requiring more substantial nourishment, is driven down by hunger to the lesser heights, and falls an easy prey to the hunters.

According to an estimate taken of the game in 1800, there were but twenty chamois in the Tegernsee district in that year, whereas in 1847 there were six hundred and fifty, and now the number in the different districts mounts up to nearly four thousand—more than enough to render the chase exciting and profitable to sportsmen and poachers. The skin of the chamois fetch a good price, its flesh—especially when young—is very palatable, and every man is only too fond of having a "chamois beard" in his cap—that is to say, a tassel formed of the long fine hairs growing down the animal's back. Not less prized are the

EAGLE AND SHEEP.

"*Krickeln*," as they call the black horns of the chamois, which are used as ornaments and for many other purposes. The balls—composed of hair and the fibres of plants—sometimes found in the stomachs of chamois, are also much sought after, as they are a preventive of giddiness, and, according to a popular superstition, a safeguard to their wearers from all hobgoblins and from the influence of the mountain spirits.

Another much smaller animal native to the mountains is the Marmot, a harmless little creature, rather like a rabbit, which is, however, only met with about Berchtesgaden near the Funtensee, and in the neighbourhood of the chaos of rocks closing in the Königssee on one side; for it is beneath such masses that they burrow out their homes, sleeping in them in the winter, and in the summer disporting themselves near them amongst the aromatic Alpine herbs, of which they are very fond, or sitting bolt upright like a hare in its form. Hunters endeavour to obtain the teeth of these little creatures to wear on their watch-

chains; the fur, too, is valuable, and the fat is used as a medicament in the mountains, and is supposed to be good for everything.

We have already spoken of the singing-birds as part of the feathered game of the mountains. We have therefore now only a few specialities to mention, such as the Red-headed Woodpecker, or the Red-legged Crow, with its shrill shriek, which latter is found in places little frequented by man, and instead of shunning is disposed to follow him inquisitively. The Auerhahn (*Tetrao Gallus*) and other gallinaceous birds that frequent the lower moors and mossy tracts are by no means rare in the mountain forests; but on the other hand, their cousins the Black Cock or Heath-fowl, the Ptarmigan, and the Red Grouse, never go down to the plains. The plumage of these three birds is as beautiful as their flesh is delicious. The red grouse is distinguished for its red beak and claws, and the ptarmigan for becoming perfectly white in winter, and for the purple streak above its eyes.

The predaceous birds of the mountains include many species of owls and eagles: the Fish-eagle or Sea-eagle (*Aquila Haliæëtos*), which has its home near rivers and lakes; the Golden Eagle (*Aquila chrysaetos*), a powerful creature, which measures more than eight feet across when its wings are outspread, and builds its eyrie in the clefts and crevices of steep precipices, so that robbing it is a dangerous feat, only to be accomplished by those bold enough to let themselves down by ropes. These fine birds are mostly found in the Berchtesgaden district, and must formerly have been very numerous, as a forester of St. Bartolomä boasted of having himself shot one hundred and twenty-seven. The still larger *Lammergeiers*, or Great Bearded Vultures, which are able to carry off a young chamois or to help himself to a lamb from a flock of sheep, were formerly to be met with pretty frequently; now, however, they no longer build eyries in the Bavarian Highlands, but only pay extremely rare passing visits.

Of the hated and uncanny race of reptiles, the Alps contain only harmless and well-known varieties of the Common Snake; but up to an elevation of 5,000 feet Vipers are seen. The Lizard, called the Black Salamander, with bright orange coloured spots, is frequently met with, and popular superstition looks upon it as a supernatural creature because of its supposed power of living uninjured in fire.

Not to forget the fishes, we must mention that the Trout frequents in great numbers the clearest and most rapid mountain streams. Most of the lakes of upper Bavaria contain some speciality of their own besides the commoner kinds, such as the Heuch (*Salmo Hucho*), the Grayling or Umber (*Thymallus vulgaris*), &c. The Starnbergersee, for instance, is famous for the so-called "*Renchen*" or "*Renke*" (one of the smaller *Salmonidæ*), the Ammersee for another variety called the "*Gangling*," the Chiemsee

for the Salmon Trout (*Salmo trutta*), and the Königssee for its "*Salblinge*" (*Salmo Alpinus*), which, when smoked, form the well-known and favourite dish called "*Schwarzreuterl*."

As we have already stated, there are many popular superstitions connected with the animal and vegetable world of the mountains. Those held by the herdsmen, hunters, Sennerins, and woodcutters have been noticed elsewhere; but many a mountain brook is worked by a solitary saw-mill, and in the heart of the forest we come to many a secluded clearing where a lonely charcoal-burner has built up his smoking pile, and awaits in his primitive hut the slow and all but imperceptible extinction of his fire. The occupation of the owner of the lonely mill and of the charcoal kiln set down in the midst of the mighty mountain solitudes are alike calculated to promote dreamy meditation, and we can well understand the rise of ghostly legends around the blackened homes of the charcoal-burners, nor shall we feel much surprise when some old mountaineer tells us of all manner of wonderful things—that there is no better protection from snakes than a staff of ash-wood, from which all animals shrink; that crumbled up "Bibernell" (*Pimpinella saxifraga*) given to cattle will save them from the "*Viehschelm*," an evil spirit which goes bellowing about the mountains in the form of an emaciated bull. It is easy, too, to understand the origin of the fable of the "*Tatzelwurm*," a creature which, according to some traditions, was a kind of dragon, and according to others only a lizard, in the claws (*Tatzen*) of which dwelt magic power, as in the wishing-hat of Fortunatus. In spite of the large reward offered, the "*Tatzelwurm*" (also called the "*Bergstutz*," or Stag of the Mountain) has never yet been found. The skeleton is said to have once hung from the ceiling in the castle of Marquartstein, and a votive tablet was formerly shown at Unken on which was represented the death of a peasant, the result of his horror at meeting two such creatures, which were depicted in the form attributed to them by the imagination of a village painter; but if Franz Kobell had not copied this work of art in his fine book on the chase, "Der Wildanger," even this trace of the "*Tatzelwurm*" would have been lost, for it disappeared from the stone pillar containing it a little time back—probably some son of Albion, in quest of curiosities, had appropriated it to himself.

THE "TATZELWURM."

GOD BLESS THEE!

WHEN travellers twain have wandered,
And the parting hour draws nigh,
With kiss and many a greeting
They bid a warm good-bye.
Now is our happy converse o'er,
Greet me the wife and child.
  "God bless thee!"

If thou this book hast pondered
With genial heart and soul,
Its thoughts perchance may lighten
Life's journey to its goal.
Now its last lines before you lie,
I too must bid a last good-bye;
  "God bless thee!"

The mountain path we've trodden,
Hamlets and lakes have seen;
Through meadows and green forests
And changeless snows we've been;
And all around so bright and glad,
Must not the parting hour be sad?
  "God bless thee!"

THE BAVARIAN MOUNTAINS.

Yet still will fancy linger
O'er scenes we learned to prize;
And when, in future summers,
Sweet memories arise,
Then think as travellers do, I pray,
On that true Guide, who led the way.
      "God bless thee!"

APPENDIX.

THE GEOGNOSTIC FORMATION OF THE BAVARIAN ALPS.

By Dr. KARL HAUSHOFER.

THE GEOGNOSTIC FORMATION OF THE BAVARIAN ALPS.

I.

WE not unfrequently hear our mountains designated as Limestone Alps. If in such a case it is not forgotten that there are elsewhere in the great district of the Alps limestone mountains—if by this designation it is not intended to mark any local limitation, but only that which is special in their nature—it may with good reason be used, for the limestone and its kindred substances prevail largely under the manifold forms of which the boundary Alps of the Bavarian Tyrol are constructed, and its peculiarities affect a considerable portion of the physiognomy of the scenery, of the articulation, the water-sheds, the vegetation, and it probably also influences the civilisation of the district under consideration.

The presence of limestone there produces a truly complicated diversity in the surface-configuration, which prevents any appearance of uniformity in the character of the mountains. Sometimes there are red compact marble walls as they rise to the pinnacles of the Untersberg, sometimes dazzlingly white or grey cliffs, whose sharply angled fragments clink under the tread like broken glass; delicately veined, speckled, or deep-black slabs, on which the stone-saws carry on their monotonous daily task; soft perforated masses of tufa, full of impressions of sedge, leaves, and snails, spread abroad on their slopes; myriads of wonderful shells of extinct creatures grown into compact masses of stone,—under all these, and many other forms, we find that Proteus of the mineral kingdom, limestone. Again, we find the same material, the same collocation—calcareous earth and carbonic acid; the white oxide of a light silvery metal and the stinging carbonic acid gas are its principal constituents.

White and light grey colours generally prevail in the limestone. The limestone mountains, therefore, do not wear on their rocky walls, their torrent-beds, and on the numerous blocks in their foreground, the glory of colour which we meet with in many valleys of the primitive mountain range; but they are indebted to this circumstance for their marvellously tender blue tones of shadow and the indescribable splendour of colour which is formed over them by the light of dawn and by the setting sun. Pure limestone is colourless, or white as the Carrara marble or the beautiful stone of Schlander. The variegated colourings depend on foreign admixtures which have nothing in common with the substance of the limestone, and frequently occur only in very small quantity. Thus many limestones contain traces of carbonate of iron. Under the influence of air and water is formed from this, of itself, a yellowish grey body, oxide of iron, which clothes such limestone rocks with a coat of reddish brown. Many waters also, which hold in solution little particles of iron, colour the surface of the rocky walls over which they drip with the deposit of oxide of iron—a deep brown—a phenomenon which may be observed frequently enough; for instance, on the Schwartzbachwachtstrasze, on the rocks on the west of the Funtensee, and which contributes not a little to the colouring of the landscape.

In the colouring of the limestone rocks, moreover, their clothing of vegetation has a certain share. This is the case not only with the various kinds of moss which creep about the grey blocks, with dark green, yellow, or rust-coloured cushions; but still more with the lichens, those wonderful leafless and flowerless excrescences which, among others, characterize the lowest grade of organized existence. Partly as a many-coloured scarf, and partly also as a thin faintly visible crust, they adhere everywhere—even far above the snow-limit—so closely and intimately to the rock that they appear to be one with it. Only by the solution of the limestone in diluted vinegar can they be separated from it. They are then left as a slimy, brownish skin, which appears under the microscope as an entangled web of exceedingly delicate threads. With them they penetrate into the white limestone, suck therefrom their frugal sustenance, and finally, when they perish, form the foundation for the settlement of new and more highly organized plants. These are the pioneers of vegetation.

On the surface of those limestone rocks which they clothe they usually produce blue-grey or greenish-grey tones of colour, which are commonly darker than the colour of the rock itself. The most beautiful kind of these lichens, however—the so-called "violet moss" (red byssus), whose fragrance pervades all the Tauern valleys, and whose burning red hue glows even on the mosses of the Riesengebirg and of the Hartz—is not met with in the limestone mountains.

Probably the question has often been ventilated whether the palm of natural beauty is to be accorded to the limestone Alps or to the mountains of the central chain. The question, if it is to be answered in its entire extent, is an idle one, as so many are on which the taste of the age exercises its capricious judgment. But single parts may perhaps be separated in thought, and an answer given. As we attempted it in respect of colouring, it may also be done in respect of the mountain forms, and in that behalf the palm certainly falls to the limestone Alps. If we must ever concede to the ice-crowned giants of the granite, gneiss, and mica-slate the pre-eminence in the grandeur and majesty of their appearance, still it is hardly difficult to show that in picturesque charms, in richness and grace of formation, they do not equal the limestone mountains.

The reason of this is found in the different way in which the rocks yield to the action of the weather. The disorganization at which weather and water are incessantly at work leads in the primitive mountain ranges preferably to the rounding off of the forms. There the tooth of time, the dissolving power of the atmospheric agencies, gnaws especially at the sharp angles of the rock, and produces shapeless lumpy blocks; a mass of fine rubbish and lumber fills up the cavities and obliterates the delicate lines in the face of the mountains.

But in the limestone, which is usually pierced by numberless delicate rifts in all directions, every winter creates new forms. The water which has penetrated into the crevices, at the moment that it is to become ice bursts the rocks asunder with irresistible force. At the coming in of the warm season the loosened fragments lose their hold, plunge down, and cover valley and slope with ruins, while above, on the airy pinnacles, new sharp angles and lines are formed. It is a strangely solemn moment when the silent loneliness of the valleys is broken and interrupted, when from the dizzy height a mass as large as a house thus rolls into the abyss. There, where in the sun-scorched desolation of the upper Wimbach valley the green-clad Griesalp rises like an oasis, seek for thyself a couch on the carpeted turf in front of the deserted hut; it is a place to surrender thy thoughts to the transporting horror of the mountain loneliness—

> "The lonely valley glows in golden sunlight:
> Below thou seest the naked pines projecting,
> Where rocky horns support their icy burden,
> Where wild white torrents foam through craggy portals.—
> There, down it thunders, sudden headlong falling,
> And roars and shatters in fierce stormy chasing,
> To leap from wall to wall in volleying crashes,
> Till in the deepest vale it downward plunges.
> Long rolls the thunder, and the mountains tremble
> With Echo's tenfold voices proudly sounding,
> And clouds of dust that sweep from forth the valley.
> From rocky crest the waterfalls drop lightly—
> Away! away! thou monstrous life and lonely!
> Wild was thy storming—long is thy reposing!"
>
> MAX HAUSHOFER.

A further reason for the greater wealth of forms in the limestone mountains is found in their construction of immense ledges of rock and slab-formed masses which here and there are scarcely connected at all, but are bent, broken, and thrown one upon another in the most heterogeneous fashion. Thence that opulence in the articulation in bold profiles and surprising lines, that definiteness in the expression which nevertheless nowhere allows stereotyped forms to arise, and which is an absolutely inexhaustible source of suggestion to the artist. How entirely different, again, is the character of the mountains in the Berchtesgaden district, and near the Kochelsee on the shores of the Salzach, and on those of the Loisach, on the Inn, and on the Walchensee; how strangely glitters the gigantic ridge of the Watzmann above the gloomy forests of the Ramsau, as we gaze up at its haughty jagged summit when seated at our mid-day meal in some one of the international hotels of Berchtesgaden. The variety of forms of one and the same mountain from different sides gives to the landscapes that surround it their peculiar stamp. It is in a certain measure their epic impulse.

The disruption of the limestone rock implies a deficiency of water, which is specially characteristic of the upper regions of the limestone mountains. It is one of the most sensible drawbacks from the triumph of the climber of the Watzmann. A slender thread of water, which trickles down from a cleft of the rock over a slip of wood stuck into it, is the only refreshment to be obtained in the burning rocky desolation in the upper portion of the mountain. The Sennerins of the Reiter Alp collect the droppings from the eaves of roofs to procure enough drinking-water for themselves and their cattle. In a network of large and small rifts which penetrate the rock the snow and rain-water sinks away everywhere without a trace into the abyss, to break forth suddenly again as a mighty brook in some other place, frequently remote. Among the eastern precipices of the Reiter Alp is situated a narrow cavern clothed with dark moss, the "Schwarzbachloch," from which gushes forth a stream and hurries in joyous leaps through the lonely valley of the same name to the Reichenhall basin. The Schrambach also, not far from St. Bartholomä on the Königssee, the Jochbach on the Kochelsee, which, according to the popular notion, brings water from the Walchensee, the source of the Partnach on the "Anger," the Gollinger Schwarzbach, which rushes down out of a rocky chasm in wildly foaming eddies, and may with great probability be regarded as a subterranean outlet of the Königssee, with many other phenomena of this kind—to which, moreover, belongs the wealth of the valley springs—may be traced back to the same natural causes.

Under special circumstances the clefts and rifts of the limestone rock become filled with other mineral masses—most usually with calcareous spar. This is in some sort a richer limestone; it consists of the same materials, but it is distinguished by the peculiar structure that crystallization gives, and which on fracture causes little smooth surfaces to appear everywhere. It has for the most part white or light grey colours, and therefore in filling up crevices it draws a delicate network of brighter lines on the mass of many a red, grey, or black limestone. By the action of the weather they frequently stand forth from the surface of the rock in small patches, because they are better able to resist the destructive action than the mass of the rock.

In specially favoured places, in protected caverns and clefts of the rock, the growth of the calcareous spar has proceeded so uninterruptedly that perfectly formed transparent crystals, as clear as water, or light yellowish in colour, have arisen therefrom. They are comparatively rare in our mountains. The most beautiful are found in the region of Berchtesgaden. More ordinary kinds, combined into groups and crystalline masses, are more frequent, and occur, for instance, in the Krossenberg, near Innzell, at Bergen, and at other places.

In a country which is so rich in stone as the Alps, it is conceivable that no great account is made of the common limestone. Stone-quarries, indeed, are everywhere met with, which are worked in the grey solid limestone to get material for road-making and for lime-burning; but for the building of houses other kinds of stone are usually preferred, which are more easily worked, and are also less liable to decay, especially certain sandstones, pudding-stones, and so on. Many limestones which, with the capability of taking a high polish, combine special colours or coloured markings and sufficient hardness, form, as marble, the subject of a not too richly developed industry. The places where marble is found are too numerous to name them all, and with little trouble new ones could easily be discovered. Every visitor from Salzburg will remember the various kinds of marble: white, rose-red, down to rusty brown, stained and veined, whose beauty in many a building would atone for even a more inartistic form. The white freestones which King Ludwig I. employed for his monumental creations come from a remarkable stratum of stone on the northern declivity of the Untersberg, which is worked in several quarries. There, moreover, the occurrence of several kinds of marble calls into existence a small branch of industry—the manufacture of those elegant balls which in popular language are called marbles, and are among the articles most coveted by us in our "dear school days." Whoever visits the marble quarries at Salzburg from Glaneck, or the "lofty throne" of Salzburg on the Untersberg, must pass the marble mills, and may then be glad for a time to look on at the work.

Moreover, the neighbourhood of Berchtesgaden (Kälberstein, Schellenberg, Barmstein) and Reichenhall (Karlstein) supplies excellent faint reddish kinds of marble in large blocks. From the marble quarries of the Haselberg, near Ruhpolding, and of the Hochgern, near Marquartstein, come the red and grey marble that we meet with in many churches and convents of the Chiemgau. The latter, in a double deposit of freestone, girdles the shore of the Frauen-Chiemsee as a protection against the enormous pressure of the drifting ice. The marble which is procured in the Weiszach valley at Egern, and is there cut into blocks and sheets, surpasses many others by its manifold variety of colour and marking. There are red, white, grey, black and variegated kinds that are quarried there. Finally, the numberless blocks that lie in the valleys and on the slopes offer a rich prize in kinds of marble that are sometimes magnificent; for instance, the blocks of the so-called marble trench at Mittenwald, which show many white spots on a red ground; the immense fragments which dash down from the Laberberg at Ettal; the red and grey masses of stone in the neighbourhood of the Wendelstein, from the Rothwand, and many others.

It might appear surprising that many marble quarries, which in earlier times were vigorously worked, at the present day lie forgotten and unused, although they contain serviceable material enough, and trade in them has become so very much easier. Can it be that in our time the love for the venerable magnificence of durable marble has declined because the art of imitation has been carried to such marvellous perfection? Can it be that in our days railways and barracks are built in preference to churches and palaces? However this may be, we cannot refuse our admiration and gratitude to the love and perseverance with which our ancestors conveyed their splendid building materials, often under the most unfavourable circumstances, from a distance of many days' journey.

The remarkable stone which is familiar under the often misunderstood name of "granite marble," and is valued as building material, belongs to another class of rock. It consists of fragments of coral and small remains of crustaceous animals which, covered with white or grey lime substance and closely cemented in its texture with numerous dark grains of sand, form a compact rock and, on account of the contrast of colour of the individual portions of the compound, manifest a remote likeness to many a grey granite. Beside the important quarries at Sinning, not far from Neubeuern, there are also stone quarries worked for several fine and coarse-grained varieties of granite marble in the district of Tölz (Bockleithe), in Leitzachthal, at Miesbach, Trauenstein, and Reichenhall.

Many limestone formations are still to be seen at the present day. Whoever has wandered along the charming forest-paths from Abwinkel, on the Tegernsee, to the "Bauern in the Meadow," must have been struck with the spring-water which at one spot, immediately at the side of the road, has clothed its channel with a yellowish white slime, and has in a short time covered branches and leaves which have fallen down into it with the same substance; this also is carbonate of lime. In waters which are rich in carbonic acid a considerable mass of carbonate of lime is dissolved when they slowly ooze through the fissures of the limestone mountains. At their appearance on the surface the lime falls to the bottom or is deposited as a crust upon all the objects which the waters of the spring trickle over. The continuance of this simple process during thousands of years may accomplish the formation of thick ledges of those porous masses of limestone which are called lime-tufa (in the popular language, "tufa" or "white-stone"). Similar deposits, which have been formed in fresh-water lakes, and therefore usually enclose a mass of shells of various fresh-water molluscs, are called fresh-water limestone, and now and then play an important part as rocks. Under some circumstances the limestone tufa may possess sufficient solidity to be available as building material; in that case it is all the better that, by virtue of its porous constitution, it is apt to be dry and of little weight. The extensive tufa quarries of Pölling and Kugelfing, near Weilheim, the quarries of Tölz, also those of the Mühlthal, near Miesbach, and countless other tufa formations of smaller extent, contain such material.

With such causes, moreover, is substantially associated the formation of the dropping-stones or stalactites, only with the modification that the lime-depositing water oozes from overhanging rock forming the vaulting of a cavern. Curious formations of stalactite, however, are among the rarities in our mountain range, although there are tufa springs in plenty. The reason of this is to be found in the surprising fact, that our mountains, notwithstanding all their disruptions, possess only few and small caverns.

Frequently the deposited particles of limestone have only an extremely loose cohesion, and then they form white friable masses of chalk-like appearance. Such tufa earth ("ground chalk," plasterer's earth) is dug in several quarries, among others at Mittenwald, Kreuth, Oberaudorf, Marquartstein, and Ruhpolding, and forms, on account of its applicability to plastering and to writing, a not unimportant article of commerce, which is sent some distance down the Isar and the Danube.

Many a one who has marvelled at the immense masses of the limestone mountains will have been led to inquire how they have come into being? And the answer that science can give him will assuredly not diminish his amazement. According to the latest views of geologists, they are mainly composed of the calcareous shells of little creatures which swim in prodigious multitudes in sea-water, and moreover lived in the ocean which formerly covered the Alpine region. The shells sink, when the tiny inhabitants have ended their ephemeral existence, to the bottom, accumulate there continually, and in the course of time become, by the pressure of the sea, and by certain chemical processes, a concreted mass. By the drying up of the sea, or by the upheaving of its bottom, they emerge again in the sunlight as solid limestone, after thousands of years' submersion. In this limestone the most rigid investigation will scarcely find even faint traces of its primitive nature. Only in such deposits as were, perhaps, not sufficiently exposed to the active powers of the deep do we find under the microscope those remarkable animal remains in numbers which transcend all our conceptions. That is the true chalk, with which, however, we do not meet in our mountains. The so-called chalk rocks of the Leonhardstein, near Krouth, owe their chalk-like constitution to the softening effect of moisture; but they are no more true chalk than the "ground chalk" of Mittenwald.

Scientific men have known how to fetch from the bottom of the sea the proof of this startling theory. Even to this day such slimy lime deposits are still being formed in the bottom of the sea; and the microscopic investigation of the specimens of slime from a depth of fourteen thousand feet has shown that they consist almost exclusively of such limestone shells. We understand thence also why many limestones contain a greater or less mass of foreign matters. In those portions of the primeval lime-depositing seas which were situated nearer to the land, where the rivers of the mainland carried out their mud many miles distance into the sea, it got among the limestone shells in very fine regular commixture—the finest portions furthest from the land, the coarser portions nearer to it. Even by means of the breakers on the coasts, the sea takes up with it a mass of finely-pulverized stone. Nay, in accordance with the inland nature of the rivers and in accordance with the stones of the coast, the slime which is brought therefrom into the limestone deposits of the sea has an argillaceous or a silicious constitution, and is the primary condition for the formation of clayey and flinty limestones. It is obvious that the deeper and larger the seas, the farther removed they are from the defilements of great streams, the purer the limestone, and that the varying relations of mass between lime, clay, and sand afford us foothold for the decision whether any sort of rock was formed in the depth of the sea or in the neighbourhood of the coasts. Nearer to the impurity of rivers there always appear coarser admixtures, and nearest to the continent is the gravel, which remains in its place as soon as the propelling power of the river becomes weaker. With the preponderance of the river-mud and sand are diminished the conditions of life of the delicate animalculæ of the limestone shells, and there are formed clay-slate, clays, and sandstones; these are formed out of the coarsest boulders, the conglomerates and pudding-stones.

Limestone rocks with little clay are called marly limestones; when the clay that they contain is more abundant, they are designated without definite limit as marl and argillaceous marl. It is conceivable that the marly limestones and the marl appear in greater mass as rocks; nay, there are in general only few limestone rocks which do not contain at least traces of clayey or silicious substances. Gradual transitions connect these rocks. Many marls cannot often be distinguished from limestones as far as their external appearance is concerned. The damp odour of clay which they emit on being breathed upon, the disposition to a slaty laminated mode of formation, and their small capacity of resistance to disintegration, may serve as indications of marly rocks. On the last-named peculiarity, however, is dependent the formation of a soil which, rich as it is in nourishment for plants, is still more favourable to the growth of the spicy herbage for cattle, and therefore affects the whole of Alpine husbandry, in our mountains at least. In every place, where especially rich and productive Alpine pasture is formed, it will be manifest that deposits of marl are the cause. We shall find there fat, deeply-based kinds of soil where such rocks appear on the surface, and in their district we meet with the name that so frequently recurs, "Kothalp," which consequently means

APPENDIX.

something better than it expresses. The utility of certain kinds of marl for the fabrication of cement has developed in many places of our mountains a lively branch of industry, which is still progressively flourishing. We need only to remind the reader of the excellent cement marl of Staudach, near Marquartstein, of Hinterwessen, and of Schöffen, near Oberaudorf, among many others.

The contingencies which have co-operated in the origination of the intermediate rocks between the limestone, sandstone, and clay-slate, were the conditions of a multiformity in their appearances which sets at naught all limitation and description.

Even in the sandstones, there are the greatest diversities in the size, substance, and colour of the granules. White or grey sharply-edged, or even-rounded granules of that hard mineral which bears the characteristic name employed by the German miner, of "quartz," forms the chief masses, more or less strongly cemented together by carbonate of lime, by marl, or clay-slime, or by the quartzy substance itself. Rocks of the last kind belong to the most solid and hardest of the whole range of mountains. The agglutinating medium itself shows now and then a reddish or yellowish brown colouring, which proceeds from some little association with iron. By the commixture of little grains of a peculiar dark green mineral are produced the green sandstones, as such occur in slight manifestation between Bichel and Tölz, on the western shore of the Tegernsee, between Breitenbach and Kaltenbrunn, at the Neureit, and in the Leitzachthal (Kaltewasser). If more clay is mingled with the sandstone rocks, they assume the laminated and slaty constitution of sandstone-slate, and finally pass over into sandy slate-clay and marl-slate.

By many rivers, moreover, as we have mentioned, might quartzy (silicious) particles be added to the limestone formations, and being commingled in exceedingly fine distribution, they give to the limestones a greater hardness and sharpness, and finally, by a definite alloy of silicious substance, make them the valuable whetstone slate. On a small belt of this stone, which extends from Unterammergau towards the west, there are more than fifty quarries on the eastern continuation of the same towards Ohlstadt, and twelve quarries for whetstone in activity, which annually supply over a hundred thousand whetstones. On the Besenbach, near Kochel, are found useful whetstone slates.

WIMBACHTHAL.

The greater the mass of the commingled finely comminuted silicious substance in the limestones, the harder they appear, and finally they form those sharp rocks which are constantly occurring in our mountains, which are characterised as lime-hornstone, or silicious limestone. On the disappearance or the withdrawal of the limestone true hornstones are produced. They strike sparks from steel, and have red, brown, and dark grey colours. Many limestone rocks contain the hornstone in roundish lumps, often marked with variegated colours; others enclose sharp splinters of it, which, as the stone is weatherworn, come to the surface and give it an extremely rough indented face; here and there also are silicified mussel-shells changed into hornstone, and especially corals, which communicate to the limestones and marls that enclose them a similar appearance. Such are met with on the Barmstein, near Berchtesgaden ("Barmstein lime"), on the northern summit of the Hochfell. On the mountain-ridge which slopes down from Hirschberg to Ringspitz, on the Tegernsee, are found limestones which enclose a mass of fragments of hornstone. Similar depositions, and hornstone in general, are numerous in the district of Berchtesgaden, in the neighbourhood of Audorf and Bayerischzell, and at many other points.

THE BAVARIAN MOUNTAINS.

Most of the limestones enclose small masses of magnesia; only a few are entirely free from it. A larger alloy of this material is the condition of certain peculiarities, which have obtained for the combination in question another name: this is the dolomite. It is frequently confounded with limestone, and *vice versâ*, because the external differences are trifling, and only discoverable to the practised eye, and because the numerous intermediate stages which may be designated as dolomitic limestone have their limits undefined. On accurate investigation, however, there are usually found some characteristic indications in the genuine dolomite; such are the somewhat greater weight and hardness of the dolomite, and, above all, a crystalline structure which in the fractured surfaces reminds one of finely grained sugar. The colour of the dolomite varies from light grey, yellowish and brownish grey, to blackish; yellowish and reddish white varieties are most rare. By the action of the weather the colour is bleached, and therewith is associated a loosening of the surface, which causes the stone to feel rough, like sandstone, and, moreover, yields more sand-like products of disintegration than the limestone.

In general the dolomite is liable to crumble more easily than the limestone, on account of its disruption. But, especially if the dolomitic limestone and marl are classed with it, it will equal in amount the limestone itself, and it may be conceived that its influence on the plastic formation of the mountain must be very great. It makes itself felt in two directions; on heights which the protecting covering of growing grass cannot reach, it gives to their wildly rugged forms extravagant projections, columns and needles, which everywhere tower aloft upon them, while on their slopes are strewn endless heaps of rubbish. The upper Wimbach, with its jagged, gravelly crest, with the Palfelhorns and with the streams of rubbish which slope down from them, gives a perfect type of the forms and of the destructions of the dolomite. If any one desires to compare others with them, let him range upwards from Weizbach on the Salach, to the "Schüttergraben"—it is not called thus for nothing—and over a saddle-back formation, between the Steinbergs, towards Hochfilzen. There extend in all directions deeply-cut ravines in the dolomite heart of the mountains, pathless and full of rubbish. Even on the far more convenient road to the Mooswacht, at the Hirschbühel, there are the magnificent Steinmuhren, which, from the foot of the Mühlsturzhörner reaching down to the road, excite the astonishment of the traveller. In both places yellowish-white dolomite has set itself free from the substratum of the above-named mountains, and has poured itself forth in gigantic streams over forest and pasture.

ENGELSTEIN.

We see the action of the dolomite in its greatest extent in the effect of a degenerate kind of dolomite, which bears the characteristic name of Rauhwacke (coarse trap). It consists of a porous corroded dolomite mass, of a yellowish grey to brown colour, containing numberless cavities which are usually clothed with little dolomitic crystals, but frequently also are filled up with fragments of dolomite or earthy dolomite substance. Besides the ruined masses peculiar in the districts of the "Rauhwacke," it deserves our attention on account of its association with gypsum deposits and sulphur-springs. Two small zones of "Rauhwacke," in many parts concealed by later rock rubbish and growing plants, extend on the northern extremity of the mountain range from the district of Ruhpolding towards the west, breaking out here and there in rough, rocky peaks, accompanied in certain places with a rich stratum of gypsum. Let him who desires to combine the study of the Rauhwacke rocks with the enjoyment of the charms of scenery, leave

APPENDIX.

the track at the Bergen Railway Station and find his way over the green meadows from Pattenberg to the Engelstein. From the rubbish heaps which he must scramble over towards a range of brown, weather-beaten colossi, the summits scantily overgrown with parched grass, here and there adorned with crystalline incrustations of brown calcareous spar. Towards the south are fragrant valleys with forest and meadow, above them the sides of the Hochfell; towards the north, the mirror of the Chiemsee in the misty level country. On the further side of the Hochfell, we meet in the Keumalp valley with the second line of the Rauhwacke; a deserted quarry, containing deposits of snow-white alabaster-like gypsum, indicates its vicinity. The gypsum quarries on the Steinbach, near Nuszdorf; the Rauhwacke, which from the Schrofen, not far from Brankenburg, unfortunately poured itself over the fields of Gemeind, and is still always likely to produce new landslips, because the soft schists on which it reposes are constantly being undermined by the Schlipfbach; the sharp rocky crests which extend from Mühlau, in the Leitzach valley, over the Aurachstein, towards the south of the Schliersee, appear again at the Baumgarten Alp, and crop up in the Stinkergruben, near the Tegernsee, in association with gypsum and sulphur springs, belong to the northern line, which continues through the gypsum quarry on the eastern shore of the Kochelsee and over Wallgau. In the wilderness of rubbish of the Fauckenschlucht at Partenkirche, the southern chain ends with a characteristic form of Rauhwacke, while the northern here and there emerges again in small masses in the west.

If the Rauhwacke, perhaps, indicates remarkable, but proportionally only unimportant, isolated features in the physiognomy of the country, the dolomite and the dolomitic limestone furnish the massive contours. A group of rocks which came into existence, according to the testimony of their few organic remains, under tolerably equal conditions, and in the same period, consists chiefly of dolomitic Rauhwacke and dolomitic limestone, and is on that account called the chief dolomite of the Alps. Among all rocks those of the chief dolomite group occupy incontestably the largest space in our mountains. An intrepid pedestrian, such as the Alpine Club produces, might make his way from the district of Reichenhall even into the streets of Partenkirche, and if it were not for the Loisach valley, might descend by Reuth into the Lechthal without coming upon any other tract of rock than that of the chief dolomite group, probably also without meeting with any great number of inns.

It is in the more central groups of the mountain range that the dolomite chiefly prevails; in many higher mountains, as the Watzmann, the Steirnerne Meer (Ocean of Stone), Untersberg on the Reiteralp, the pedestal alone consists of the stones of the chief dolomite group. Therewith are associated characteristic features which are rarely disguised. If the higher dolomite mountains are not distinguished for their wonderfully rugged rocky crests and peaks, or for uniformly picturesque beauty of landscape, the middle and lower dolomite mountains are also remarkable for a certain poverty of form only too evident. To the friend of the mountains we need only name a few more prominent familiar names from the region of the chief dolomite to prove that to him. Mountains such as the uncouth Ristfeuchtkogel, or the Hochplatte, near Marquartstein; the Geigelstein (or Wechsel), near Sacharung; the Hochrisz, the Kranzhorn, Jägerkamp, Wallberg, Wiesing, and Planberg, appear typical of the middle heights, which are composed of the chief dolomite. Long descending slopes of rubbish, cemented together again in process of time, and covered over with "Krummholz," or crooked-stem pines, or brown grasses, afford pasturage even on the summit of the mountains. The bottom of the valley and the mountain-top become linked together by long-drawn expressionless curved lines, and one seldom meets with the articulation, the delicate architecture which is peculiar to the limestone rocks over other formations, and even the colours, which are almost confined to browns and greys, add to the monotony of the impression produced. If exceptions occur, as, for instance, the boldly constructed range of dolomite which reaches from Sonntagshorn to the

Wildalpenhorn, and over the Dürnbachschneide to the Schwarzlofer, the Schinder, the Herzogstand, or the Walchensee, and other stately mountains, yet the character of the chief dolomite districts is always the same, as we see between Bayerischzell and in the country on either side of the Brandenberg valley; the Jachenau; in the Isarthal, from Länggries to Mittenwald; in the Sacharanger valley, from the Vorderreisz. The mountain forests which extend between Eibsee and Ammerthal, those which are reflected in the lonely Walchensee, the heights around Reit in Winkel, and those which attend the wayfarer in desperate monotony from Kössen to Erpfendorf, consist almost exclusively of rocks of the chief dolomite group. Of the origination of the dolomite less is known than of that of the limestone, but the relationship, the similarity, and the transitions between the two make the supposition probable that the dolomite also was produced directly or indirectly by the action of great floods. The Rauhwacke, on the other hand, may with tolerable certainty be regarded as a tufa formation corresponding to the lime-tufa formation, because dolomite tufas are deposited from many waters before our eyes.

Still more frequently than in the limestones there appears in the dolomite a varying alloy of carbonate of iron. If it attains a certain magnitude it may confer on the rock the value of an iron ore, which is fitted for working, especially if it is weather-worn into brown ironstone. Under the Wendelstein occur such iron dolomites at several points: for instance, not far from the Dickelalp, the utilization of them certainly is lessened by local circumstances, whilst a similar deposit at Werfen is rather energetically worked. Moreover, the Anzmoosalp by its very name suggests the occurrence of such ores. The dark colouring of the dolomites, and also of the limestones and marl, is usually derived from the admixture of a finely divided residuum of animal and vegetable bodies, or from a product of their decomposition—the so-called bitumen. The presence of the latter is not unfrequently betrayed by the peculiar burnt smell that such stones emit on being rubbed or broken, and which has procured for them the trivial name of "Stinkstein." In many marl-slates, especially from the group of the chief dolomite, the alloy of bitumen (also called asphalt and mineral pitch) is of such importance that it is worth while to submit it to a distillation in order to get the bitumen from it. At Seefeld in Tyrol, in the Oelgraben in the Vorderreisz, on the Kramer and Griesberg near Garnisch, and on the Seinsbach near Mittenwald, appear asphalt slates of the kind (oil-slates, bituminous slates), of which the two first yield considerable profit. The distillation, which is carried on upon the spot, supplies the asphalt of the Munich pavements, and liquid earth-oil, a kind of petroleum, the application of which, nevertheless, is limited to the fabrication of cart-grease and for consumption in the domestic dispensary of the peasant. Where such asphalt permeates the rocks in a sufficiently fluid condition, and the circumstances of the deposit are fitted for it, it may trickle spontaneously from the soil as the well-known Quirinus oil of the Tegernsee, which on the western shore of the Finner comes to light so plentifully, as a deep brown oil mixture of petroleum and asphalt, that nearly four hundred measures can be annually obtained. As the boring experiments which were then set on foot attest, it must proceed from a stratum of rock which is deeply entombed beneath accretions and later deposits. Along the whole western shore, as far as Wiessee, traces of petroleum show themselves. We can still the less doubt of the derivation of the asphalt from the bodies of preadamite animals and plants, for the numberless impressions of fishes that occur—for instance, in the slates of the Oelgraben, or the carbonized remains of plants in other formations—witness to it with sufficient plainness.

The material which the living activity of preadamite existence contributed to the building up of the mountains is generally more important and of greater extent than we are at the first glance disposed to believe. Apart from the compact limestones whose origination has already been discussed, many other kinds of rocks are met with which directly declare themselves as an accumulation of the remains of preadamite creatures. Among others must not be forgotten those remarkable limestone rocks which owe their existence to coral animals and their love of building. The petrified fragments of their dwellings, the coral lodges, are indeed less frequently met with in our Alps than in other lands, yet they are not wanting, and they appear pretty plainly, for instance, in the rocky masses of the Barmstein and Eckerfürst, in the Göhlgruppe and in the northern ridge of the Hochfell, as light grey limestone, whose weather-worn surface appears rugged and uneven in consequence of numerous projecting partially silicated coral remains. To this head, moreover, are to be referred the so-called Lithodendron limestones, a beautiful kind of rock consisting of a dark grey or red-brown mass of limestone interwoven with light cylindrical bodies in the same direction, which appear on a diagonal fracture as roundish spots on a dark ground, and are nothing else than the branches of coral changed into calcareous spar.

The beautiful marble already mentioned, which is found on the northern declivity of the Untersberg, belongs to the Hippurite or Rudisten limestone, a kind of rock sparingly distributed indeed, but very remarkable. It consists for the most part of the well-preserved tapering or seed-shaped dwellings of a perfectly extinct family of crustaceous animals, the hippurite, cemented by pulverized portions of themselves, and it extends from the well-known Kugelmühle to the Nagelstein on the Hullthurmpasz. Even on the summit of the Lattengebirg we find it again, certainly not in that distinctness which made the "Nagelwand" above the Ruins-Plain a true place of pilgrimage for geologists.

In much greater extent appear the so-called Nummulite limestones and sandstones, which likewise are conglomerations for the most part from the exuviæ of animals. On the northern verge of the Alps numberless larger and smaller nummulites, of the form of flat lentils or little pieces of money (penny-stones), form the chief mass of these, mingled with grains of sand, clay, little dark green atoms of *Glauconiæ*, and various fragments of mussels. In the Höllgraben at Adelholzen, at the foot of the Marineckberg at Bergen, they appear in easily accessible brittle rocky masses. On the crumbling of the rocks the nummulites, consisting of limestone, get into the sand and gravel, whereby they become so polished that the delicate architecture of their chambers comes forward in fine outline. In this condition the popular belief regards them as a remedy for the eyes, which, being introduced under the eyelid, attracts to itself foreign substances that are mischievous. Thence it is called also "Augenstein" (eye-stone).

In many limestones is observed, by means of some little attention, a round-grained arrangement of the parts, which suggests as the best companion for it the roe of a fish. Numberless little globules of lime cemented by the substance of the limestone, or even by clay-marl, are found lying together, and form compact banks of rock, which are called "Rogenstein" (roe-stone) or oolite. In most of the oolites the globules vary in size, from a millet seed to a pea; in many they possess a hardly measurable circumference, in others they reach the size of a man's head; but in the last case they are generally only indicated in the surface of the rock by circular outlines. If the pellets are cut through, the centre is not unfrequently found, especially in the medium and small-grained oolites, to be indicated by a tiny fragment of a mussel-shell—a diminutive grain of sand.

Distinctly marked oolite limestones are met with in numerous parts of the mountain-range; among others, at the Roszstein near Kreuth, near Bergen, on the Hochgern, near the "Weber an der Wand," in the stone quarry of the Pichler near Innzell, &c. The oolite structure may easily be overlooked, especially in newly broken fragments of rock; but the action of the weather brings to light the granules on the upper surface.

II.

The limestone rocks of our mountains came into existence neither in respect of time nor place in uninterrupted continuity. What may be concluded from the manner of deposition from the often repeated attenuation of limestone layers—layers of marl-clay and sandstone, from the animal and vegetable exuviæ peculiar to each successive stratification—is that in different parts of the mountain land deep seas, tracts of coast, large, low river-flats, and continents followed one another in incalculable periods. Hence has been learned the method of distinguishing a great number of limestone formations of various age, which, as to external appearance as to colour and structure, are often indeed so similar that without reference to the sequence of their petrifaction and deposition they must absolutely be confounded.

If we ask ourselves about the share taken by the several limestone rocks in the building up of the mountains, it will be found that only the few formative epochs attain to any influential development. Such a group of rocks we are already acquainted with—those of the chief dolomite of the Alps. Under the chief dolomite we meet in normal succession usually with a not very strong zone of marly and clay-slates which are clothed with the richest vesture of verdure. They are called "Raibler" deposits. Under these, however, are deposited immense ledges of a clear, close limestone, which has been called "Wetterstein lime" and "Hallstädter limestone," because in these places it develops itself with special distinctness. The Wetterstein limestone rocks are pre-eminently white, light yellowish, also indistinctly stratified, moderately sized, and very poor in petrifaction; the Hallstädter limestones are usually well stratified and rich in petrifactions, and show prevailing reddish, yellowish, or spotted colouring, and not unfrequently contain enclosed variegated lumps of hornstone. The nature of the Hallstädter limestone is best seen in the quarries of the Külberstein and Draxlchen near Berchtesgaden, where reddish and white strata of limestone are deposited with numberless petrified mussels, the quarries near Schellenberg, and finally the rocks of the Kapellchen near Hallein, which contain an abundance of ammonites and numerous scattered rocky blocks. Some mountain sides and tops of the Berchtesgaden district consist of Hallstadt limestones. In the Jenner it raises itself to a stately mountain crest, appearing always plainer and grander towards the east; in the west of our mountain range it is displaced by the Wetterstein limestone. A chain of mountains, whose beauty of form delights us, ranges from the Staufen near Reichenhall over the Rauschenberg towards the west, and is indebted to the Wetterstein limestone for the craggy, shining walls, which can be seen far away in the Chiemgau. The old master of landscape might well class them with the Greek and Italian mountains, so justly famous for their beauty of outline.

Rocky ledges of Wetterstein limestone forced upwards break through in the ragged Kampenwand, Gedererwand and *Ueberhangenden Wand*, near Aschau, in the loftily-reared Wendelstein and Breitenstein, Fockenstein and Geigerstein, in the Steinwand near Fischbachau, the Benediktenwand, and in the "Stein" on the Kochelsee, with the covering of more recent rocks; their names betraying to us their form and surface-constitution. Above all, however, glitter the towering white Wetterstein limestone masses of the Kaisergebirge, of the Uunitz and Guffert, of the many-crested threefold tops of the Kurwendel chain from beyond the frontiers. They attain the greatest development in the group of the Wetterstein mountain range: Wettersteinwand, Wetterschroffen, Dreithorspitz, which, from base to crest, are almost completely built up of the rocks from which they take their names.

To the Wetterstein limestones and the adjacent rocks are closely joined, with the exception of the iron, those few and unimportant patches of ore which our mountains possess. The lead and zinc ores in irregularly scattered beds, on many points of the mountain range, were the subject of an extremely vigorously

APPENDIX.

prosecuted mining enterprise. More than fifty drifts intersected the mass of the Rauschenberg in all directions; in every peak beneath the jagged crown of the Kampenwand some forgotten and half-blocked-up mine leads into the abyss, and a dozen old drift-openings are found in the Wetterstein limestone of the Loisach region. It was, however, but a deceptive treasure. Rich quarryings and brisk profits alternated with dead stones and loss. The final drying up of the "Moor of Ore," after a long struggle and repeated vain attempts, brought the working to a standstill, and the spots where in the olden time hundreds of busy hands were employed, are now deserted solitudes, the ruins of the old workmen's sheds alone telling of former activity, whilst upon the slopes grows the crooked mountain pine. It is the same with the old mines in the Staufen, in the Königsberg near Berchtesgaden, and in the Höllenthal near Garnisch. In them to the poverty and uncertainty of the beds of ore was added the inhospitality of Nature in those rugged mountain heights, which was such as only to allow the working to be prosecuted during a few months in the year. In general also the depreciation of the value of metals may have aggravated the ruin of mining speculations. Only at the "Silberleithen," near Bieberwier, and in several points near Nassereit, some little mining is still carried on.

Limestones, other than the Wetterstein limestone, would therefore in normal sequence of stratification be deposited beneath it, and play only an altogether subordinate part in the construction of our mountains. Where the valleys cut deeply enough into the mountain range, or where single portions of the shattered crust of the earth are pushed up sufficiently high, we usually strike, first of all, under the Wetterstein limestone, upon dark-coloured clayey slate and sandstone with impressions of plants. There are the rocks through which the Partnach has had to force its way near Graseck in order to reach the valley basin of Garnisch. Above the narrow path which leads the

WETTERSTEIN LIMESTONE.

wayfarer into the Partnach defile, the blackish, thin, leaflike masses of slate are built up into crumbling walls. Their sombre colouring, which the sunlight touches with a strange, dim glimmer, their flat tops and rounded forms, with the dark green herbage clothing their slopes, make them a strong contrast to the bald, white, gigantic forms of the Wetterstein limestone, which gaze down upon us in a white circle when we step out of the twilight of the defile on to the sunny declivity before the forester's house.

Dark grey limestone rocks, mostly permeated by veins of white calcareous spar, usually underlie the Partnach slates; in the Graseeker gorge they alternate twice with the steep and erect Partnach slates; on the terrible southern precipice of the Zugspitze at Ehrwald they run up tolerably high above the bottom of the valley. To this limestone formation, but little diffused in our Alps, commonly called "Guttenstein limestone" (mussel limestone of the Alps), belong the black marble slabs from the quarries, near Bach, on the Tegernsee Weiszach, the limestone rocks of Hohenwaldeck on the Schliersee, the northern declivity of the Aurachstein near Neuhaus, and other similar rocks of smaller magnitude and development. This then, is about the oldest limestone of our mountains. It lies on a peculiar group of rocks, likewise but rarely and to a limited extent uncovered, concocted chiefly of red, violet, greenish grey sandstones and sandy marl slates. In the district of Werfen, however, they attain to a considerable development, and have therefore been named the Werfen bed. The petrifactions which they enclose have a certain similarity with those of

3 E

the variegated sandstone in the Vosges and on the Neckar, and they are therefore regarded as coeval with the latter, although it cannot be asserted that they appeared in absolutely the same millenary. More important than this question, at least from the commercial point of view, appears the circumstance that they embrace the most valuable mineral treasures of the Alps, the strata of rock-salt of Berchtesgaden, Hallien, and Hall. In the uppermost divisions of the group are found the grey or brown slate-clays, usually dolomitic, called "Haselgebirge," which contain the salt partly in fine admixture, but partly also, especially towards the bottom, in large masses. Side by side with it they also contain gypsum, anhydrite, and fragments of limestone, often of immense size, which latter may have been tumbled down when the whole mass was of the consistency of pap.

The salt is thus procured from the salt clay:—Spring-water is brought from outside and in large spaces—"Sinkwerken"—it washes out the salt, and reappears as water impregnated with salt—"brine." In a few places brine-springs are found, the reparation of which is attended to by Nature herself in the salt-springs of Reichenhall. By the boiling of the brine in large pans the salt is obtained after the brine, by trickling through highly piled-up brushwood in the so-called drying-houses, has lost a part of its watery contents by evaporation. A portion of the brine is driven in pipe-channels, with the help of admirable force-pumps (Ilsang, Reichenhall) to Traunstein and Rosenheim, there to be boiled away. Besides these is procured in the lower parts of the mountains solid rock-salt of white, grey, brown, and red colour; as a rarity, portions of rock-salt are found that are distinguished by a beautiful blue colour. The most faithful associate of the rock-salt is the gypsum, of which graceful crystalline groups are found in abundance, and are offered among other specimens to the visitor as a memorial. The Berchtesgaden mines are distinguished above others for their excessive cleanliness and dryness; "Selbstwässer" are the chief foes of the salt miners. A visit to the mine is quite worth the while of the traveller. It even has its grand moments. An altogether prodigious effect is produced by the thunder of a shot in the vast gloomy vaults; the earth trembles to its foundations to a great distance; and one involuntarily casts an inquiring glance upwards to the roof.

In the Werfen beds we have reached the lowest limits of the familiar rock-deposits in our mountains, without having anywhere lighted upon the genuine rock of the primitive mountain. On clay-slates void of petrification are no gneiss or granite.

After having followed the course of the rocks from the chief dolomite downwards to the oldest deposits, we choose the same point of departure, as being the principal mass of the mountain region, in order to carry on our review of the order of formation of the rock upwards as it was built up in time.

The upper limit of the chief dolomite is generally indicated by light grey limestones, which, on account of their deposition in beds clearly marked off from one another, are called the slab limestones of the chief dolomite. Their stratification and constitution is nowhere better to be observed than in the upper quarries of the Wallberg, near Tegernsee. Already visible from the Rottachthal from the east, it develops itself, if the summit itself is reached, into a characteristic formation. Divided by deep ravines, the vertical surface rears itself upwards from out a countless number of white limestone slabs, which lie over one another like the bricks of a wall, and in part appear to be only loosely connected together. With somewhat more trouble, but with even higher recompense, the platten limestone may be followed up on the broad back of the Watzmann, which declines, arching, gradually towards the north, and in that respect generally follows the prevailing curvature of the stratification. On the east and west flanks of the mountain, which rigidly slope off towards the Konigssee and Wimbachthal, the rent-off strata of the platten limestone express themselves in the numberless lines that run high up on the walls on both sides in a similar direction, and, by means of their staircase-like construction—especially after a recent fall of snow—stand out most plainly. They belong to the physiognomical features of this and many other mountains in our Alps, and, according to the position of the sun, develop an abundance of picturesque peculiarities. It scarcely needs to be observed that other deposits of rock besides the platten limestone present this peculiarity of form, only perhaps not in so expressive a manner.

The upper limit of the chief dolomite group is usually indicated by a system of grey marl ledges and clayey slates, which, indeed, only appear in small quantities, and therefore contribute but in a small degree to the characterization of the mountain lines, but in general by their weather-wear beget soft watery clay soils, and produce, according to the constitution of the mountains, either flourishing Alpine pastures or marshy mountain holes. In special places, where they are laid bare or cut through by mountain floods, a multitude of petrified Testacea has been revealed which gave them among geologists a brilliant reputation. The Kothalp between Breitenstein and Wendelstein, the Eipelgraben, which reaches up from Staudach to the foot of the Hockgern, fringed with stately forests, meadow grounds and rocky banks—the meadows of the Unken Heuthal, the much-visited Himmelmoosalp, near Oberaudorf, and above all, the gorge of the Schwartzlofer, near Kössen, which latter has given to the system the name of the Kössen deposits, are places which may not only reward the lovers of fossils, but even satisfy the mountaineer.

The next rock-deposit in order of time above the Kössen strata is formed of dazzlingly white, to grey, more rarely reddish, limestone rocks and ledges of marl, which have been named in accordance with the point at which they have been chiefly developed, Dachstein limestone. A peculiar bivalve mussel, the Dachstein bivalve, whose cross section on weatherworn blocks often appears as a heart-shaped outline, and grey or reddish Lithodendron limestone, symmetrically spotted with white spar, belong to the characteristics of our rock. In the east of the Alps, just as strongly developed as belemnite limestone and the chief dolomite, it fuses with these, by the shrinking together of the Kössen and Raibler deposits, into immense limestone blocks, in which the limits of the individual members of the rock can seldom be sharply defined. Hence the pecu‑

LIMESTONE OF THE WATZMANN.

liarly magnificent development of mountain forms in the chain between Saalach and Salzach and farther to the east. Those masses of limestone—strongly connected together—were too inflexible to be able to assume undulatory curvatures, and were therefore pushed upward, by the powers which in the Alps formed mountain and valley, in the form of immense slabs of rock, fractured and warped here and there. We see such formations in the Reiteralp, in the Untersberg, Lottengebirge, Göhl, Haagengebirge, and, above all, in the Steinerne Meer (the Ocean of Stone), near the Königssee. There may have been a time when the Watzmann, also the Hochkalten, and their southern neighbours, were connected with the great mass of the Steinerne Meer in one gigantic smooth dome. Yawning, upbursting chasms, gnawed out into valleys by the destruction of thousands of years, separate them now; the Wimbachthal, the Königssee, the gorge of the Schrambach, of the Funtensee, the ravines of Eiskapelle, and those between the block-like Gjaidköpfen. On their table-lands is diffused the Dachstein limestone, here and there overlaid by more recent red limestones in those immense rocky wildernesses which in the salt district are so significantly called "dead mountain"—in scientific language "Cartfields" (Karrenfelder).

It appears a pardonable endeavour to seek to retain a satisfactory representation of the grandeur of this Nature by pen or pencil: grey, bald, rocky ridges, deeply furrowed by the channels of snow and rain-water, rise up by thousands in all directions, ranged one above another over a vast extent, with only here and there a scanty parched-up moss clinging in their crevices; fathom-wide fissures, plunging down into bottomless abysses; funnel-shaped, washed-out rocky basins; gigantic blocks, and sharp-angled masses of rubbish, &c. Here towers a colossal mountain peak in daring profile, hiding its crest in the shadow of the low-lying clouds; there emerges, in some deeply-indented gap, a meadow of the most exquisite green, the "Schönbühel;" there again we see a weather-beaten, dilapidated cabin, which can scarcely be believed capable of harbouring a man for several weeks, and bears witness to the fact that the human species belongs to the most easily satisfied in creation. The ox, the goat, could not find subsistence here; and even the chamois forsakes this barren wilderness, in part perhaps driven away by the sheep, to which it appears to entertain an invincible repugnance. Let him who seeks cheerful pictures avoid these heights, for here there is neither beauty of colouring nor delicacy and richness of landscape scenery, but only the vast, lonely, desolate masses; these are the gigantic features of the countenance of Nature, the inanimate heights producing a petrifying terror, which the shuddering soul will never forget. The artist will not attempt to fix this upon his canvas; and yet the memory of the lover of

DACHSTEIN LIMESTONE.

mountain scenery will retain such pictures for ever, for they belong to the most magnificent in the domain of the Alps—whether the deep blue heaven expands over the wide solitude which glows and trembles in the sunlight, or whether the black cloud-shadows fly over it, or brown-grey mist-wreaths eddy from every abyss and hang on every crag; the whistling of the wind in the rocky walls, the shrill scream of a "Mankei," are the only sounds of these regions.

The question as to the causes of the "Waggon-field" formations (Karrenfeldbildung) is not to be exhausted in a sentence. Many circumstances combined to their magnificent combination. The forcing upwards of the immense masses of limestone, to begin with, originated a multitude of rifts extending in all directions; numberless slabs pushed themselves up above others which remained behind; the watery deposits of the atmosphere dug out for themselves wonderful furrows, till they reached the nearest fissure and plunged into the abyss. No herbaceous plant clings to the parched, soilless crags; and only where marly and clayey masses have floated together and closed up the clefts of the limestone can water remain, and in such places a growth of grass is developed which appears luxuriant when contrasted with the surrounding barrenness.

Beyond the vast districts occupied by the Dachstein limestone in the eastern portion of our Alps, its

APPENDIX.

appearance is limited in a westerly direction by the Saalach—except in the Loferer Steinberg—to several small parallel lines from west to east, which have generally found only slight elevations; yet even there the rock is mindful of its lofty Alpine nature, and bursts out into steep, rocky, erect rifts, which have all the more effectual an influence on the scenery of the mountains that they are better able to defy the action of the weather than the softer stones of the Kössen deposits, washed around as they are by water.

The northern precipice of the Hochstein with its coral formations, the white limestone rocks with which the foot of the Hochlerch near Marquartstein is welded into the valley bed, the "rough needle" near Oberwossen, the Spitzstein near Sacharang, the rocky crown of the Heuberg, the Brünnelstein, the Bodenspitze, the great Roszstein, Leonhardstein, and Plattenstein, the Bürstling near Ammergau, and many other picturesque mountain-forms characterize the Dachstein limestone within the lines above mentioned. In rich succession are ranged more recent rock formations of all kind, one above another; but in that part of the Alps now under review none of them has attained the majestic development of the high mountains, such as the belemnite limestone, the group of the chief dolomite, and the Dachstein limestone. There are, first of all, the red kinds of marble, so rich in ammonites, of Aduet and Hiorlatz, which gave

FONTENSEE.

their names to the Rothwand not far from the Spitzingsee, to the Röthelwand near Wessen, to the Rothpalfen near the Hirschbühlerbach, and others; there are, further, the red Jura limestones of the Haselberg near Ruhpolding, Tegernsee, Weiszach, and the grey and spotted whetstone slates which are deposited thereupon, especially developed in the Ammergau. Then follow greenish sandstones, sandy marls, and limestone-slates; a smaller strip of this rock extends from Woghausköchel in the Eschenloh Moss above Grub near Schweiganger, the Geistbühel near Bichel, to the Stallauereck near Tölz, and appears also in the east, here and there, in the mountain-spurs; for instance, at the Neureit and Gindelalp in the "Nase," at the Jägerhaus near the Schliersee; they are designated as the older chalk formations (Galt, Neocom). After their deposition extensive changes must have taken place in our mountain land in the arrangement of mountain and valley. For while they occur everywhere where they appear in harmonious deposition with the older series of rocks, it is manifest that the next most recent rocks—the breccias, the limestone conglomerates, marl-slates, and clay-marl of the so-called Eocene formation—are no longer imbedded in conformity with, but altogether independently of, the stratification of the older rocks in their trough-shaped curvatures. The greatest part of the upheavings and depressions which are the original causes of our Alpine land may have taken place subsequently to the deposition of those green sandstones and marls. With this is associated the fact that they appear to be wanting in the west of our Alps. In the east, moreover, they occur only in a limited extent. To them belong the "Urschelauer" deposits near Ruhpolding, the celebrated cement marl of Schwaig near Kufstein, certain rock deposits on the margin of the Reichenhall valley basin, the southern declivity of the Staufen, the Müllnerberg, and, above all, the already mentioned Nagelwand on the Untersberg (near Plain), &c.

The limestone and sandstone rocks rich in nummulites, following one another according to age, the clayey, sandy, and conglomerate-like formations which are attached to them, called "Flysch" by the Swiss, no longer upraise themselves above the present valley bottom; and, moreover, they prove, by their relative deposition, that the principal outlines of the mountains already subsisted at the time of their formation. Only here and there do we see the cloud-topped rugged chains of mountain-peaks, so numerous on the northern ridge of the high mountains. In the structure and formation of these rocks are found the conditions of life necessary to stately forests and luxuriant Alpine meadows; and the abundance of springs and of lofty rounded hills which greet the mountaineer, like a crowned gateway, are due to the same cause. In this district we meet with the oft-recurring name of "Gschwendt," which signifies the rooting up of the forest and the common result of cultivation. Useful rocks contained in this strata also deserve mention. Besides the remarkable oolite-like iron ores of the Kressenberg, which are smelted in the Max smelting-houses near Bergen; we must not forget the granite, marble, and the numberless cement-stone, mill-stone, and building-stone quarries which are found in the nummulite and Flysch formations. From the circumstance that in the interior of the mountain land they appear but rarely and in small quantities, it is again manifest that the mountains that were upheaved at that remote time held back the waters from which the former were deposited like a wall; moreover, we here notice curvatures suggestive of a coast-line, such as in the basins of Reichenhall, Reit in the Winkel, Niederndorf, and Oberaudorf. At Häring these Flysch formations contain rich beds of brown coal or peat.

Where they slope down towards the frontiers of Bavaria, they are, for the most part, overlaid by "Molasses," as the rocks of the last (tertiary) formation are called, which were formed before the surface of the earth and its organisms received that configuration which in general they still retain. Here we find alternate marl and clay-slates, clays, sandstone, and pudding-stones in varied series, being partly formations of the sea, partly of great fresh-water lakes. Although they attain here and there an elevation of 3,000 feet, the upheavings of which they formed part, when compared with the lofty position of the land and of the Alpine chain, appear merely as hills. But what calls special attention to them is the occurrence of excellent brown coal (pitch-coal), which, as far as external appearance is concerned, cannot be distinguished from the genuine anthracite coal. Numerous, although often not very extensive, strata of pitch-coal are profitably worked near Au, Miesbach, and Tölz, near Penzberg, and on the Peissenberg, and along the whole of the northern mountain verge between Salzach and Lech are found traces of similar coal formations accompanied by sandstones and shelly marls, in which fresh-water snails play a prominent part.

And, finally, were deposited the masses of débris which cover the wide plains down as far as the Danube. This was the "Looss," the fertile loam to which entire provinces owe the blessings of harvest; and here were strewn the huge, mighty blocks of the primitive mountain-rock, which rise in scattered groups in the border provinces. Who is able to say how and whence?

It is conjectured, that in an epoch which lies proportionately near to the historic era, the whole of our Alpine land was to a great extent covered by immense glacial masses, probably sloping down into vast expanses of water. The giant foundlings floated down on their backs; but it remains to be decided whether they slid down to the solid earth, like the glaciers of the high Alps, or whether—borne up by huge slabs of ice—they floated forth to a distance, and finally sank down, on the annihilation of the support on which they rested. If the first supposition be decided on, there ensues the necessity of making the glaciers of that epoch extend over the Starnberger, Ammer, and Chiem lakes, and over the Innthal down as far as Attel. Everywhere are, or rather were, these stone-wanderers of the ice period to be seen; but on account of the poverty of the table-land in building-stones they are daily becoming scarcer; the dark greenish gray colour, or the glistening crystal laminæ of the mixed varieties of stone betray their presence in many an old wall. The ice period ended with a depression of the Alpine district, which took place so suddenly, or at least in so short a time, that the enormous ice-masses were immediately dissolved. Everywhere vast deluges broke through the wall of the mountains, rolling with them millions of cubic feet of rubbish and boulders. The land was finally slowly once more raised to its present elevation. The waters subsided into the sea-basins which even to this day fringe the mountains, but the circumference of which was lessened even in the historical period. At the foot of the rocky peak on which is built the castle of Marquartstein some imbedded iron rings are shown, which must have served in the remote antiquity for the making fast of ships, when the blue waves of the Chiemsee extended as far as this. We see that the ice also played no insignificant a part in geology, and therefore is rightly included among the forces which co-operated in the formation of the earth's surfaces. Probably the remains of the moraines may still be traced out which the gigantic glaciers of the ice period pushed before them, even as at many points the traces of their onward gliding motion have been discovered in the so-called glacier-polish on the strangely worn-down rocky walls. At the present day, none but few and small ice-masses are found in the limestone Alps. In our district we see the well-known Plattach glaciers of the Zugspitze, the little glaciers of the neighbouring Höllthal, and the "Blaueis" (blue ice) in the Hochkalter, which, although only of small extent, yet, in beauty of the colouring of the blue green rifts of the ice, rivals the glaciers of the Central Alps. A deeply rent ravine extends from the Hintersee upwards between the masses of the Hochkalter and the Steinberg, partly filled up with the forest débris. When

BLUE ICE.

the vast plateau of the Watzmann group split open, and the Wimbachthal came into existence, the rocky mass from the north-west side of the Hochkalter may have been set free, the fragments of which were flung across the Hirschbüchler valley and dammed up the Hintersee. The "Blaueis" is imbedded in an immense cavity, protected by high rocky walls and a northern position against the sun's rays. It sinks abruptly down in a chaos of grey limestone blocks, vaulted in the centre, and at the lower and more precipitous end torn by yawning fissures, through which all are able to gaze into the blue crystal depth. The rest of the glacier, however, consists of smooth white ice, which can hardly be trodden upon by a foot not well protected.

After the ice period, the upheaving of mountains forming the earth's crust appears to have ceased. No investigations as to whether our mountains are still rising or sinking are being carried on; but it appears that the geological activity of the present time is limited to the continual but imperceptible advance of the levelling of the mountain range—the sinking of the heights and the filling up of the valleys and sea-basins. Yet there are not wanting vast new creations of rock which are coming into existence before our eyes, although but slowly. We have but to recall the formations of tufa, the masses of boulders and rubbish which are heaped up everywhere in the valleys. Floods, holding carbonic acid, and rich in limestone, percolate through them and gradually cement them together, and after a few thousand years they will perhaps appear as compact conglomerates and breccias.

And so we may call up a picture before our minds of the great lakes of the limestone formations—the shores and the river deltas with their sandstone depositions of the olden time—and make to ourselves types of the gradual destruction of the rocks already formed, because the analogous events of the present day are familiar to us; but for the true estimation of the forces which lifted up the deposited layers of rock, folded or fractured them, which shoved over one another single slabs of the earth's crust, overturned them, or let them sink down, the standard is altogether wanting to us. From many indications, especially from the peculiarity of the preadamite organisms in the Alps, the conclusion has been come to that formerly an enormous mountain-wall extended from the Bohemian forests to the Bodensee, which separated the seas of the Alps from those of the middle and north of Europe. It has sunk down without a trace! When the mass of the Central Alps that runs from west to east was forced upwards out of the abyss, the strata of the Alpine rocks that were in the meanwhile deposited, held up from the one side and pressed forward by the other, must have been pushed up and folded together like wet pasteboard. Therefore most of the high ridges of the limestone Alps run from east to west, like the waves of a sea impelled by the south wind. The most magnificent instances of this are found in the Kaiser group and in the parallel ranges of the Karwendelgebirg. Only a few more important mountain ridges make an exception to this. Hence it is that many of our mountains which rear themselves up as broad masses if we approach them from the north, appear as sharp pyramids from the west or east. The Benediktenwand, with its broad northern declivity, characteristic of the Loisachthal; the long, extended Hochrisz, which runs alongside of the wayfarer from Nuszdorf to Aschau in an almost uninterrupted line; the broad, rocky walls of the Schinder, of the Bernhardjoch, and of the Wettersteingebirg are not recognised again from any point situated in a western or eastern direction—for example, from the Ratzinger mountain at Endorf,—because their profiles emerge as bold peaks from the sea of mountain summits.

It will, however, appear surprising that the more important valleys do not follow the direction indicated above. On closer investigation, however, it will be found that there are valleys of eruption through which the Lech, the Loisach, the Isar, the Weissach, the Inn, the Prien, the Kitzbühler Achen, the Traun, the Saalach, and Salzach come forth into the plains, and that the deposits of rock continue on the one shore in the same stratification in which they broke off on the other. Much more numerous are the earth-folds of the direction from east to west; and if they appear to us unimportant, the reason is that in general they lie higher, and because for traffic they are of but small importance as compared with those which lead into the mountain range.

To the causes already enumerated of the mountain formation, which are found in their stratification and in their manifold curvatures, must be added the powers of destruction. If the effects of air and water even at the present day are sufficiently great to leave behind remarkable traces of their agency, they must needs—even if we are unwilling to conceive of them as more powerful in the earlier ages—have so accumulated in the course of time, that a larger share in the moulding of the Alpine land may be attributed to them. Many facts of this kind may be pursued in their causal connection; as, for instance, the formation of the rocky gorges of the landslips. High above, on the walls of the Unken gorge we see the trace of the waves, where, at the present day, a brook hurries forth from the depth of the rock; we still see the shores which formerly fringed the wide sea-basin of Kössen, and which fall off like a dam. Deeper and deeper the drainage cut its way into the rocks of the Klobenstein pass, till finally it sank beneath the level of the valley, and the lake was perfectly drained. We can explain the displacement of the Isar from its ancient bed, which led to the Walchen- and Kochelsee, by the masses of detritus which diverted it to the eastward, and in this recognise the traces of the landslip between Schliersee and Valepp which compels the Spitzingsee and the streams of the Valepp to flow aside to the south. We shall be still more startled by the results of destruction if we do not seek counsel of the geognostic profiles, and with their aid follow out the process of the rock deposition. We find how the mightiest systems of stratification suddenly cease, and their expected continuance has abruptly come to an end, leaving no trace; and we are compelled to think of the movements of water which could carry away whole lines of mountain such as are constructed by the natural course of stratification.

It has been said of science, that it takes from things the charm of what is legendary, the breath of poetry. We submit the decision of the question whether this reproach extends also to the knowledge of the nature of the mountains to the judgment of any person who, high above on some lonely peak, directs his gaze over the Alps, over their glittering heights and their blue, hazy valleys, and, in so doing, remembers what these lines have related to him of their origin, of their seas and their inhabitants, of their earth-movements, and the whole of their prodigious past.

www.ingramcontent.com/pod-product-compliance
Lightning Source LLC
Chambersburg PA
CBHW031945230426
43672CB00010B/2061